Reluctant Reformer

Reluctant Reformer

Nathan Sanford in the Era of the Early Republic

Ann Sandford

Don,
I hope I got
most things
straight!
Best,
Ann

ee
excelsior editions
AN IMPRINT OF STATE UNIVERSITY OF NEW YORK PRESS

Cover art: Portrait of Nathan Sanford. An 1880 copy of the circa 1825–1830 original. Court of Appeals Collection. Courtesy of the Historical Society of the New York Courts.

Published by State University of New York Press, Albany

Printed in the United States of America

Excelsior Editions is an imprint of State University of New York Press

For information, contact State University of New York Press, Albany, NY
www.sunypress.edu

Production, Jenn Bennett
Marketing, Michael Campochiaro

Library of Congress Cataloging-in-Publication Data

Names: Sandford, Ann, author.
Title: Reluctant reformer : Nathan Sanford in the era of the early republic / by Ann Sandford.
Other titles: Nathan Sanford in the era of the early republic.
Description: Albany, NY : State University of New York Press, [2018] | Series: Excelsior editions | Includes bibliographical references and index.
Identifiers: LCCN 2016052229 (print) | LCCN 2016059186 (ebook) | ISBN 9781438466934 (hardcover : alk. paper) | ISBN 9781438466958 (ebook)
Subjects: LCSH: Sanford, Nathan, 1777–1838. | Legislators—United States—Biography. | United States. Congress. Senate—Biography. | Lawyers—New York (State)—New York—Biography.
Classification: LCC E165 .S247 2015 (print) | LCC E165 (ebook) | DDC 328.73/092 [B]—dc23
LC record available at https://lccn.loc.gov/2016052229

10 9 8 7 6 5 4 3 2 1

To Ezekiel's Descendants

Contents

Illustrations

Acknowledgments

The origins of this book rest in my family's history on eastern Long Island, New York, where I grew up, like my cousin Nathan Sanford.[1] The idea of writing a biography is recent. It began to take form about twenty years ago, when, in roaming through the stacks of Harvard University's Widener Library, I located the section devoted to New York State history. Among the volumes were the proceedings of the constitutional convention of 1821. Finding Sanford in the index, I realized that much of what I had heard as a child about a famous relative could be true. I became convinced of his significance as a politician and that ample material awaited my research.

I wish to thank the knowledgeable and helpful staffs at the archives and libraries that hold Sanford's correspondence, his account books, and other documents, including the New-York Historical Society, the New York Public Library, and the New York State Library. I am grateful to Jim D. Folts, Head of Reference Services at the New York State Archives, for sharing his knowledge of court documents and for his discovery of Sanford's estate settlement. Staff at the New York Genealogical and Biographical Society and the Butler Library at Columbia University helped in guiding me to important material that was dispersed among multiple collections.

Online newspaper databases, with their skillful design, helped me uncover unique material and sped my research. I benefited from Readex's *America's Historical Newspapers*, *Chronicling America—Historic American Newspapers* (Library of Congress), and *NYS Historic Newspapers* (Northern New York Library Network with the Empire State Library Network).

I thank the dedicated staff at the fine institutions on the South Fork of Long Island: Gina Piastuck, head of the Long Island Collection, East Hampton Free Library, was always a helpful resource; Richard Barons,

Executive Director of the East Hampton Historical Society, and Rosanne Barons, Registrar, always supportive of my research, assembled a collection of holdings on Clinton Academy for my use; Julia Greene, archivist, Bridgehampton Museum, promptly answered my diverse requests.

Scholars appeared unexpectedly during my years of research. I want to thank Bethany Berger, a legal historian and professor at Wayne State University Law School at the time, who in a 2005 telephone call asked me wide-ranging questions about Nathan Sanford and alerted me to recent research on the *Pierson v. Post* case. I am especially grateful to Angela Fernandez, Faculty of Law at the University of Toronto. Her phone call on August 25, 2009, began a series of exchanges that has helped me sort out legal and other matters pertaining to Sanford.

J. Kirk Flack, Suzanne McNear, and Donald Roper made time to read the manuscript and suggest improvements, while Natalie Naylor reviewed and corrected the notes—to them I owe a special thank you. Georgia Rose, another Sandford cousin, and Jerry Rose shared their enthusiasm for the project and pointed the way to my locating a rare illustration of Sanford Hall.

I am also grateful to the anonymous readers for the State University of New York (SUNY) Press who made constructive criticisms and suggestions. I thank Amanda Lanne-Camilli, acquisitions editor, who encouraged me to submit a proposal, and Jenn Bennett, who then guided me through the production process.

I appreciate the encouragement and assistance from family—Paul Sandford Guggenheim and Nancy Hansen McCaffrey—and from friends, Arona Gvaryahu, Ellen Karp, and Carol Mellor. Most of all, my appreciation goes to Jerry Korman, who shared his insights chapter by chapter, as well as his enthusiastic support for this project all along the way.

Introduction

Nathan Sanford's heritage was rooted in eastern Long Island, New York, where he was born into a family of farmers and tradesmen. Becoming a lawyer, he benefitted from the Republicans' national electoral victories in 1800. Three years later, President Thomas Jefferson appointed him federal attorney for the District of New York, which encompassed all of the state. Sanford soon began to engage in politics and faced the challenge of navigating amidst factional tensions among followers of Republican leaders—DeWitt Clinton, Aaron Burr, and Martin Van Buren—first in New York City, and then in the state and the nation. When he ran for the state assembly in 1808, he could not have imagined a future as state legislator, United States senator, or chancellor of New York.

Sanford reached the height of his political influence in the years following the War of 1812, beginning with his first term in the Senate. His courage and informed thinking were evident. He rejected the compromise with slavery passed by Congress and voted against the admission of Missouri into the United States as a slave state. Seeking to extend democracy, he supported a proposal for the popular election of presidential electors in all states. (It would have diminished the power of many state legislatures, including New York's.) After he lost his bid for reelection, Sanford became a delegate to the state constitutional convention of 1821: there, he voted for a ban on slavery in the state and led the effort to secure universal manhood suffrage, free of a property requirement. Both resolutions lost, and at the end of the suffrage debate, he supported the compromise that left the freehold requirement in place for African Americans.

Although his influence had waned, powerful factional leaders continued to promote his candidacy for office. In 1823, he accepted the appointment of chancellor for the state.[2] Around the same time, he was encouraged to join gubernatorial races. He agreed to run as Henry Clay's vice presidential candidate in the election of 1824. Finally, he regained his Senate seat for a second term. During that period, between 1826 and 1831, he augmented his fortune with investments in property and financial assets. His political career ended when he lost his bid for reelection.

The senator's lasting impact on the young Republic has been little noticed. After his death in 1838, historians offered only sparse commentary on the lawyer-politician's political achievements, and delivered mixed judgments on his character and legacy. Although not published until the 1970s, comments made about Sanford by the jurist James Kent in his *Necrologies*, written over many years, expressed the criticisms of a retired chief justice of the court of New York State Supreme Court. He labeled Sanford, who had succeeded him at the chancery, a "hard, avaricious, heartless Demagogue."[3] In his multivolume classic on the political history of New York published in 1906, Congressman DeAlva Stanwood Alexander described Sanford as a mere "pet of the Martling Men,"[4] the Republican faction that aimed to control New York City politics during the first decade of the nineteenth century and met at Abraham Martling's tavern.[5]

But Sanford, endowed with strong intellectual abilities, remarkable ambition, and extraordinary discipline, also displayed political skills—during his first Senate term and at New York's constitutional convention in 1821, in particular. On Long Island, his use of the title chancellor guaranteed public admiration in Queens County, where he retired, and his reputation earned him tributes from regional historians. Henry A. Reeves, in the *Bi-Centennial History of Suffolk County* (1885), lauded the "eminent services rendered to his country" by the "Suffolk County statesman."[6] In the May 21, 1908, issue of the *Sag-Harbor (NY) Express*, William S. Pelletreau summarized the life of the "distinguished and eminent man," while emphasizing his "greatness and his fame."

Many factors help to explain Sanford's omission from the historiography of the early Republic. For example, he never held an executive post: Governor DeWitt Clinton, or President Martin Van Buren, might be more appealing to scholars interested in the most impactful of New York's politicians. As a legislator, Sanford's influence would have been less obvious to public opinion. His public persona, moreover, characterized by rapid career mobility and, eventually, abundant wealth, may have obscured his achievements to historians: perhaps it was reasonable to attribute them to consummate ambition and associations he cultivated in the backrooms of power. Then there was his health: he was limited throughout his career by a lung disease that curtailed his public speaking. As early as 1806, while addressing a jury, the young district attorney of New York commented on his condition. Over the years, he would occasionally excuse himself from public forums, citing his persistent cough. When he did speak he was often barely audible, and he was never able to sustain eloquence as an orator at a time when soaring oratory was highly valued[7] and attracting the limelight.

Finally, contingency participated in the construction of his reputation. When he died at his newly built mansion on October 17, 1838, "after a long and lingering indisposition,"[8] he left no record of political thought captured in pamphlets, and no diaries with insightful observations. Nor did he leave extensive correspondences with prominent men of his day. His written legacy survives, in the main, through recorded legal arguments and court judgments, in legislative records, and in the few pieces of political correspondence that remain. Moreover, when examining the judiciary, attention is more often given to judges' decisions than to the arguments of lawyers. Even when the office of United States attorney for the District of New York celebrated its 225th anniversary at the Plaza Hotel in New York in 2014, the court's website persisted in referencing judges, ignoring the names of past district attorneys [9] who served in the office Sanford held from 1803 to 1815.

As my research progressed in archives, libraries, and on the Internet, my findings led me to realize that Sanford's beginnings in his particular rural community helped equip him to enter the governing and economic elites of New York State and the nation. He rose in prominence, traveling on the periphery of the highest centers of power in the land, becoming a tenacious attorney, competent officeholder, and effective legislator. This book presents Nathan Sanford, the lawyer-politician from Long Island who lived through the major events of the early national period. His life made an important impact; he deserves recognition and our attention.

Chapter 1

Rural Heritage of an Ambitious Son, 1750–1795

Nathan Sanford was born in 1777, a year after the start of the American Revolution and the British occupation of Long Island, New York. His parents had descended from seventeenth-century colonists, who left him a rich heritage. In his lifetime, Sanford would purchase grazing land in Montauk, where herds of cattle were driven onto the eastern tip of Long Island in a seasonal migration. The pastures were near the spot on the Atlantic Ocean where the second Congress had authorized a lighthouse in 1792, the first to be built in New York State. A fifth-generation American, Nathan spent his boyhood in Bridgehampton, a hamlet first settled in 1656 and located in the Town of Southampton, established in 1640.

On his father's side, Sanford descended from a family of tradesmen, farmers, whalers, and officeholders, a past Nathan would have heard about on visits to his cousins who lived in the ancestral homestead. They descended from one of three Sandford brothers who had disembarked in Boston from England during the first Puritan migration to Massachusetts. The brothers had traveled with an uncle, soon to become a deacon in the first church in Cambridge, a member of its town board, and a proprietor[1] who owned rights to purchase land in the town—rights that were inheritable and could be sold to others. One nephew, Robert Sandford, moved to Hartford, and around 1670, one of his sons, Ezekiel, made his way down the Connecticut River and across the Sound onto Long Island, until he came ashore at Southampton.

He was twenty-three years old and eager to join in expanding the settlement east of the town center when certain large landowners, the proprietors of Southampton, exercised their public authority as trustees and granted him land in exchange for a contract to set up a wheelwright shop to make and repair carts.[2] A married Ezekiel built a large shingled house in 1680[3] on his home lot near the boundary of the land grant. Six years later, the town recruited him to build a bridge over the large pond nearby to the east. This bridge connected his area to Sagaponack, already a settlement.[4] Shortly, the entire area became known as Bridgehampton.

One of Ezekiel's sons, a cooper—and Nathan's grandfather—prospered from a whaling "Company"[5] while Nathan's father, Thomas, rejected both the cooper's trade and whaling. Prominent in the public life of the town, Thomas Sandford was among the men who surveyed land for future subdivisions; he appeared in the town records as a justice of the peace. He was one of the "layers out" of a large tract of land that would include the right for proprietors of the town to excavate clay and build "brick kilns."[6] The elder Sandford did well by his family, which in time provided Nathan with a significant inheritance. In his 1785 will,

Figure 1.1. Sandford Homestead, Bridgehampton, New York. Built circa 1680 by Ezekiel Sandford, Nathan Sanford's great-grandfather. Photograph by Sally Spanbough, 2011.

he gave his "Negres . . . and two of the best horses . . . and the sum of five hundred and fifty pounds York money," among other assets, to his wife Phebe "to support herself and family." Besides bequests to children and grandchildren from his first marriage, Sandford left Nathan "all my lands and buildings and rights of land that I have in the Township of Southampton and Easthampton."[7]

Much of the stability of Thomas's assets, however, came from his acquiescence to British rule during the seven-year occupation. On October 2, 1778, Sandford was one of two administrators who assembled a list of refugees from the Town of Southampton who had left for Connecticut. A month later, Sandford's name appeared on a list of those "who took the oath of allegiance and peaceable behavior before Governor Tryon," the royal governor of New York.[8] While a large portion of the oath-takers were never diehard Loyalists, many factors may have led Thomas Sandford down this path. Like other colonists, he stayed to protect his family with young children—Nathan was a year old—and no doubt succumbed to the military's intimidation tactics. In Sandford's case, moreover, there was property to protect.[9]

In contrast to his substantial cash legacy to his wife, Thomas Sandford's first cousin left a meager sum to his family. "Ezekiel Sandford, ye Third" owned the homestead and was among the earliest in the town to rebel against British rule. He and his family had fled to Connecticut as refugees in 1776 and suffered the disruptions of losing household goods and his livelihood. Economically diminished, Ezekiel Sandford left his wife Sarah only "twenty pounds current money of New York" in 1789.[10] Clearly, Nathan's father was a yeoman of means, a position from which his son benefitted after his death. Thomas's farm had benefitted from slavery: he possessed at least two slaves when he died in 1787, but their status may have changed in Widow Sandford's household. There, the 1790 federal census lists two free persons (African American) and one (African American) slave.[11]

The political prominence and deference accorded Widow Phebe Baker Sandford's ancestors in East Hampton began early: town records note that one was already a magistrate in 1653. Five years later, Phebe's ancestor, Thomas Baker, would join two other local justices to investigate charges of witchcraft in the town.[12] Nathan was well aware of this heritage of exercising local authority. Shortly after 1791, twice widowed, Phebe married David Hedges, a widower, slaveholder, and deacon of the Presbyterian Church in Bridgehampton.[13] A powerful politician, Hedges lived in Sagaponack and became Nathan's stepfather. He and his extended family would help cement some of the social relationships that supported his new son's ambitions.

Nathan's stepfather was a dairyman who processed large quantities of cheese, which he often sold on the New York market, most likely transporting his goods by packet boat on Long Island Sound leaving from Sag Harbor, a gateway to New York, New England, and the Caribbean. In 1793, the Southampton town trustees granted Hedges and a partner the right to build a fulling mill next to the deacon's water mill on nearby Sagg Swamp, using slave labor. At the time, Hedges owned four slaves. The soon to be profitable new mill was used to wash, stretch, and press the rumpled woolen fabric brought to the owners by household weavers.[14] Hedges also gained political prominence. Large landowners and merchants in the wealthier eastern part of Southampton town supported his frequent reelection as supervisor. The town meeting elected him during some of the same years that he was representing Suffolk County in the New York State Assembly, in the late 1780s, and again in the early 1800s.[15] In June 1788, he attended the convention in Poughkeepsie, joining in the vote whereby New York State adopted the Constitution of the United States.[16]

In the assembly, Hedges could feel assured that he represented a significant jurisdiction on Long Island. Based on the state census, the number of delegates apportioned to the assembly in 1802 assigned three seats each to Suffolk County and to Queens County. In contrast, King's County garnered only one seat.[17] The population and the wealth of Long Island still weighed toward the eastern end around 1800, an important demographic fact for any politician in New York. In this context, Nathan would receive an early education in politics, government, and slavery in his stepfather's household until his mother's death in 1796 and his move to New York City to read law.

Bridgehampton had offered Nathan other experiences. Its population, roughly 1,250 in 1800, accounted for about one-third of Southampton town and included fifty-two free African Americans and forty-two slaves. The federal census also included Native Americans, such as the Stephen Cuffee family that resided outside the land leased from the town in 1703 by the Shinnecock tribe—for a thousand years. The Shinnecocks who lived on the tribal land were not counted. As a boy, Nathan would have come into contact with Indians and blacks, many of whom would be slaves in his Bridgehampton, a substantial rural hamlet for its time.[18]

The community occasionally drew prominent visitors from New England to the South Fork of eastern Long Island. Their travel accounts describe the setting of Sanford's youth in the 1780s through the early '90s. Yale College president and Congregational minister Timothy Dwight, whom Nathan would likely encounter at Yale, traveled on horseback from the Town of East Hampton west, through Bridgehampton, in May 1804 on a trip from New Haven to record local customs on Long Island. He observed that Bridgehampton's "surface is agreeably undulating; the soil better, or better cultivated, than any tract, of the same extent, on our journey; and the houses are in more instances neat in their appearance." Dwight ranked its farm fields among the best on Long Island.[19] His visual assessment of material life in the community fitted a larger purpose. Dwight wanted to persuade settlers, like Nathan's ancestors, that Christianity and private property, considered New England institutions, must be replicated everywhere. As one historian has suggested, they were the "means through which to transform the 'savage' into 'civilized men.' "[20] Given Dwight's assumptions about the culture of Native Americans, such as the nearby Shinnecock tribe, in contrast to the culture of New England settlers, Bridgehampton's well-tended landscape and dwellings were the achievements of advancing civilization, an attitude widely held but rarely articulated in young Nathan's surroundings.

When Dwight wrote in 1804 that "We saw no village in this parish," his standard for comparison to Bridgehampton was, perhaps, Sag Harbor, to the north, a federal port of entry authorized in 1789 to collect import duties. The commercial activities and ships at the port would not be visible from the vantage point of a horseback rider traveling eastward on the "Main Road to East Hampton," today's Montauk Highway.[21] Or, Dwight may have had in mind the village of East Hampton, where he visited with the Presbyterian minister, Lyman Beecher. These two villages boasted densely laid out house lots along main streets. Dwight described East Hampton as "compactly built" and estimated it had "about one hundred dwelling houses." In contrast, Bridgehampton, whose center was known as Bull Head, was spread out. The houses noted by Dwight were scattered throughout six distinct settlements and covered about twenty-five square miles.[22] The Sagaponack settlement, for example, was oriented toward the Atlantic Ocean beach, where the land just north of the dunes provided a cartway for settlers' use in farming and fishing. Like the Hedges family's Sagaponack, the area known as Scuttle Hole, where Nathan was born, was distinguished by a commons. Only Bull Head and Sagaponack had some clustering of houses. The boundaries of Bridgehampton, in evidence in documents by the start of the eighteenth century, included all of the settlements.[23]

Its people were optimistic. The Triangular Commons anchored the center of the hamlet. A new meeting house south of the Commons and a grammar school, built about 1720 near the Commons, reflected the confidence residents held in a future oriented toward commerce, as well as agriculture. Commercial activity was becoming more valuable than ocean fishing; travel along the cart path north of the dunes lessened. Merchants now depended on the deep harbors built on the bays.[24] Trade and communications largely depended on water routes, especially through the Long Island Sound that bounded the north shore of the island. During the eighteenth century, Bridgehampton's center had shifted northward, closer to Sag Harbor, and was adjacent to the crossroads of the Main Road to East Hampton, running east-west, and the north-south intersection of "Beach Road" and "Sag Harbor Road." Militia companies from Bridgehampton, Sag Harbor, Southampton, and East Hampton had trained there prior to the Revolution because it was centrally located on the South Fork. Captain John Sandford, Nathan's uncle, led Bridgehampton's Ninth Company, and in February 1776 its formation was reported to the New York Provincial Congress. After learning of General George Washington's defeat in the Battle of Long Island, he and his family would join his first cousin Ezekiel in the evacuation to Connecticut. Nathan's father and his future father-in-law, Hedges, were never listed as refugees,[25] although the deacon is reported to have wavered; then he elected to stay in Sagaponack.

In the 1790s, some Bridgehampton families came to understand that the future required more education for young people in order to prepare them for business activities, commerce, and the rights and obligations of citizenship in the new Republic. They were helped by schoolmaster Stephen Burroughs, who arrived in Bridgehampton from New Hampshire in 1791, well before Timothy Dwight's journey through the hamlet. Fourteen-year-old Nathan would have known of him in Bridgehampton through his mother and stepfather. The youth no doubt learned about the schoolteacher's reputation as a counterfeiter only later in life, since Burroughs's criminal history in New England would remain unknown to residents until he published his *Memoirs* in 1798.[26]

Burroughs made an impact on life in the hamlet, but it was not without controversy, about which Nathan would have heard. During the school year 1792–93, in addition to the day school, where he taught reading, writing, and numbers, Burroughs opened an "evening school" in the old schoolhouse. But the flamboyant teacher had also spearheaded a drive to organize a subscription-based library,[27] a project that aroused tensions between the local minister, the evangelical Aaron Woolworth, and the free-thinking Burroughs. Woolworth, a Yale graduate and former student of Timothy Dwight, had been ordained after the Revolutionary War. In 1787, he contracted with "Subscribers" from the "Parish of Bridge Hampton" to serve as minister. He had also begun teaching the classics and mathematics to scholars,[28] perhaps in his home. A precocious Nathan had learned about the arguments between the minister and schoolmaster over selecting books for the new library, and he may have attended Woolworth's classes before he went to the academy in East Hampton.

For young Nathan, the minister probably inspired the quest for a future education at Yale. Pastor Woolworth had recently married Mary Buell, daughter of Samuel Buell, another Yale graduate and the influential revivalist minister at the East Hampton Presbyterian Church.[29] By 1789, Nathan's mother had enrolled her diligent son in Clinton Academy, influenced in her decision, no doubt, by Woolworth, and by James Brown,

Figure 1.2. Clinton Academy, East Hampton, New York, opened 1785. Photograph by the author, 2011.

the long-retired Bridgehampton minister who had preceded him and another Yale graduate.[30] Twelve-year-old Nathan continued his classical education at the academy with Buell. The reverend had led in organizing the coeducational school; Deacon David Hedges was among the largest contributors to his fundraising efforts.[31] According to an advertisement in the *New York Gazette of the United States* on May 5, 1790, the academy was "determined to renounce corporal punishments." It was written by the academy's first teacher, William Payne. While "Rev. Mr. Buell," the principal, would attend to the "religious improvement of the Scholars," another teacher would instruct students in Latin, Greek, and French.[32] In addition to the classics, Nathan would have studied "English and Writing" and the curriculum of a common school under Payne.[33] Buell drew talented students from throughout Long Island and Connecticut. Nathan appears to have boarded in East Hampton with the family of Jeremiah Miller, the widower of Nathan's half-sister, Mary Sandford. Having completed his preparatory studies for college in the summer of 1793, he was ready for Yale.[34] By then, he probably knew about his substantial inheritance of properties in both the Southampton and East Hampton townships.[35]

The contents of the Burroughs's library in Bridgehampton offer an indication of the reading interests of the hamlet's residents. Nathan would have shared some of them, carrying those interests across the Sound to New Haven. Even though Pastor Woolworth's choices, emphasizing ethics, formed the basis for its core holdings, Nathan would have had access to the secular books that Burroughs contributed, which stressed history and geography. Not surprisingly, travel was well represented. The library's book list included Sparrman's *Voyage to the Cape of Good Hope* and Cook's *Travels*. It also offered novels. It circulated Samuel Richardson's *Clarissa Harlowe*, a source of social rules and advice. In reading fiction, the wealthier, literate locals, including young Nathan, were learning the manners and practice of civility that might improve their social standing.[36] Roughly forty households subscribed, and the library was one of 266 subscription or social libraries organized in the United States between 1791 and 1800.[37] Library patrons followed politics and international events as well. For example, they could read editor David Frothingham's *Long Island Herald*, published weekly in Sag Harbor from 1791 to 1798 and the first newspaper on Long Island.[38]

In the fall of 1793, sixteen-year-old Nathan Sanford left Bridgehampton for Yale,[39] where he would meet Lyman Beecher, a classmate who[40] recounted his college experiences later in life. In his autobiography, Pastor Beecher criticized the college for allowing a decline in church membership and an explosion of religious infidelity. For Sanford, equipped with an education from Clinton Academy and an exposure to debates over the library that had surfaced in Bridgehampton, Yale presented different opportunities. He pursued advanced liberal studies to prepare for a secular career. A student notebook from 1794–95 lists topics for the weekly disputations required of junior and senior students. Sanford no doubt attended these debates as a freshman and a sophomore. He encountered such questions as "Whether Democratic societies are beneficial" and "Ought property to be a necessary qualification for public office."[41] With exposure to such topics, lectures in political philosophy, and other studies in the classics, languages, and history, Sanford's perspective broadened, and with good reason he came to envision himself as a lawyer.

Ezra Stiles may have influenced Nathan's leanings. An eminent president at Yale, Stiles was known to defend the offering of undergraduate law studies. He argued that a republic could not be enslaved if its citizens learned "their Laws, Rights and Liberties."[42] Deacon David Hedges would have encouraged his stepson in his professional aspirations as well. He had served in the state assembly in the late 1780s and met prosperous lawyers. By the 1790s, moreover, the demand for lawyers in New York City had swelled. The growth was driven by the business needs of its export economy and the presence of major tribunals, including the New York State Supreme Court, the mayor's court that heard civil cases, and the federal court for the District of New York. In 1800, about 300 lawyers were licensed to practice at the supreme court alone.[43]

Even when he began to read law in New York City in 1796, Sanford would keep up with the news of political events that occurred in his hometown, perhaps from his stepfather Hedges or his Sandford relatives in Bridgehampton or East Hampton. In particular, the raising of a Liberty Tree on Bridgehampton's commons must have attracted his attention. The local event reflected national tensions between Republicans—farmers and small businessmen who championed the growing market society and political participation, including a popularly elected government—and the governing Federalists who sought to further strengthen the central government and maintain a hierarchical society with proprietary wealth "held together by patronage and dominated by a leisured few."[44] With Federalist John Adams as president, the United States government had begun preparations for war with France. The president aimed to retaliate against France for its recent attacks on American merchant ships. Republicans at home, however, like the French abroad, had objected to the recent treaty settling differences with Great Britain, France's enemy. Local opposition on Long Island to the federal government's actions rested on the memory of the harsh British occupation and on merchants' need for trade with the French after Britain had closed both its home market and its West Indian colonies to American vessels. Readers of the *Long Island Herald* had already found arguments to defend Republican positions against the Federalists, who had begun to levy new taxes to raise money for the war effort.[45] Further inciting discontent, Congress passed the Sedition Act in July 1798—the Act severely restricted public criticism of the government's policies.

Soon, Republican opponents of these policies from Bridgehampton and surrounding communities followed the example of other New York Republicans who had raised liberty poles in their towns to protest.[46] With growing support throughout Suffolk County, Republicans organized a political rally to defend "Liberty." The rally was called for Wednesday, December 19, on the Triangular Commons in Bridgehampton. The event depended on the political connections among local leaders, county politicians, and other Republicans.

Hundreds of people converged on the commons for the rally. Aaron Burr, the New York City lawyer, a leading Republican in the state, and the next vice president, attended and may have addressed the gathering. An account of the events that took place on the commons was published by Thomas Greenleaf in his *New York Journal and Patriotic Register*.[47] The rally celebrants raised a seventy-six-foot "Liberty Tree," shorn of its

Figure 1.3. Sandford Homestead and farm where Nathan Sanford would have visited his cousins as a boy, Bridgehampton, New York. Photograph, circa 1904. Courtesy of the Bridgehampton Museum.

branches. A vane on the top read "Liberty" on one side and displayed an eagle, an American flag, and a "Liberty Cap" on the other. Mottoes, apparently carved into the trunk, read, "No unconstitutional act, no unequal taxes, Liberty of the Press, speech, and sentiment."[48] According to the newspaper account, the crowd sang the "celebrated song of the 'Liberty Tree,' " and its leaders raised their glasses and delivered "patriotic toasts" (a way of communicating messages) while they drank rum, perhaps bought at nearby Bull Head Tavern. They toasted "The Tree of Liberty . . . The People of the United States . . . [and] The Constitution," and they honored George Washington and those who had lost their lives in the Revolution. The most cheers were reserved, however, for a toast to

> Thomas Jefferson, our worthy Vice-President; may his republican Virtues, bless our Country, by raising him soon to the first office of government and may the tongue and hand of the slanderer who would injure his honest fame be palsied.[49]

The rally expressed fervent and early support for a Jefferson campaign for president in 1800.

In their toasts, Republicans showed their optimism for the future, even though some may have been troubled by a collective rhetoric that declared an intent to paralyze the "tongue and hand" of any "slanderer . . . [of Jefferson's] fame."[50] As their cheers bore witness, residents held strong anti-Federalist feelings, many of which Nathan would come to share. A Republican, his views were consistent with those in his family and held by other men in his hometown. Sanford's republicanism was principled and grounded in his youth. Over his lifetime, he would engage these communities in a web of connections made during his early years; in turn, these contacts would support him on his political journey.

Chapter 2

Legal Training and Law Practice, 1795–1806

After two years at Yale, Sanford left to read law in Manhattan, but in 1798 he traveled back to Connecticut to attend the prestigious Litchfield School of Law.[1] Known for studies that would improve one's chances to gain public office,[2] Litchfield offered courses in topics relevant to Sanford's interests, such as business law, including "Real Property." Most frequently, students pursued lectures entitled "The Law Merchant, Contracts, etc.," and took courses in "Criminal Law" the least often.[3] Sanford would participate at moot court and attend talks on political issues during the fifteen-month course. Some constitutional law was also taught. He would pay a $100 fee for the first twelve months.[4] Students had the opportunity to make lasting relationships while boarding with a local family, giving Sanford the chance to refine his manners and in the future to participate in a "nationally expansive [Litchfield] network of advice, information, and patronage."[5]

His formal student days over, Sanford returned to the city in 1799. During the next few years he earned the certifications required of a lawyer, his time interspersed with periods of reading law and establishing his private practice; he obtained an influential position with the federal government; and he participated in important court cases. Sanford probably studied with the Federalist Samuel Jones when Jones was the state controller. Given the preponderance of Federalists at Litchfield, Sanford may have been referred to Jones by someone at the law school.[6] He earned his first licenses to practice as an "attorney" in 1801. Early in that year he was admitted to the Supreme Court of Judicature of New York State as an attorney, and was accepted as a "solicitor" at the court of chancery, the state civil court held over from colonial times where the chancellor presided, usually issuing rulings without juries.[7] As reported in the March 3, 1801, issue of the *Albany Centinel*, Sanford was admitted as a "counsellor" to practice at the court of common pleas, called the mayor's court, along with Daniel D. Tompkins, a future governor and vice president, and Peter A. Jay, son of the Federalist governor of New York, John Jay. On May 1, appearing with three other candidates, including Tompkins, he passed the examination at the supreme court and was licensed to argue cases as a counselor at that court.[8] Sanford had practiced as a solicitor for about three years at the court of chancery when, on April 2, 1805, he arrived at City Hall to be examined for his "Learning, Competency and Ability" to become a counselor there. He received his license.[9]

Sanford was educated well beyond the level of any of his ancestors and was typical of the young, ambitious, and public-minded lawyers who came from rural backgrounds. He began to practice in New York City in 1800. A man on the go, Sanford had already dropped the first "d" in his surname in order to save time, he later said. With his family background in colonial Connecticut, the twenty-three-year-old's educational experiences in that state, and his familiarity with nautical culture and the commercial bustle he had experienced as a boy in Sag Harbor, a port of call on the northern coast of the South Fork of Long Island, Sanford unsurprisingly thrived in the changing city. There, New England emigrants had joined the older merchants who dominated the wharves, and lawyers, as a percentage of the population, had come to far outnumber their counterparts in New England.[10]

According to the May 6, 1800 issue of the *New York Mercantile Advertiser*, Sanford had recently purchased a "dwelling house and lot . . . nearly opposite to the French Church" at 25 Pine Street and had moved his law office there. Called King Street before the Revolution, the location was east of Broadway and just north of Wall Street, already home to most of the city's banks. The lot measured twenty-five by seventy-five feet.[11] The density of buildings on Pine Street and the neighborhood's proximity to businesses and federal and city institutions in lower Manhattan created a compact world where Sanford would grow his new law practice, serve out his early federal appointments made by President Thomas Jefferson, and run for state office. His house and office were within walking distance of City Hall. Refurbished and converted to Federal Hall to accommodate George Washington's inauguration on April 30, 1789, the first session of Congress also met there. When the nation's capital was moved to Philadelphia in 1790, the colonial building reverted back to City Hall.

The law practice and rental income from his inheritance offered the financial stability and self-confidence that allowed Sanford to marry early, which he did, in an Episcopal church with a wealthy and influential congregation. According to the records of Trinity parish, located near the intersection of Wall and Broadway, he wed New Yorker Eliza Van Horne in early May of 1801. The couple took up residence at the Pine Street address.[12] The house, in the city's second ward at the time of purchase, placed Nathan and Eliza in a central location between William Street and Nassau Street. By the mid-eighteenth century, these routes had been extended north and laid out for commercial and residential use. Dutch building styles with stepped gable-end houses now appeared less often in the streetscape, replaced by the larger English structures that helped accommodate the growing city population of 33,131 inhabitants recorded in the first federal census of 1790. In that year 19 percent of the city's households headed by white men owned slaves. Two decades later, 40 percent of New York City's households included slaves;[13] Nathan Sanford's, marked in the 1810 federal census at the Pine Street address, would include two free African Americans. In 1820, it included one free African American, the year the city counted a population of 123,706 inhabitants.

Sanford had already opened his law office when he received his commission as a public notary on August 26, 1801—a lucrative new source of income that allowed him to charge additional fees.[14] His appointment as federal attorney for the District of New York in November 1803 did not deter him from expanding his profitable private practice. As a young attorney, he represented clients in two lawsuits that stand out. Both cases involved Southampton town, where his attachment to his rural roots and his interest and practical understanding of local issues of property stood him in good stead. In 1803, Sanford led the appeal to the state supreme court in *Pierson v. Post*, the landmark case that became popularly known as the Fox Case.[15] The second case came in 1806, when he aided proprietors from Southampton in a case brought by the Shinnecocks and decided in the town court.

Sanford, who had been appointed a commissioner of bankruptcy in the city of New York, was not involved in the initial trial in the Fox Case but only as an attorney for the appeal. The court proceedings began on December 30, 1802, in a house located in the village center of Southampton on the busy southwest corner of Main Street and Jobs Lane. The presiding justice of the peace, John N. Fordham, recorded the depositions of the twenty-five-year-old plaintiff, Lodowick Post from Bridgehampton, and the defendant from Sagaponack, Jesse Pierson, who was twenty-two.

The owner of the house, Hugh Gelston Jr., son of a judge and a sergeant during the Revolution who had fled to Connecticut during the occupation, may have been present, along with his two slaves.[16] Post stated that on December 10, he and some friends had gone foxhunting on horseback near the "beach" in Sagaponack[17] "with dogs and hounds,"[18] when they were thwarted in their proper pursuit of a wild animal, a fox. Apparently walking along the beach or behind the dunes, Pierson spotted the hunters, snatched and killed the fox, perhaps with a "broken [fence] rail," and took the fox home.[19] Shortly thereafter, Post, believing the fox in the chase was his, took Pierson to court for knowingly interfering with his pursuit. The jury of six men chosen from the twelve called for jury duty decided in favor of Post and awarded him seventy-five cents "for his damages," while the justice of the peace calculated the costs of the trial at five dollars.[20]

The financial settlement was minuscule, given the status of Lodowick Post's family. Unlike that of Jesse Pierson, Post's wealth came largely from his father's commercial activities after the Revolutionary War. A magistrate, merchant, and farmer, then militia officer and privateer, Captain Nathan Post had fled Bridgehampton for Connecticut early in the British occupation of Long Island. By the 1790s, he had assumed part ownership in a brig that engaged in the West India trade, an investment that produced substantial profits for the captain.[21] Captain David Pierson, Jesse's father, also possessed rural riches, some passed down, no doubt, from his great-grandfather, Lieutenant Colonel Henry Pierson, a wealthy farmer, investor in a whaling company, and by 1700, a representative to the Colonial Assembly of New York from Suffolk County.[22] Also a farmer, David Pierson had served as captain of Bridgehampton's Company of Minute Men in 1776 and had been elected to numerous town offices. By family background alone Jesse, a schoolteacher, would possess substantial social status, enough for him to treat the loss in the first round of Post's lawsuit as an insult to his honor—one to be redressed.[23]

Pierson had always denied that he acted with malicious intent in killing the fox, and in early 1803 he appealed the judgment in Southampton to the state supreme court, which had the authority to review the records of any lower court. He engaged Nathan Sanford as his lawyer, perhaps acting on a recommendation from Sanford's stepfather Hedges, who lived near the Pierson family. The young lawyer may have accepted the case, in part, as a favor to his cousin Jesse.[24] Twenty-six at the time and a counselor at the supreme court, the case afforded Sanford an opportunity

Figure 2.1. Pierson House, home to Jesse Pierson's cousins, Sagaponack, New York. Built circa 1740. Photograph by the author, 2011.

for visibility before the court. His legal strategy began by alleging that the justice of the peace had erred in many instances in the conduct of the trial.

For example, the attorney objected to the short amount of time allowed for Pierson to respond to his summons, a matter of hours rather than the six to twelve days required by the law. When the appeal was finally decided in September 1805, Pierson received a "recovery" against Lodowick Post for $126.37, more than $2,100 in 2006 dollars.[25] The two sets of proceedings, in 1802 and 1803, with a ruling in 1805, became known as the Fox Case.

In the United States of 1800, critical property law debates dealt more often with movable than real property. According to legal historian Angela Fernandez, in dealing with how to "establish possession over wild animals on land that belonged to no one," the case addressed one of the most controversial movable property issues.[26] In the 1803 appeal, Post's lawyer argued that pursuit (of the fox) was ownership. Sanford, using Roman law and other sources of civil law claimed that capture was possession, the basis for title. It was Sanford who convinced the court, which adopted his argument; his client won the judgment. Professor Bethany Berger has stated the issue of the case by asking: "what is the best rule [to use] for converting unowned resources into individual property." She maintains that by 1800 or so, New York State courts had begun to accept legal "principles designed to serve the new Republic."[27] An expanding national economy required a basis for the certainty of ownership of particular resources. Pursuit as the basis for property rights could include many claimants, whereas possession would be much clearer, and certain. Fernandez has viewed it similarly: civil law, she has written, "provided a way of thinking about property in absolute rather than feudal terms," with its often-conflicting property claims.[28]

Fernandez has sought to explain why the "eminent attorney"[29] Sanford, and the other lawyers and judges in the case, remained involved with the appeal for more than two and a half years, as it was held over by the court, term after term. She argues that rather than to reverse the case "on pedestrian procedural grounds or on trite common law,"[30] the participants saw a chance to use their training in the classics, allowing the learned Sanford to quote and argue from the codes of Roman jurist Justinian, among others.[31] Justice Daniel Tompkins, who had received his counselor's license for the supreme court with Sanford,[32] wrote the majority opinion for the court following Sanford's arguments.[33]

In 1802, the legacy of the case was uncertain. To participants, it must have seemed to be a purely local dispute based on the Sagaponack and Bridgehampton connections of the litigants. With the appeal, it became clear that several other local circumstances would help propel the case from minor trial to grand debate. Among them were the rural wealth that by 1800 allowed men to pursue the leisure activity of foxhunting on eastern Long Island and a confluence of events that brought together a fox, a sometime Atlantic Ocean beach walker, Jesse Pierson, and an open field. Also, in 1803, the village schoolteacher felt wronged strongly enough to appeal; the family of the aspiring country squire, Post, enjoyed sufficient prosperity to hire a good lawyer; and Sanford, the ambitious attorney who practiced in the city, agreed to take his cousin's case. The case added clarity to the legal question—how is property not already owned acquired?—and gradually became widely known among lawyers in the nineteenth and early twentieth centuries. In 1804, James Kent, a future critic of Sanford, became chief justice of the New York Supreme Court, and one may speculate whether he influenced the court's decision on the appeal along the lines Sanford had argued. In his widely read *Commentaries on American Law* published in 1827, the influential law professor wrote at length about *Pierson v. Post* in his section on property law, bringing the case to a wider audience.[34]

For Sanford, instances where he could examine and interpret different dimensions of property law presaged a lifelong interest. A year or so after the *Pierson v. Post* judgment, Shinnecocks on eastern Long Island challenged a group of Southampton town trustees and wealthy white proprietors before town justices over the proprietors' regulation of activities in pasturing sheep, cattle, and horses on land that the tribe had leased from them in 1703. The trustees and proprietors had continued to own certain rights in the town's remaining common lands, and they hired Nathan Sanford to examine the rights detailed in the lease. His opinion maintained that only Indians "properly so-called" had rights to the land covered by the lease contract and it specifically excluded "Negroes, Mulattoes (and) Whites."[35] The opinion persuaded the town justices to deny at least two Indians of mixed ethnic ancestry their participation rights as leaseholders. The Shinnecocks' complaint had responded less to the white proprietors' use of their ancestral land than to the "often arbitrary regulations and demands imposed on them" by the town trustees and proprietors, according to one historian.[36] Sanford's detailed technical analysis of the language in the lease was not unlike the approach he used in his opening arguments in the *Pierson v. Post* appeal that focused on the procedural errors committed during the initial trial.[37] The two cases involved legal dimensions of property and their economic implications—the first case added to the law of property, while the second defended the interests of the powerful white elite in Southampton over those of the members of an Indian tribe resident in this Long Island area for thousands of years.

Chapter 3

United States Attorney for New York, 1803–1815

With a Republican as president, Nathan Sanford could reasonably set his sights on a patronage appointment in the federal judiciary. In Manhattan, he counted on state senator DeWitt Clinton, one of New York's leading Republicans, to use his influence to steer President Jefferson's selection of commissioners in bankruptcy, an office authorized under the Bankruptcy Act of 1800.[1] Sanford's name had already appeared in a May 1801 "Memorandum" addressed to Secretary of the Treasury Albert Gallatin—bankruptcy commissioners came under his authority.[2] When Clinton became a United States senator the following year, he recommended Sanford to the president as a commissioner for New York.[3] Sanford accepted the position from Jefferson and held it until the fall of 1803, when he resigned to become the federal district attorney for New York, a jurisdiction that encompassed the entire state. Sanford's experience with bankruptcy cases made him an attractive candidate to replace Edward Livingston, a member of a politically prominent New York family. President Jefferson's appointment letter of November 18, 1803 read, in part:

> Know ye. The reposing special trust and confidence in the Integrity, Ability and Learning of Nathan Sanford, of New York, I have nominated, and by and with the advice and consent of the Senate do appoint him Attorney of the United States in and for the District of New York. . . .[4]

It was a fortuitous opportunity for the newcomer since the number of federal cases at New York's district court, particularly in admiralty law, had multiplied during the first decade of the nineteenth century. They provided additional sources of fees to be collected by the U.S. attorney, especially after the start of the War of 1812. Sanford's work there reveals the workings of the large organization and how personal contacts shaped his success.

Among the lawsuits the newly appointed federal attorney filed at court were those triggered by events related to ongoing conflicts on the high seas. These civil suits were heard in the federal courts, given that admiralty jurisdiction covered all of the states. Even before President Jefferson's administration, maritime cases had become more frequent in response to the growth in exports during the 1790s and the accompanying interference by Britain and France with the neutral merchant ships of the United States. The expansion of American maritime trade with the West Indies was an example of the enriching international trade that had long been impacted by war. Trade had grown, even though British ports in the West Indies, like in Canada, had been officially closed to American shipping. In response to the attacks, politicians began to threaten Great Britain with tariffs and other trade restrictions. In 1795, however, the British government agreed to give access to its ports in the West Indies to small trading vessels from the United States, while continuing to reject the principle of neutral rights for American merchant ships to trade with belligerents. Seeing a degree of American cooperation with the British, the French began to seize America's neutral ships and confiscate their cargoes.[5] When Napoleon Bonaparte, First Consul of France, declared war on Britain in 1803, it was an indication that the European wars were continuing to intrude on the Republic's affairs. The war was the latest in a series that had ravaged the continent in the preceding decade. By the summer of 1805, seizures of vessels had multiplied, as indicated by the resultant quadrupling of insurance rates for merchants.[6] The stage was set for continued violence at sea—and a jump in the number of maritime cases at the federal district court.

Sanford's court sessions as district attorney met four times a year. He earned five dollars for each day at court and ten cents per mile for travel expenses. Instead of receiving a salary, the federal attorney's earnings were based on a fee-for-service system established by Congress. By 1799, for example, the fee for "drawing and exhibiting libel, [the complaint], claim or answer in each cause was six dollars. In addition to fees, it became customary for the federal attorney to receive a percentage of the payments made to the court for the cases he won.[7] Sanford's aggressive, and successful, pursuit of fees and a cut of the fines and remedies he won were legitimate business practices, although they were, no doubt, resented by other officials and lawyers.

After President Jefferson appointed Matthias B. Tallmadge judge of the District Court for the District of New York in 1805, administrative changes there began to favor Republicans. The judge replaced the Federalist-dominated Bank of the United States with the Manhattan Company to fulfill the court's banking needs. Established as a water company in 1799 by the already prominent Republican, Aaron Burr, it also possessed banking powers. In addition, Tallmadge transferred the business of publishing the court's legal notices from the *New York Daily Advertiser* to the *New York American Advertiser*, a "staunch Jeffersonian sheet" according to one historian.[8]

Besides conflicts on the high seas, the jurisdiction of the district court covered the illegal activities to supply a ship in support of a foreign power, bankruptcy cases, improprieties in collecting the revenue from tariffs at ports of call, violations of customs and navigation laws that often led to the seizure of imported goods, and certain suits involving aliens.[9] In what must have been among Sanford's first cases, the November 23, 1803, issue of the *New York Daily Advertiser* notified the public that William S. Smith, the Surveyor of the Customs, had issued a libel at the court involving weapons. This use of the term "libel," that is, a complaint that initiated a prize case in maritime law, accused Samuel Newton of fitting out the British sloop *Admiral Duncan* with gunpowder and muskets for the "King of the United Kingdom of Great Britain" in order to engage in hostilities against the French Republic. It asked the court to forfeit the ship (a prize) to the federal government under the Neutrality Act of 1794, noting that the United States was at peace with France.

The *New York Daily Advertiser* also listed numerous notices of customs infractions and declarations of bankruptcy made by the district court. As district attorney, Sanford implemented the judicial decisions in bankruptcy cases: from January through July 1806 he signed a series of receipts "Nathan Sanford Atty. U.S." for debt payments made out to aggrieved lenders. The bankrupts' lawyer in all cases, John T. Irving, had kept them.[10] Unlike Sanford, the brother of writer Washington Irving earned a degree of praise from James Kent when he wrote in his *Necrologies* that Irving was an "amiable, worthy man, not of very strong Intellect." Irving and Sanford probably transacted their business at the court clerk's house at 49 Dey Street,[11] even though court sessions presided over by Judge Tallmadge were held at City Hall.

The Republican newspaper *American Advertiser* also published notices of customs violations. The indirect customs tax was paid at ports, where collectors boarded ships and assessed the cargoes for duties that would be paid by the merchant importers. As a boy, Sanford would have relished watching these activities at Sag Harbor, designated a federal port of entry in 1789. Alexander Hamilton, the Republic's first secretary of the treasury, largely created the Customs Service on his own. By 1790 or so, import duties paid to the United State Treasury supplied 90 percent of government revenues, used to support banks and to fund the debt, largely a result of the Revolutionary War. With three-quarters of the payments coming from British imports, maintenance of trade with Great Britain was critical. In order to track receipts at the ports, Hamilton required weekly reports from his collectors.[12] Perhaps the practice was discontinued by the time President Jefferson appointed David Gelston as collector for the port of New York in 1802, since customhouses had become more loosely bound to the central administration by then.[13]

Some of Gelston's activities provide a window into the political environment that surrounded Sanford's work as a federal attorney. A merchant in New York by 1786, David Gelston came from Bridgehampton and would have known Sanford's father. He was an early patriot. A brother, John, had been appointed to the same federal office at the Port of Sag Harbor by President Washington in 1789.[14] Another brother, Hugh Gelston Jr., owned the house in Southampton that served as the site of the first trial in the *Pierson v. Post* case. When the Surrogate's Court was established in 1787, David Gelston was appointed surrogate of New York County.[15] He may have been recommended for the post of collector by James Monroe, a protégé of Jefferson and a former U.S. Senator from Virginia, whom early fellow Republican Gelston had known since the late 1790s. The collector would serve under Secretary of the Treasury Albert Gallatin in a customs service that employed 707 people in 1801.[16] In New York City, customs offices were in Government House, which was located at Bowling Green near the southern tip of Manhattan—a short walk from the district court.[17]

Gelston's decisions often involved assets worth tens of thousands of dollars to the Treasury. In 1810, he refused to seize the ship *American Eagle*, despite indications that the vessel was being fit out as an armed ship for a rebel leader intent on leading a rebellion against the French in their Caribbean sugar colony, Saint-Domingue, in violation of the Neutrality Act of 1794. But President James Madison instructed the collector to reverse his decision. Gelston was soon overruled again: Judge Tallmadge refused to issue a "certificate of probable ground of seizure," apparently challenging the evidence Gelston himself had once questioned. The judge restored the ship to its no doubt politically well-connected owner, who sued the collector for damages, eventually winning a judgment against him. In 1818, a House committee held Gelston responsible for his initial failure to seize the *American Eagle*, although the government soon came to his rescue by covering the damages assessed against him in the course of his legal battles. The case illustrates the personal risks collectors faced in carrying out their responsibilities, given that they were held financially responsible for the decisions they made.[18]

Shortly after the incident with the armed ship, Congress passed a new Non-Importation Act. The law stipulated that British ships and goods would be turned away from American ports. In an effort to enforce the February 1811 law, Collector Gelston wrote to Sanford informing him that he had ordered the seizure of the British schooner *Union*, with its cargo. Gelston's enumerated list of goods included forty-one barrels of sugar and four bags of coffee. The vessel had arrived from Martinique, one of the sugar islands in the Caribbean taken by the British during the ongoing Napoleonic wars. In closing his note, the collector ordered Sanford to "proceed against the same as the law directs"[19]; the courageous old revolutionary outranked Sanford, the ambitious and well-educated young lawyer.

In a few months, President Madison would call Congress together to consider preparations for war with Great Britain. The growing frequency of seizures at the port of New York epitomized what was at stake for the nation. In his book *Empire of Liberty*, Gordon Wood summed up the issue: "Could Americans establish their separate identity only by fighting and killing Britons to whom they were cultural kin and whom they so much resembled?"[20] In June 1812, Americans found out: Congress declared war on Great Britain.

While the maritime cases in 1803 and 1810 that addressed the illegal arming of ships were heard in the federal district court of New York, at least one violation of the Neutrality Act of 1794 was deemed sufficiently menacing to the international position of the young Republic that it was prosecuted in the circuit court. In April 1806, Sanford brought criminal indictments against William S. Smith and Samuel G. Ogden in the Circuit Court of the United States, District of New York, in the second circuit. Smith, a College of New Jersey (now Princeton) graduate, was a former Revolutionary War officer given to engaging in failed speculative schemes while always searching for a higher-ranking government job. A Federalist, he gained prestige through marriage. His brother-in-law, and future president, John Quincy Adams, found the colonel financially extravagant.[21] During President John Adams last days in office in 1800, he had appointed his son-in-law Surveyor of the Customs for New York. With mounting debts, Smith was sentenced to prison in 1805 for indebtedness.[22] By the time court proceedings began against him in the new case, the Jefferson administration had removed Smith from his office at the port. Charged at the same time as Smith, Samuel G. Ogden was tried separately. The son of a clergyman, the wealthy merchant had established his own shipping business on Pearl Street in 1800. The legal team of five for the defense was led by Cadwallader D. Colden, a Federalist and Nathan Post's lawyer in the 1803 appeal in the Fox Case. At court, the required two justices presided; they were William Paterson, who had been appointed to the United States Supreme Court by President Washington in 1793, and district judge Tallmadge.[23] Paterson participated little in the case, since he was suffering from the aftereffects of a debilitating injury sustained in 1804 while riding circuit. He died soon after the trials ended.[24]

Addressing the court and the jury during Colonel Smith's trial on July 18, 1806, Sanford summarized the charges: Colonel Smith had "provided the means for a military expedition, to be carried on from the city of New-York, against the dominions of Spain in South America, the United States and Spain being at peace."[25] American sympathies for schemes like this one to aid Francisco de Miranda, a Venezuelan general dedicated to freeing South American colonies from the Spanish Empire, had a long history. In 1798, Alexander Hamilton had become involved in one of Miranda's plans, which included a role for American soldiers. The former treasury secretary had already persuaded President John Adams to upgrade the military, a project that would also prepare the country for the anticipated hostilities with France. During the military expansion, the president took the opportunity to give his son-in-law, Smith, already a friend of Miranda, a promotion in the army. Miranda's project floundered. When the general resurfaced in New York in the fall of 1805, he located Smith, who recruited Ogden for his latest venture. Miranda persuaded the merchant that during his recent trip to Washington, President Jefferson and Secretary of State Madison had lauded the cause of independence in South America. Convinced of government support, Ogden joined Smith in the scheme to fight Spain.[26]

At their trials, the defendants acknowledged their involvement in the plot, but their lawyers argued that the chartering and provisioning of the *Leander*, a merchant vessel owned by Ogden, according to Collector David Gelston's testimony,[27] was authorized by department secretaries in the Jefferson administration. Therefore, Smith and Ogden were not guilty as charged. From the start, Sanford warned of the political ramifications of the case. In a letter to Judge Tallmadge dated February 19, 1806, he described the alleged activities of "individuals" to carry out a "hostile expedition against the dominions of a foreign State" as a "high offence against the laws of the United States . . . [and] also an affair involving important public consideration." He requested that the charges be brought before a judge "in the first instance"[28]—that is, a circuit court. In a letter to Secretary Gallatin after the proceedings had begun, Sanford described the political intent of the "enemies of the administration," the Federalist defendants who had asserted that the "government either assented to the expedition of Miranda or connived at his preparations."[29]

Besides the popular argument from the defense lawyers that support for the mission came from the Republican administration, Sanford was soon discouraged about the prospects of an "impartial trial" because of the "political attachments of a great majority of the petty jury." He estimated that among the forty-eight petty jurors, "a few were Republicans[,] a few were Burrites [followers of Aaron Burr][,] and a large majority Federalists." Moreover, the defense requested the court to subpoena Gallatin, Madison, and Henry Dearborn, the secretary of war, among others, to bolster its case. In addition, Sanford wrote that the grand jury had contacted Jacob Radcliff, a "gentleman of federal politics" because the jurors had inquired about paths of redress for their grievances against Judge Tallmadge. Radcliff, a former justice of the supreme court, outlined the steps for impeachment, which the jurors did not pursue. Instead, they filed a complaint, which stated that Tallmadge had proceeded "in a manner unusual oppressive and contrary to law,"[30] a typical objection from political opponents at the time.

In a response to Sanford's message, Gallatin included a copy of a letter he had sent to the court and "a press copy" that requested that "evidence of the heads of departments be taken by commission" so they would not have to travel to New York. Gallatin feared that if the subpoena was granted, the precedent would encourage anyone accused of a crime to "arrest the whole administration." In an act of subtle subterfuge, the secretary asked Sanford to deliver the copy of his letter to the press "as if the copy had been obtained in court."[31] Whether public opinion from this particular newspaper article influenced subsequent events is unknown. The trial of Smith, which convened on July 14 without the secretaries, ended ten days later. In his instructions to the jury, Judge Tallmadge explained that the case "is not a question of party politics." He emphasized that the country must conduct its foreign affairs in a "harmonious" manner and must enforce its laws. Unpersuaded of the merits of the government's case, and politicized, the jury returned a verdict of not guilty.[32]

With Ogden, Sanford and his assisting lawyer decided to proceed with the trial just as the defendant had been charged: he acknowledged to Gallatin that "it will be merely a farce," but it seemed more "prudent than any other course." On July 26, Ogden, like Smith, was found not guilty.[33] In a letter from Jefferson at Monticello to Gallatin, the president cut through the complexity of the Miranda project and the Smith-Ogden trials. He praised the government's lawyers, and rationalized the verdicts: "The skill and spirit with which Mr. Sandford [*sic*] and Mr. Edwards conducted the prosecution give perfect satisfaction, nor am I dissatisfied with the result. I had no wish to see Smith imprisoned; he has been a man of integrity and honor, led astray by distress. Ogden was too small an insect to excite any feelings."[34]

The case illustrated the continued use of the federal courts for political positioning by the Federalists—and the Republicans. It also offered a record of Nathan Sanford's public acknowledgment of his lung disease. In July 1806, the trial recorder captured Sanford's comparison of his voice to that of Smith's counsels: "I shall certainly not be so loud; for my lungs would fail in the attempt." He further remarked with a note of sarcasm that "if I should not exhaust my subject, I should, at least, exhaust myself in less time than any one of . . . [the counsels] has occupied in addressing you."[35]

As the country eased toward war in the spring 1812, Sanford's responsibility as federal attorney for the District of New York weighed more heavily than at any time since his appointment in 1803. He led the federal prosecution of cases where American naval vessels fought and captured belligerents' ships. In these cases, Americans were responding to British violations of American maritime rights as they were understood—specifically, for the right of the United States, as a neutral nation, to pursue international commerce with belligerents in wartime. The leading naval power, Great Britain had never agreed with the Americans' pursuit of the trade, which the British saw as benefiting their enemies. British seizures, however, were perceived by Republicans as attacks on United States' sovereignty, particularly as they affected the lucrative wartime carrying trade, in sugar, for example. Of the merchant fleets that sailed from ports in the Northeast and engaged in carrying goods between French and Spanish colonies in the Caribbean, and European ports, many were only harassed by the British. Nonetheless, from 1803 until the outbreak of the War of 1812, Britain and France seized roughly 1,500 American ships at sea.[36]

When war finally came in June 1812, it dealt with Indian attacks on settlers in the Northwest, American efforts to annex the Canadian territories, and battles waged in the naval war fought, in the main, on the Atlantic Ocean and the Great Lakes, the waterway used by the British in their defense of Canada. There were other fronts: Sanford would experience the war as a resident of the Port of New York, where Mayor Clinton fought off the threats of a British invasion. Sanford's friend Henry Dering, the customs collector in Sag Harbor, would witness engagements near the wharf between British ships and volunteer soldiers under General Abraham Rose, the officer in charge of the defense of eastern Long Island. Through newspaper accounts and family connections, Sanford would learn about the general's deeds—Rose was a brother-in-law of Sanford's sister. In April 1813, a letter from Congressman Ebenezer Sage of Sag Harbor to James Madison alerted the president to the threat: "We have quite a fleet of british [*sic*] ships off this port," Sage reported. He went on to explain that the British navy had "two purposes—blockading the sound [the waterway between the north coast of Long Island and Connecticut], & driving a trade with their Connecticut friends. . . ." an allusion to the Federalist merchants in that state. Three months later, in his official report, General Rose noted that "no lives were lost or injury done except to the vessels. . . ." The strong defenses along Sag Harbor's wharves succeeded in helping to repel the heavy cannon assault launched from British ships.[37]

When armed American ships seized or destroyed enemy vessels and their cargoes in wartime, adjudication of the disputes landed in federal court under Article 3, section 2 of the Constitution. Sessions of a "Special District Court" that became known as the prize court decided the legitimacy of the seizure and the disposition of the ship and its cargo as lawful prizes, with the net proceeds of sales usually distributed to the officers and the crew. Forfeited ships and their cargoes were most often auctioned. Deductions from the proceeds included fees paid to the marshal and the clerk of the court, the federal attorney's fees, and wharf and warehouse charges. By statute, the federal government took half of the money for a navy pension fund. The court allocated the remainder to the captain and crew in specified fractions.[38] Prize law offered an incentive to seize and bring enemy vessels and cargoes into American ports rather than destroy the assets at sea; it served to encourage the preservation of captured property. It also provided a degree of certainty within the chaos of war for international merchants because the property captured came with clear title and, therefore, could be insured. The law benefitted insurance companies that began to see a degree of predictability in their assessments of risk factors, and it favored the captains and crews who would likely receive compensation. During the war, American ships took roughly 750 British merchant vessels into U.S. ports.[39] Many of the seizures ended up in prize court.

In 1812, the court under Judge Tallmadge appointed a committee to set the rules for New York's "Prize Causes." The five-member committee included Nathan Sanford and John Irving. One administrative recommendation, later adopted, was a form designed for "interrogatories" to set out the basic facts of a case. Another form, known as a writ, showed two names with titles printed on the form: "Clerk" is on the lower right side, and below that, at the lower left, appears "NATHAN SANFORD, Att'y U.S." The document included a brief description of the capture and

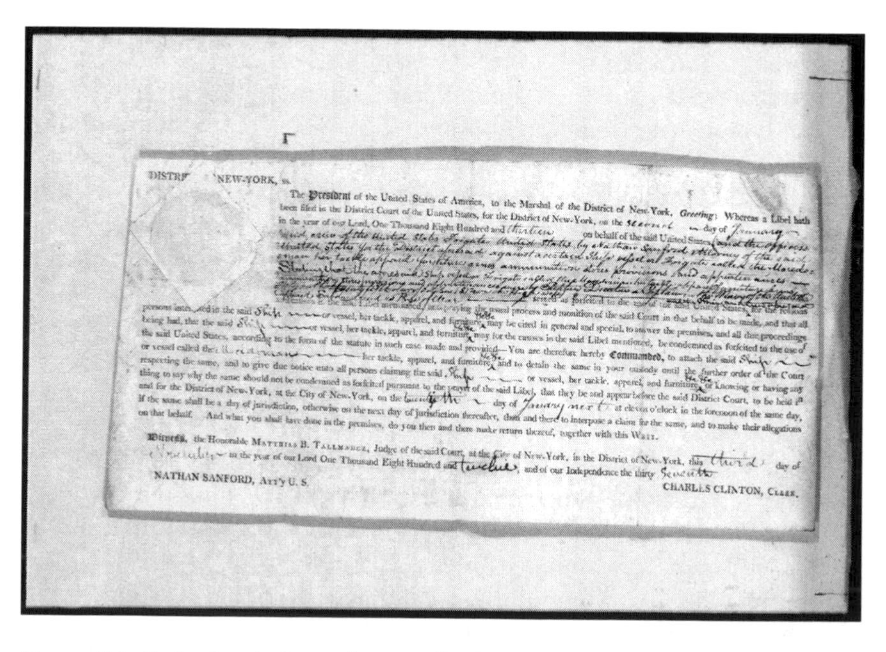

DISTR[illegible] NEW-YORK, ss.

The President of the United States of America, to the Marshal of the District of New-York, Greeting: Whereas a Libel hath been filed in the District Court of the United States, for the District of New-York, on the second day of January in the year of our Lord, One Thousand Eight Hundred and thirteen [illegible] on behalf of the said United States [illegible] by Nathan Sanford [illegible] [illegible] seized as forfeited to the use of the said United States [illegible] persons interested in the said Ship or vessel, her tackle, apparel, and furniture, may be cited in general and special, to answer the premises, and all due proceedings being had, that the said Ship or vessel, her tackle, apparel, and furniture, may for the causes in the said Libel mentioned, be condemned as forfeited to the use of the said United States, according to the form of the statute in such case made and provided—You are therefore hereby Commanded, to attach the said Ship or vessel called the [illegible] her tackle, apparel, and furniture, and to detain the same in your custody until the further order of the Court respecting the same, and to give due notice unto all persons claiming the said Ship or vessel, her tackle, apparel, and furniture, or knowing or having any thing to say why the same should not be condemned as forfeited pursuant to the prayer of the said Libel, that they be and appear before the said District Court, to be held in and for the District of New-York, at the City of New-York, on the twentieth day of January next at eleven o'clock in the forenoon of the same day, if the same shall be a day of jurisdiction, otherwise on the next day of jurisdiction thereafter, then and there to interpose a claim for the same, and to make their allegations on that behalf. And what you shall have done in the premises, do you then and there make return thereof, together with this Writ.

Witness, the Honorable Matthias B. Tallmadge, Judge of the said Court, at the City of New-York, in the District of New-York, this third day of November in the year of our Lord One Thousand Eight Hundred and twelve, and of our Independence the thirty seventh

NATHAN SANFORD, Att'y U. S.

CHARLES CLINTON, Clerk.

Figure 3.1. Federal writ form showing "NATHAN SANFORD, Att'y U.S.," dated November 3, 1812, and describing the *Macedonian*, "Captured Subdued said as Prize of War" on October 25, 1812. National Archives, Record Group 21. Fold3.com.

its date, the date and name of the judge as witness to the seized vessel in the custody of the court, the date and an outline of the libel, that is, the initial pleading filed by a federal attorney, and the date the court would convene. Besides Sanford, the officers of the court included Judge Tallmadge and, after 1812, Judge William P. Van Ness; the clerk; the marshal, who was responsible for moving the judicial process forward; the collector of customs; a naval officer; and federal commissioners who took testimony in prize cases.[40] The collector throughout the war years was David Gelston, who had come to know Sanford well after their involvement in the Smith-Ogden trial in 1806.

Addressed to the marshal, the writ was a public notice intended for all interested persons. It summarized the circumstances of the capture and the lawsuit being brought against the property, not its owners. Sanford filed the libel on behalf of the United States government and the captors, most often a navy captain and the crew. At the district court on December 22, 1812, Sanford elaborated on the charges in the case "Jesse Elliott *et al.* (U.S. ship *Eliza*) v. *Caledonia*." The attorney outlined the reasons for the requested forfeiture of the ship and its goods as a "lawful prize": first, that "open and public war" existed between the United States and Great Britain; second, that Lieutenant Elliott was an officer in the United States Navy; third, that Elliot followed the instructions of the president when he "subdued[,] seize and take as prize of war a certain Brig or vessel called the *Caledonia*" and its cargo, 390 "packages of Skins," on October 9, 1812, on Lake Erie; fourth, that the *Caledonia* belonged to the king of "Great Britain and Ireland and was employed in his service"; fifth, that the skins were "employed in trade and commerce" by subjects of the king who were enemies of the United States; sixth, that the vessel and its cargo had been forfeited to the United States and the "officers and crews concerned in the capture," and "ought to be condemned as prize of war for their use"; and, last, the Honorable Court was urged to adjudge the *Caledonia* and the skins to be a "lawful prize" after public comments on the libel were heard.[41]

The American naval victories illustrate the geographic breadth of the chaos on the high seas; in litigating the prize cases, Sanford would expand his knowledge of the operations of the U.S. Navy, international trade, commercial business practices, and maritime law. Cases extended from the Niagara Frontier to the coast of Africa and the South Pacific. In the defeat of the Brig *Caledonia* by the *Eliza* captained by Lieutenant Elliot, the date of the seizure has reordered historians' chronology of the important early battles on the Niagara Frontier. In his book *Don't Give*

Up the Ship! Myths of the War of 1812, Donald Hickey argues that the encounter was the first battle in the planned invasion of Canada by the United States since it took place four days before the American defeat at the Battle of Queenston Heights. Like other captures at the start of the war, it reflected the new Republic's initial superior naval performance.[42]

The reach of the prize court was global. On October 25, 1812, in a battle waged about 600 miles west of the Canary Islands in the North Atlantic Ocean off of the northwestern coast of Africa, Captain Stephen Decatur, with the U.S. Frigate *United States*, captured H.M. Ship *Macedonian*. Already a naval hero, Decatur "showed brilliant seamanship."[43] For Sanford, the American victory resulted in one of his best-known cases. He may have known Decatur. In late August 1811, he had informed the commodore that because of ill health he could not serve with him on the

Figure 3.2. U.S.S. *United States* and British frigate *Macedonian* (October 25, 1812). PR100, Maritime History Collection, Box 11, folder 17, no. 65; image #92594d. Courtesy of the New-York Historical Society.

Court of Inquiry, to which they both had been appointed by the secretary of the navy.[44] Sanford issued the libel on January 2, 1813, two months after the *Macedonian* was placed in the custody of the court. At court proceedings, referees appointed by the Navy Department valued the prize at $200,000, to be paid to the captain and crew: Captain Decatur's three-twentieths share came to $30,000. Decatur may have received more prize money during the war than any other United States naval officer—a total of about $34,500. His wartime earnings would roughly equate to $517,500 today.[45] In short time, the U.S. Navy brought the British ship into service as the U.S. *Macedonian*. It was not decommissioned until 1828.[46]

While these captures engaged the enemy in the Great Lakes and the North Atlantic, the U.S. frigate *Essex* traversed the South Pacific. By the end of 1813, the ship was the most global in its voyages among American naval vessels. In 1800, during a period of trade embargo with France and turmoil on the high seas, the *Essex* had journeyed around the Cape of Good Hope, becoming the first American warship to sail in the Indian Ocean, and in 1813, it became the first to sail around Cape Horn and cruise the Pacific. According to the libel filed by Sanford on July 20, 1814, at the court presided over by Judge Van Ness, Captain David Porter had seized the British whaler "*Atlantic* otherwise called the *Essex Junior*" on May 30, 1813, in the South Pacific Ocean near the Galapagos Islands. Less than a year later, two British warships would capture Porter and the Frigate *Essex* off the Chilean coast. By then, the captain had spent months in the Pacific inflicting damage and securing the seizure of seven, relatively small, British whaling ships. The value of the smaller vessels captured by Porter totaled about $300,000, an amount of money larger than the $200,000 prize assessment awarded for the *Macedonian* under Captain Decatur.[47]

Meanwhile, soldiers and their families living near the Great Lakes continued to suffer disruptions in their livelihoods from the devastating attacks by the British along the Niagara frontier. In late 1814, New York City residents managed to raise funds from the common council, private subscriptions, and church-goers to help them with their everyday needs. Sanford's (second) wife, Mary Esther Isaacs, joined the "ladies' association," composed of women "prominent in social position in the city," who raised the money to buy needed clothing.[48] As the months wore on, the lengthy military stalemate on other fronts helped end the war; it was followed by the Treaty of Ghent, signed on December 24. In 1815, Nathan Sanford had long ago entered politics; like other lawyer-politicians, he would hold federal office and a political position at the same time.

Chapter 4

State Politician and Legislator, 1800–1815

Although the federal government had lost the Smith-Ogden case in 1806 in a show of Federalist strength that had politicized a New York City jury, Thomas Jefferson's "perfect satisfaction" with Sanford's "skill and spirit" as prosecutor signaled his continued support for the young Republican. Jefferson, victorious in the election of 1800 and soon to be inaugurated as third president of the United States, had helped launch Sanford's career in New York's Republican politics. Decided in the House of Representatives in February 1801, Jefferson was elected president, and Aaron Burr, the well-educated but secretive leader of New York Republicans who had fought Jefferson during the election, became vice president. For the president, like Sanford later, the ideals of democracy that propelled an expansion in voter turnout also boosted Republican candidates' chances for victory at the polls.[1] With this context in mind, James Kent would write after Sanford's death that "in the Election in April 1800 . . . [Sanford] suddenly abandoned the federal & joined the democratic Party, & became an admirer of Jefferson. . . ."[2] While there is no direct evidence that Sanford was ever a Federalist, Kent rightly implied that the young lawyer's civic interests under Republican dominance had improved his chances for an appointive federal office and led him into politics. To boost his chances of success in these pursuits, he worked to build personal relationships.

In 1801, Sanford accepted membership in the Holland Lodge of the Masons, which met in the extravagantly decorated City Hotel on lower Broadway.[3] Like City Hall, it was also close to his home. At the lodge he was introduced to leading men in the city and state. They included DeWitt Clinton who, at thirty-two, was nearly a decade older than Sanford. He led the Republican Party in the state and was serving as a state senator from the southern legislative district that included New York City.[4] Republicans like Sanford and Clinton with their emphasis on individual merit and representative government saw the lodge as offering a setting for their political discussions and politicking. By the early 1800s, connections between Free Masons and Federalists, who favored social order and a strong central government, had weakened.[5] In 1802, again following Clinton's example, Sanford joined New York's Society of St. Tammany, launching a lifelong political association. Initially, the organization had advocated for the cultural uplift of its membership and the city but over time dropped its nonpartisanship. Sanford would also meet men of his rising social position in the Third New York Regiment, where he was promoted to the rank of captain, an achievement noted in the April 7, 1803, issue of the *Chronicle Express*.[6]

Governing and politics, however, raised different issues for Sanford from those he addressed in court cases and legal debates; among them was the use of patronage. President Jefferson defined patronage as "appointing people to office and creating clients." He was torn between his belief that patronage was corruption and demands from Republican colleagues that he bestow appointments on them in return for their past support.[7] But Republican patronage was already alive and well. In 1801, the jobs available in Jefferson's administration numbered about 3,000. Among the widely sought federal positions were those of nearly 900 deputy postmasters.[8] State senator DeWitt Clinton held no moral reservations like those of the president. After Republicans won in the New York legislative elections of 1800, the senator led the effort to appoint Republicans to government offices from his position on the Council of Appointment, a board composed of state legislators.[9]

Beginning in February 1802, after the state senate had elected him to the United States Senate, Clinton often sent lists of men he recommended for patronage appointments to Secretary of State Madison and to President Jefferson. In a document addressed to the Department of State dated May 3, 1802, Clinton provided names under the heading "Protests against the appt of the following as Commss. of Bankruptcy," writing privately to explain his reasoning for rejecting certain candidates: two were "Bankrupts," and another two were men who already held "lucrative" state offices. In an attachment, the senator concluded with a third reason for some rejections: "On account of their being incurable members of the little faction." By "little faction," Clinton meant his enemies, Aaron Burr and his followers. A few weeks later, Clinton recommended Nathan Sanford and Daniel Tompkins, among others, for the posts.[10]

With the Federalists greatly weakened by the victory of Jefferson, and the Republicans holding majorities in the House and the Senate, beginning in 1801, the Clintonian and Burrite factions in New York became even more divided. As Evan Cornog explains in *The Birth of Empire, DeWitt Clinton and the American Experience, 1769–1828*, "that weakness [of the Federalists] allowed existing rivalries within the Republican ranks to sharpen into public discord and even bloodshed."[11] The factions hit hard. Clinton wrote the president again to emphasize the political importance of filling federal offices in New York City with Republicans.[12] A reluctant Jefferson agreed and proceeded to replace most Federalists with Republicans, but in New York, although he appointed Republicans, they were sometimes Burr loyalists.[13]

In late 1803, DeWitt Clinton resigned his Senate seat to become mayor of New York, a city that remained a "Federalist bastion."[14] He would earn over $10,000 a year. As Sanford's mentor, Clinton soon wrote the president regarding Sanford's appointment as federal attorney. Citing "principle," the mayor informed Jefferson that Sanford "intends to resign his office of Commissioner of Bankruptcy—upon the principle that honorary and lucrative offices ought not to be too much confined to a few."[15] Holding multiple offices was a controversial issue in the young Republic. During his career, Sanford never held two appointive offices at the same time, but as a federal officeholder he continued to pursue his private practice and the politics of elective office in New York State.

Unlike Mayor Clinton, who generously bestowed offices on his supporters,[16] Sanford never occupied an executive office, therefore lacking the sources of patronage. He was able to use his contacts to further the Republican cause in other ways. The March 19, 1804, issue of the *New York American Citizen*, considered a Clintonian newspaper, reported that Sanford had become an "elector." He held sufficient property to vote and would be among the delegates from the city and county of New York who would help decide the Republican nominees in the upcoming election for governor and lieutenant governor.[17] In a letter to Henry P. Dering, the collector at the bustling Port of Sag Harbor, Sanford addressed the upcoming election for the House seat in District One on Long Island and shared that he had "private information from Queens" that assured a Republican majority in that county. In an effort to emphasize the importance of Dering's Suffolk County, he noted that the election would "depend entirely on the Electors of Suffolk," and then added that he thought it "perfectly safe."[18] Sanford's reassuring comments confirmed the political realities that Suffolk was largely Republican and that, as late as the early nineteenth century, the population of Long Island tended to be distributed more heavily toward the east than the west. These advantages influenced elections for members of both the House and the state assembly.

In the Republicans' factional positioning, Sanford allied himself with DeWitt Clinton, who was moving to unite New York's Republicans under his leadership by bringing Burrites and a few Federalists into his fold. By 1805, Aaron Burr, who had attended the rally in Bridgehampton in 1798 in support of a future Jefferson candidacy for president, had killed Alexander Hamilton in a duel and become alienated from the Jefferson administration. He had even begun defending Federalist policies.[19] Mayor Clinton, with his adversary's reputation tarnished but still with followers, felt confident in promising offices to Burr's political sympathizers in exchange for loyalty: certain politicians decided to organize a celebration of Clinton's reconciliation with Burr and his followers. When details about the event that took place in February 1806 and the realignment became more widely known, the Clintonians and Burrites involved became even more fractured in their opinions of Clinton's attempted alliance. As news of the meeting circulated, discontented Clintonians and some other Republicans gathered at Abraham Martling's tavern.[20] A Clinton supporter, Sanford attended the February 25 meeting. Two days later, he sent the mayor his assessment of the efforts at unity and their aftermath. The letter was addressed to the senate in Albany, where Clinton had been urging the reconciliation. In glowing terms, Sanford described the situation that existed before the two meetings: "Ten days ago our politics in this City were a most favorable aspect. Our friends were united and confident in each other[,] great numbers of the Federalists were friendly[,] the Burrites were well disposed." At Martling's, "A thousand lies were circulated," he continued, and a "spirit of jealousy and suspicion among some of our best friends" was created. The underlying accusations about corruption that involved Burr's Manhattan Company, and Clinton's clumsy attempts to reconcile the factions, led to charges of opportunism and manipulation by colleagues who then turned on Clinton. In the process, he lost control of the legislature in the April 1806 elections. Early in the following year, Clinton's opponents on the state's Council of Appointment united to remove him from the mayoralty. Standing apart from the intense factional loyalties, Sanford declined to join the Martling Men who opposed Clinton—at least for the moment.[21]

In the same letter to his friend Clinton, Sanford illustrated his hands-off approach to patronage when he was approached by a candidate for the position of inspector of flour. While withholding any recommendation for the man, he wrote that he had learned of two other interested persons, one of whom was a flour merchant and "I presume very competent to fill the office for which he asks. His political principles are correct and his private character is I believe fair."[22] With this stance, Sanford became an observer of the patronage deal even though patronage, coupled with merit, had helped his own career.

In an annual ritual, the New York City Council assigned inspectors to polling locations for local elections. While most polling places were in taverns, in the election that took place on November 3, 1806, Nathan Sanford and two other civic-minded residents were appointed to the polling station at City Hall, on Wall Street in the first ward.[23] Oversight of the polls was a serious mission in the new Republic, requiring vigilance to minimize fraud and ensure voter access. Republicans like Sanford had followed earlier cases of corruption. During city elections in 1801, Federalist inspectors had blocked many Republicans. They were defending the city charter that dated from the colonial period. It stipulated that suffrage was granted to freemen and to those men who met a financial requirement. The Federalists in charge of the granting corporation only gave temporary freeman status to their "merchant friends," refusing to give grants to many artisans and mechanics. In response, a group of cartmen petitioned the Federalist mayor, Richard Varick, for redress. They charged that the corporation aimed to stifle the political participation of Republicans. Shortly after the scandal erupted and unwilling to challenge the petition, the mayor retired from public life; Varick moved into a new house—near Sanford at 7 Pine Street.[24] In Sanford's time, voter fraud in New York County favored Republicans. As one historian has concluded, their politicians were "notorious for the fabrication of Republican voters, temporarily qualified to vote for governor or assembly, by means of temporary deeds and loans. . . ."[25] Poll duty had offered Sanford one of his earliest encounters with manipulative urban politics.

By the time he ran for the state assembly in 1808, Sanford's exposure to the intricacies of patronage and voter fraud would equip him with the savvy and experience needed to deal with Republican factions and their Federalist opponents. During the Smith-Ogden trial he had corresponded with Secretary Gallatin, communicating his observations of the political groupings at work. At the same time, the *New York Republican Watch-Tower* reported in its April 29, 1806, issue that "republican citizens" in a meeting at Martling's tavern had nominated candidates for the state legislature and for Congress. They had also appointed a committee of correspondence of three that included Sanford. Its purpose was to pressure voters in the congressional district to support the party's nominees for the state senate. In writing to Collector Dering in Sag Harbor two years before, Sanford had engaged in those activities. In 1808, soon after he had been appointed by the city's Republican-dominated common council as a poll inspector, Sanford joined the Republican ticket to run for a seat in the assembly.[26] Federal attorney Sanford won election to the assembly in 1808, and again in 1810, when the Federalists dominated the state legislature. He had no doubt benefitted from the practice of voter fraud and, as a poll inspector, may have looked the other way. As assemblyman, he was following in the footsteps of his stepfather, who had served many terms in the assembly from Suffolk County.[27]

The young lawyer-politician served in the fall session, one marked by Federalist gains. That resurgence was largely driven by voter opposition to the Jefferson administration's Embargo Act of December 1807. Farmers, in particular, suffered from the closing of ports to agricultural exports and began to vote for Federalists in greater numbers. Soon the embargo came under siege in New York and throughout the Northeast, even by Republicans, and Congress repealed the law in March 1809. In that period, according to estimates, exports had dropped from $108 million in 1807 to $22 million in 1808, and customs receipts[28] and merchants' profits had plummeted accordingly. Tradesmen lost their jobs and income. After the repeal, Republican candidates won about two-thirds of the assembly's seats. The number of Republican voters had also increased with the expansion of New York State's population; it soon exceeded that of Virginia, until then the most populous state.[29]

In the assembly, perhaps in the fall of 1808, Sanford had voiced his support for the embargo. He maintained that the ocean had become a "place of robbery and national disgrace," since "England had blockaded one-half of Europe and France the other half." A trade embargo would force a change in British and French policies. According to Sanford, it should be in place "until England felt the need of additional supplies, and France awoke to the loss of its luxuries."[30] In these positions, the assemblyman had overestimated the embargo's impact on Europe and underestimated popular opposition to it. As enforcement regulations against smuggling were tightened under Jefferson, the federal government increasingly required American shippers to get permits and post bonds in case their vessels were captured.[31] Serious violations of the embargo—the departure of American ships engaged in international trade, for example—went to the district court, where confiscations and fines were ordered. Sanford would follow Secretary of the Treasury Gallatin's directives since the secretary was responsible for certifying customs duties.[32]

Two years after repeal, federal attorney Sanford's political career was boosted again by the confidence Republicans placed in him. Elected speaker of the assembly by the Republican majority during the winter session of 1811, on the first ballot, Sanford's brief tenure extended from January 29 until his resignation on February 14 for reasons of health. He may have been best remembered for wearing a cocked hat,[33] with the brims turned up to form two or, perhaps, three points. The gesture acknowledged tradition while creating a personal identity for Sanford in a new Republican world, far from his rural roots on eastern Long Island. He had won by a thirty-one vote margin over his opponent, out of one hundred assemblymen present. In early May, federal attorney Sanford ran for office again. This time he barely defeated the Federalist candidate in the election for senator from the southern legislative district. He gained the seat once held by DeWitt Clinton. His strength came from Suffolk County, especially the Town of Southampton, his birthplace, and from the Town of Jamaica in Queens County.[34] He served a single four-year term as state senator, and with the coming of war faced a mounting caseload as district attorney.

Sanford's nomination for state senator had surprised Clinton's supporters, who assumed his loyalty to their leader, and signaled a divergence in the two politicians' political paths. Unlike Sanford, the reappointed mayor had opposed the embargo, at least during its early stages, and beginning in 1808, Clinton began to advance his own candidacy for president in a challenge to James Madison, Sanford's choice. By the end of May 1812, the fractured Republicans had two candidates for president: Madison and Clinton. With the declaration of war against Great Britain in June, Clinton and his Federalist allies continued to favor a more energetic pursuit of peace, while Sanford, like Governor Tompkins, supported the war.[35] Within a year or two, Sanford, Tompkins, and Martin Van Buren, all of whom had been mentored by Clinton, had split from him.[36]

According to the October 6, 1812 issue of Boston's *Pilot*, the convention of the Republican Committee, having met in New York City on September 9, nominated DeWitt Clinton for president. Two leading state senators did not attend: Nathan Sanford and Morgan Lewis, a former governor and one-time Clinton supporter. The reporter thought the two men beholden to the president, given their "lucrative offices under Mr. Madison." Perhaps, but other factors also distanced Sanford from Clinton:

policy differences and the effectiveness of the political operations to which each belonged. Senator Sanford's political success had become dependent on the backing of the powerful Martling Men who had supported him for elective office in 1808, maybe earlier. In the years ahead, use of the Martling label waned and was replaced with "Tammany Hall," denoting the same Republican faction.[37]

With the close of the state senate's spring session in Albany in April 1812, and continuing for the next three years, Senator Sanford would still spend most of his time in the city. With two children and two servants in 1810, different members of the Sanford household could take advantage of the elegant retail stores and booksellers on Broadway, west of their Pine Street house.[38] They might frequent the bootmakers' and jewelers' workshops to the east, on Pearl Street, built decades before on landfill extended into the East River. In this city neighborhood, Pearl Street held the largest concentration of wholesale firms among America's seaport cities. It was where the Bank of New York had opened in 1784. Merchants purchased goods, such as crockery and hardware from importers, and sold them to shopkeepers. Sanford's housekeeper would arrange for grocery deliveries from markets nearby on Water Street and South Street. Livery stables were plentiful for local transport, and stagecoaches had fixed routes and fares, leaving from Fraunces Tavern on Pearl Street for Albany—the district attorney would no doubt have availed himself of the stage after his election to the state legislature in 1808. It took two to three days in the summer, and an additional day or two in winter.[39] Regular travel by steamboat would have to wait, even though Robert Fulton's *Clermon*t had traveled the 120-mile route up the Hudson River from New York to Albany in 1807.[40]

Sanford's three sessions in the state senate at Albany from 1812 to 1815 averaged about three months annually in length, with a short, or no, fall term and longer spring terms that lasted, roughly, from late January to mid-April. He would serve with Martin Van Buren, the son of a tavern keeper and, briefly, a slaveholder. He owed his senate nomination to DeWitt Clinton, but would soon also break his ties with the mayor. With a Republican majority in the state senate, Van Buren emerged as leader, in support of the war. Concluded one historian, he had "moved carefully and deliberately to rise to the leadership of New York's Democratic Party [by 1828]." Van Buren led the Republicans' Bucktail faction, called Bucktails for the emblem—the tail of a buck—that they wore on their hats to their meetings. He allied his followers with Governor Daniel Tompkins who, like Van Buren, had severed his ties with Clinton.[41] Sanford supported Van

Figure 4.1. *View of Broadway, looking North from Ann Street, New York, as it appeared in 1819*. By Carl Fredrik Akrell after Leonhard Klinckowstrom, 1824. Etching/aquatint, 8 inches x 15 inches. PR058, printmaker file, flat: Akrell; image #76379. Courtesy of the New-York Historical Society.

Buren and stood among the moderate Bucktails who prioritized legislative authority, in contrast to Clinton's emphasis on executive authority.

In 1808 and again in 1811, the Council of Appointment named the state senator a director of the Bank of New York, a bank that had operated since 1784 and been incorporated by the state legislature in 1791. It had favored Federalist interests during the commercial expansion of the 1790s, years that saw the demand for credit and capital skyrocket. The bank participated in what historian John Brooke calls a "politics of development through state-chartered private corporations."[42] The appointing council was composed of Governor Tompkins and four senators, with the assembly electing one senator from each of the state's senatorial districts to the council. Republicans dominated in 1808, and again in 1811.[43]

A few years later, Sanford would broaden his bank board participation. The directors of the Mechanics' Bank of New York "unanimously elected" Sanford to fill a vacancy on its board, according to the January 3, 1815, issue of the *New York Evening Post*. By then a United States senator, Sanford was reelected to the board in April of 1816, 1817, and 1819, according to newspaper reports. Documents show him on the board again in 1822, shortly before he was appointed chancellor of the state.[44] As an investor, Sanford would have benefitted from relationship building on the boards, and he may have favored Republican businessmen in their requests for loans. As evidenced by his personal investing, he also had a genuine interest in finance, stimulated by his years of experience with banks. Like other educated politicians, he knew the phrase "political economy," current for decades before the publication of Adam Smith's *The Wealth of Nations* in 1776. The concept brought together principles dear to the senator and evidenced in his career, such as the pursuit of self-interest, a reverence for private property, and the supremacy of contract.[45]

Entering the last year of his term as state senator in January 1814, Sanford sought a seat on the politically powerful Council of Appointment but lost a close election in the assembly.[46] Meanwhile, in the state legislature, the war had continued to push difficult issues to the fore. Among them was the growing inability of the states to recruit soldiers. That fall, legislators authorized the organization of two regiments of blacks. Democratic-Republican Jabez D. Hammond, a lawyer, state senator (1817–1821), and chronicler of New York's political history, described the legislation: it would be effective for three years, and slaves could enlist with their masters' consent; if a slave received an honorable discharge, the soldier was promised manumission (freedom).[47] Sanford and two other Republicans in the senate opposed the bill, although they knew that black sailors had been serving effectively during the war on naval vessels on the Great Lakes. New York's *Commercial Advertiser* noted that "Martin Van Buren reported the bill," but there was no explanation for the opposition from the three other Republicans. Sanford may have considered the bill unnecessary given the stalemate in the war. Perhaps he suspected that slaveholders wouldn't follow through on their commitment to manumission, leading to unrest, even though most of the recruits would have been free blacks. Experienced with guns himself, he may have feared repercussions from having armed black men in the state militia.

Implying hypocrisy by another Republican legislator, Hammond noted that Colonel Samuel Young supported the legislation in October 1814, but at the constitutional convention of 1821, he adamantly opposed black male suffrage without a freehold requirement.[48] The Council of Revision, however, where James Kent sat as the newly appointed chancellor, approved the bill. Kent, the newspaper article continued, "had only one objection to the bill. He thought the negroes should elect their own officers, which by the law were to be white men. . . ."[49] Sanford and Kent stood on opposite sides of the legislation. They would clash again, at the constitutional convention in 1821, over the issue of property qualifications for the suffrage. There, both men would explain their views at greater length.

Martin Van Buren had proven to be a formidable colleague in the state senate. In December 1814, the federal attorney discussed the start of the next term of the legislature with him in a return letter he addressed to "My Dear Friend." Sanford's confidential style, reflecting a close relationship, came with the scent of patronage. As he alluded to the "other subject" they needed to discuss, he mentioned that he had hoped to confer with Van Buren about a "friend" who desired a public office. Sanford may have also been thinking about his new job just as Van Buren was about to change his, prompting the federal attorney to comment on his younger friend's "rapid advance." In early February 1815, the legislature elected Sanford to the United States Senate in a vote of eighty-nine to forty, with Van Buren's support. At about the same time, Governor Tompkins appointed Van Buren state attorney general.[50]

Chapter 5

Wealth and Charges of Corruption, 1800–1820

The return of relative peace made clear that the economy had changed, particularly in the northeast of the United States. The war that ended in 1815 had enriched many large merchants and other investors who were buoyed by an infrastructure of new banks and insurance companies organized to support commerce. Moreover, the Embargo of 1807 and other laws that had served to restrict British imports, coupled with the taking of American merchant vessels on the high seas, had motivated certain investors to shift some of their capital from overseas shipping to internal trade and small-scale manufacturing on American soil. By the 1820s, with expanding markets in the west and the south, New York City was the center of a "national market in ready-made clothes" and other goods. Investments in newly valuable urban real estate became profitable. During the new nation's first two decades of the nineteenth century, its agricultural economy had been transformed into a commerce-driven powerhouse stimulated by a citizen preoccupation with moneymaking.[1]

Nathan Sanford thrived in this environment of self-confidence and individual enterprise. Already possessed of a family inheritance that provided rental income, and a private law practice, Sanford augmented his income when he accepted the appointment as federal attorney. Together with his other sources, the addition of the government income, at age twenty-six, would place him near the top tier of the middling economic groupings in the population. According to Thomas Sandford's 1785 will, Sanford had inherited all of the land and buildings his father had owned in the towns of Southampton and East Hampton. Although the properties were not specified, tax assessment rolls for the Town of Southampton show that for the years 1800, 1801, and 1802, the assessed values of Sanford's farmhouse and land were, respectively, $2,394, $2,000, and $2,000. In 1803 and 1805, the property was listed under two names, Sanford and farmer Silas White Jr.; the assessed value for both years was $2,800, an appreciation of 40 percent. In the receipt book that he kept from 1802 to 1835, the most detailed record of his paths to wealth, Sanford noted on October 8, 1802, that he had let his farm to White for three years for an annual rent of $100.[2]

The federal attorney also found time and ways to add to his Long Island holdings. In April 1804, the Southampton town records showed that he purchased about two-thirds of an acre of land that bordered his farm in Bridgehampton. He paid eleven pounds sterling, six shillings for the property. Sanford also appears to have inherited Montauk commonage from his father, which would have been the land in the Town of East Hampton referenced in Thomas's will. On October 8, 1807, the compulsive record-keeper noted in his receipt book that he had received thirty dollars and forty-five cents from Timothy Halsey Jr. for a year's rent. Halsey, a Bridgehampton farmer, would drive his cattle to Montauk in the spring to graze, a distance of about thirty miles, and have them returned in the fall.[3] The following year, Sanford was the likely drafter of a bill that David Hedges, his stepfather and a member of the state assembly in 1808, shepherded into law. It authorized the proprietors of Montauk, who oversaw the seasonal migration of the cattle drives to the grasslands, to organize into a corporation. The law changed how the owners of the common land were represented in the governance over the land and the drives. Instead of the traditional single vote for each shareholder, the corporation's new law designated one vote for each proprietor and one vote for each one-eighth of a share owned by all shareholders. No single investor could cast more than eight votes.[4] On balance, the law favored the landed elite, an outcome consistent with Sanford's interpretation of the 1703 lease between Southampton's town trustees and proprietors, and the Shinnecocks, two years earlier. The town court's ruling had denied lease participation to two tribal leaders of mixed ancestry.

On three occasions, Sanford bought additional half shares in the Montauk land, "now undivided and held in common among the owners," according to the deeds. In 1808, 1817, and again in 1819, his purchases provided four votes for each half share. Merchant Jeremiah Miller, a veteran of the War of 1812, and his wife Phebe sold Sanford the shares. A close relative, the attorney may have boarded in the Miller household while he studied at Clinton Academy as a youngster. Perhaps the Millers sold because they needed the money: Sanford paid $1,700, $1,350, and $1,350, respectively, for each of the half shares.[5] Miller also acted as a middleman: Sanford noted in his receipt book on June 16, 1809, that he had received his annual rent, twenty dollars, from Miller, "on account of" Timothy Halsey Jr. Given his new purchases, his total rent received on May 17, 1819, for fewer than six months was $293.53—a solid return on his investment.

In 1815, Sanford extended his real estate holdings in the city beyond his home and office on Pine Street by purchasing property on the west side of Manhattan. A deed dated July 12 between the Rector, Wardens, and Vestrymen of Grace Church transferred five lots to Nathan Sanford. The lots, including a house, faced the Hudson River and backed up to Washington Street in the eighth ward. James Kent, then chancellor of the state, had ordered the "religious corporation" to sell the foreclosed property; it appears that the church had held a mortgage from an earlier sale, and the mortgagee's payments had lapsed. Sanford paid $8,850 for the "house and five lots of land." As noted in his receipt book on June 27, 1820, he received $125 in rent for the latest six-month period.[6] By then, Sanford had bought additional rural properties.

Throughout his political career, Sanford kept returning to activities that reminded him of his rural roots. On September 22, 1817, he summarized the operations of the farm he had purchased in Flushing, Long Island, in his receipt book; he had settled the accounts for "products and profits" with tenant farmer William Smith. Only seventy bushels of oats remained "on hand," unsold. The profitability of the farm was sustained during the economic downturn of the early 1820s. In 1824, Smith gave his landlord a note for a balance due of $1,072.24. Sanford would own the Flushing farm at his time of death.

In the city, Sanford was taxed on personal property, as well as real estate; in 1815, his material possessions were assessed at $60,000. They included, for example, numerous pieces of silver brought to his first marriage in 1801 by Eliza Van Horne and listed, much later, in his estate inventory. The sterling would have been included in the tax assessment, and among the items were nearly three dozen spoons inscribed "E.V.H.," a dozen unmarked spoons, and eight larger pieces, including a coffee pot. In 1820 and 1822, the total assessment was dropped to $40,000, a far lower valuation from just a few years before.[7] It reflected a reduction in the value of luxury possessions that echoed among the economic repercussions of the speculative bubble that followed the War of 1812 and evolved into the shortly thereafter named Panic of 1819.

The tough times were reflected in the assessments for his long-held city properties as well. In 1820, the city tax list documented a house at 27 Pine Street assessed at $5,000 and an office at 29 Pine Street assessed for $3,000: two years later the value of the house had dropped to $4,000 and the office to $2,500. Sanford's building at 25 Pine, purchased in 1800, was most likely rented in 1820. In 1826, all three Pine Street properties were rented, and Sanford's name does not appear on the tax assessment roll.[8] Three years before, Sanford had moved his family to Albany. Based on the tax valuations of his real property in the city and Bridgehampton, and on the prices paid for the Montauk shares and the lots from Grace Church, Sanford's real estate by 1820 was worth in the range of $27,000 to $30,000. The estimate does not include the farm in Flushing. With the addition of personal property of $40,000, at age forty-three, this portion of his estate would have reached at least $70,000.

In addition to his federal attorney's fees and his rural and urban rents, Sanford derived income from his private law practice. Near the close of the war in 1814, he would engage Abraham T. Rose as a law clerk, probably not his first. Young Rose, a recent Yale graduate and nephew of General Abraham Rose, the defender of Sag Harbor during the War of 1812, remained in Sanford's office through 1817 and, like his mentor, descended from one of Bridgehampton's modestly wealthy proprietor families.[9] Rose may have boarded in Sanford's household. The private law practice prospered from the start. Soon to be a counselor at law and a notary, Sanford worked from his office on Pine Street, beginning in 1800, and carefully noted payments for his services in his receipt book. On August 3, 1802, he informed a client that his charge for arguing a claim made to a New York Insurance Company would be $20, roughly $300 today. A few months later, he received payment of $96 for his defense of William Nicolls, a large landowner on Long Island. During 1803 and '04, payments included $2 for preparing four affidavits, $4 for assignments, $8 for his defense in a suit that went to court, and $10 for drawing up a "bond and mortgage." Sanford understood well how to value consulting services: on one occasion, he charged $5 for "several consultations." In 1806 and '07, a single deed cost $3, while "two deeds and advice" brought $15. On July 14, 1808, he received $100, a final payment for his "services as Counsel" for the Trustees of the Town of Huntington, Long Island, in their appeal to the court of errors (a state court that reviewed decisions made in a lower court).[10] That fall, voters elected the federal attorney to the state assembly, the victory that launched his political career. He served in the state legislature until 1815.

Besides his domestic needs, Sanford's earnings made possible investments in banks, insurance companies, and additional properties. A sampling of his receipts in the receipt book for the years 1808 to 1815 indicates that the state legislator recorded relatively fewer payments for his legal services and courtroom activities than in earlier years, and many more notations that record the receipt of dividends. Sanford would gain substantial knowledge about investment opportunities from his colleagues while participating in legislative debates that dealt with applications for bank charters. They were required because banks were a form of joint-stock company,[11] involving a grant of authority from the state to fulfill certain purposes. The period also bracketed his first appointment to the board of the Bank of New York by state Republicans and his election in 1815 to his first term as director of the Mechanics' Bank of New York.

Sanford became an avid investor in securities as early as 1802, receiving dividend and interest payments from 1803 through the early 1820s. He saw opportunity when business owners used capital borrowed from commercial banks and insurance companies to grow their businesses—the astute Sanford would follow them and invest. In all, it appears that he invested in ten insurance companies and nine banks over a period of roughly two decades. With the exception of the Mutual Insurance Company, his investments in insurance, a business he would have understood well given his experience at the prize court, were short-lived.

According to his receipt book, Sanford collected fairly consistent dividends over a number of years from three banks: the Manhattan Company, the Merchants' Bank, and the Mechanics' Bank. For all of his investments in financial institutions, dividends ranged from $45 to $472.50, with $225 the most often paid. They were most frequently noted as received after six months, especially those from the insurance companies. Sanford's heyday for stock returns appears to have been unaffected by the Panic of 1819. His first bank stock purchase took place in late 1802, for shares in the Manhattan Company; he received his first dividend on February 19, 1803, for forty-five dollars. The state legislature had granted the bank a charter in 1799, guided by the manipulations of Republican assemblyman Aaron Burr. Sanford may have been encouraged to invest by DeWitt Clinton, the federal senator who had recommended the young lawyer for a position as commissioner of bankruptcy in 1802. Clinton would join the bank's board when he became mayor. The more recently organized Merchants' Bank was Sanford's second venture into bank securities. A group of Federalist investors had launched the bank in April 1803 with articles of association while they sought a state charter. In the following year, newspapers saw corruption: they reported accusations that backers of the bank had bought votes in the state legislature to ensure the charter grant. In time, the charter bill was passed, and the bank operated independently for nearly a century.[12] My sampling of the receipt book entries from 1806 to 1820 indicates that the Merchants' Bank paid Sanford a steady stream of dividends, usually $225, every six months.

A comparison of aspects of the finances of the older John Quincy Adams, like Sanford a commissioner of bankruptcy early in the Jefferson administration, indicates that each politician made comparable investment decisions, although on different scales. Both men became lawyers, and by 1801 they understood the fee basis of income from certain federal offices. By 1809, the diplomat and former United States senator from Massachusetts had garnered income from his law practice, heavily mortgaged real estate investments, and stocks. As minister to Great Britain in 1815, Adams would earn a salary of $9,000 a year and $25,000 when he became president in 1824. Nonetheless, according to one biographer, he stretched to support his family and was always in debt.[13] While Adams, from a nationally known family, became a more prominent statesman, Sanford may have achieved greater wealth—initially made possible by his appointive federal office. Sanford had also prospered as a lawyer, used his inheritance wisely, and invested profitably in the growth industries of banking, insurance, and real estate.

Given his range of activities by 1808, Sanford could not avoid becoming a target of the financial interest politics swirling around the legislature, where bank charters were granted and holding multiple offices was denounced. Questions were raised publicly about the Tammany-connected lawyer-politician and his wealth after his death in 1838. His level of income drew numerous attacks from commentators who agreed that his federal office had become lucrative beyond its base sources of income. Although it was not published at the time, Federalist Kent, Sanford's chastiser on many fronts, delivered a blistering critique. He charged that as federal attorney, Sanford "made a fortune . . . by his multiplied & vexatious Prosecutions during the Embargo times. His Charges were enormous. . . ."[14]

In a veiled rebuke of Sanford for his alleged financial abuse of office, Jabez Hammond described in the 1840s how Tammany Hall had backed the lawyer-politician for the state senate in 1811. Describing him as a "prudent man," Hammond also maintained that Sanford's federal office "produced him annually . . . more than thirty thousand dollars."[15] The figure was comparable to Captain Stephen Decatur's prize award for the capture of the *Macedonian* in 1812, but the accusation against Sanford referred to an annual income and, if true, would involve much more accumulated income. In a diary entry on February 23, 1841, the wealthy

New York merchant and Federalist Philip Hone complained that the House of Representatives had provided high "salaries and "emoluments" to the Republicans, the party in power for forty years. Hone charged that "Nathan Sanford made $100,000 a year" as district attorney. He also noted that Congress had recently reduced the "fees of the district attorney for the southern district" to $6,000. Clearly, he was implying that fees had reached higher annual totals in earlier years—during Sanford's tenure, for example. Kent even claimed that Sanford "was deemed worth $300,000." Years later, journalists picked up the charges. In the first edition of *The History of Tammany Hall*, his book published in the late nineteenth century, journalist Gustavus Myers described Sanford as "credited with making his office . . . yield as high as $30,000 a year." An article in the November 7, 1909, issue of *The Washington Herald* repeated the story. A booklet printed in 1989 for the bicentennial celebration of the office of federal attorney stated that Sanford "reportedly received $100,000 annually in fees from the Office."[16]

Given the lack of data for a comparative analysis with Sanford's of the fees and other court payments received by federal attorneys in other states, it seems reasonable to conclude that most of his increased income resulted from the growth in his caseload of prosecutions. His fees were an administrative response to turbulent times: the attorney's maritime suits had exploded in number even before the war, due to violations of the Embargo Act of 1807 and because the enforcement of customs laws had been tightened. With the quadrupling of the population of New York State between 1790 and 1820,[17] and significant expansion in the number of settlers into the northern and western parts of the state, even more work, such as bankruptcy cases, came to the district court. With the war, forfeitures at sea adjudicated in the prize court mounted further. Congress was finally moved to address the increased volume; in 1812, it created a second district court in the state. The Northern District became operational in 1815. The new district, like the southern district court, used the fee system based on services rendered in each case prosecuted. The system had a long life, lasting until 1896, when it was replaced by salaries for the federal attorneys, ranging from $2,500 to $5,000. Until 1953, attorneys were allowed to retain their private law practices.[18]

While criticism of abuse of his public office for personal gain appears to have surfaced widely only after Sanford's death, accusations of corruption for holding multiple offices were voiced as early as 1808, the year he entered state politics. A reporter for the Federalist-leaning *New-York Herald*, having just read an article about a recent meeting of the General

Committee of Republican Young Men, wrote in his column on April 27, 1808, that leaders of the ward meetings "egg the people on against the Federalists, whom they modestly call *gnawing vipers*." In the tradition of the partisan rhetoric at the time, the reporter adopted a term of derision, "democrats," and offered his own list of "*Gnawing Vipers*" among the Republicans. The list started with DeWitt Clinton, head of the "democratic Party," a state senator, and mayor of New York, with earnings of "nearly 15,000 dollars a year." Next the reporter listed Judge Tallmadge, the chair of the fifth ward's "democratic meeting," who earned a "good fat salary" as judge of the district court. Nathan Sanford appeared sixth on the list.[19] Besides the charges of financial corruption, Sanford drew rebuke from the reporter for seeking an assembly seat while he held a federal office, for having "never repented of being an apostate from federalism," and for belonging to the "black Cockade gentry," the label often applied to Federalists. According to the article, Sanford and other "democrats" not only enriched themselves from government appointments and elective offices, they benefitted from President Jefferson's embargo: "All these Officers are EMBARGO MEN, and well they may be, for not a soul of them feels it." "Gentlemen" held onto their offices, while many sailors and mechanics lost their jobs when vessels remained in their slips.[20]

Three years later, Sanford encountered even broader attacks, not from a Federalist newspaper but from one in the DeWitt Clinton camp. The March 21, 1811, issue of the *Public Advertiser*, a newspaper controlled by the anti-Clinton Tammany Republicans, reported that the Republican General Meeting held at A.B. Martling's Long-Room had nominated Nathan Sanford for state senator to replace Clinton. The decision drew opprobrium from the *New York Columbian*, a paper loyal to Clinton. In an article on April 3, the paper pointed out that Sanford, like Clinton, had benefitted from accumulating offices. In a subsequent issue, using the pseudonym Columella, a reporter argued that the "district attorney for the United States (at present the most lucrative office in the gift of the general government) [is a] member, and at the same time speaker of the assembly of this date!!!" Columella continued, informing readers that Sanford had also been proposed for mayor, and if that had occurred, the legislator would have

> united in his person, legislative, judicial, and executive authority, a combination of power characterizing tyranny itself. And at this very moment, this same Mr. Sanford, who is district

> attorney of the United States, an office requiring uninterrupted attention, is recommended for our suffrages, as senator from this district!![21]

While Sanford kept his political ambitions intact during this period of scathing criticism in early 1811, he endured crises in his family life, and with his health. His wife Eliza had recently died from complications related to childbirth.[22] According to the January 8 issue of the *New York Columbian*, Sanford, now a widower with three children, led the funeral procession for Eliza from his house at 25 Pine Street. About three weeks later, as speaker of the assembly in Albany, he absented himself from the session in mid-February because of his reoccurring lung disorder. The disease had caused him to abbreviate his presentation during the Smith-Ogden trial in 1806 and to decline the navy's invitation to serve on a Court of Inquiry soon after. It did not cause him to curtail other political pursuits, however. In May, he won election to the state senate. Fewer than four years later, the same senate chose "Nathan Sanford, an acute and vigorous advocate," according to one early twentieth-century historian, [23] to represent New York in the Senate of the United States. At that point, Sanford resigned from his post as federal attorney.

Among his generation of well-educated professionals from rural backgrounds in the early Republic, Sanford stood out, becoming a lawyer-politician and a successful investor in traditional as well as new forms of wealth. Largely for this, he raised the ire of some politicians, voters, and reporters who viewed holding two offices as expressions of personal gain and the accumulation of political power. For the times, it was a common practice. Combined with growing fees boosted by the circumstances of his federal office, and not from a broad manipulation of that office, Sanford was made a target of derision. Yet, by intellect, his classical and legal education, and his experience in the practice of bankruptcy, property, and admiralty law, Sanford was equipped to fulfill a national role, joining those in the Senate who performed the broadest legislative duties in the land.

Chapter 6

United States Senator and the Politics of Commerce, 1815–1821

While in the United States Senate, Nathan Sanford became adept at reporting petitions and appeals from his constituents, as well as the bills that asked the government for various kinds of relief. In early January 1820, painter John Trumbull, now in New York following his stay in Europe, was tracking down a payment he expected to receive for having executed the third of four large paintings Congress had commissioned from him in 1817. The works, on subjects from the American Revolution, were to decorate the walls of the rebuilt Capitol, which had been severely damaged by the British occupation forces in 1814. Trumbull addressed his letter to Sanford, assuming his senator could solve the payment problem since he chaired the Senate's finance committee. As a young man, Trumbull had dedicated himself to raising the status of painting above the arena of portraiture; he sought to paint works capable of earning viewers' respect and professionalizing his field. Trumbull came to realize that subjects based on the American Revolution would provide appropriate themes. In 1789, for example, he informed his friend Thomas Jefferson of his artistic intent: he wanted, the artist wrote, "to diffuse the knowledge and preserve the Memory of the noblest series of Actions which have ever dignified the History of Man. . . ."[1] With the government's commission, Trumbull had traveled far in achieving his goal.

Sanford had recently returned to Washington when he answered Trumbull's inquiry about the appropriation for the painting, *The Surrender of Lord Cornwallis at Yorktown.* In his letter, the senator explained that he had contacted Secretary of State John Quincy Adams and learned that "no provision for its expense had been made. . . ." Sanford assured Trumbull that he would "make my efforts to obtain the appropriation," even though he held "apprehensions." In his response to the senator a few days later Trumbull, somewhat defensively, described his work habits and his need for money; he outlined his contract with the secretary of state; and he wrote of himself: "I fulfil my engagement by working indefatigably, & with my best Skill." He reminded Sanford that the price was $6,000 for each painting, but he couldn't deliver the Cornwallis work until summer. He also complained that "it will be hard to wait for my stipulated reward until another Session of Congress." In closing, the patriotic and flamboyant Trumbull declared that he would "rely entirely for the result upon that regard for Justice, & the public Faith which I trust will always control the government of my Country." Fortunately for the painter, Sanford's skepticism about an appropriation for the payment during the spring was unfounded. In April, Congress approved it.[2]

Sanford grew to become an effective senator. He enjoyed advantages from the strength of New York's Republicans, but he mostly left behind

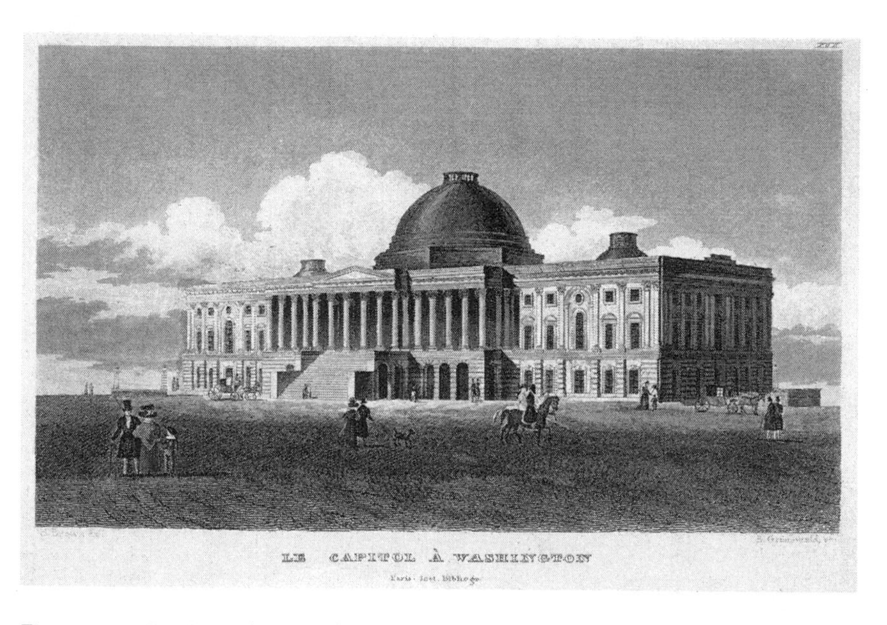

Figure 6.1. *Le Capitol à Washington*, where Nathan Sanford attended sessions in the Senate wing after 1819. By Eoban Grünewald after H. Brown, circa 1830. Catalog no. 38.00042. Courtesy of the U.S. Senate Collection.

their factional disputes. The opportunity to serve in the Senate would help him gain greater autonomy as a leader. In February 1815, he soundly defeated his lead opponent in the state legislature, Federalist assemblyman James Emott. Buoyed by the victories of Republicans in state elections the previous April, his candidacy also benefited from the factional politics of the times. Governor Tompkins, for example, had placed the prestige he had gained from his support for President Madison's national war effort behind Sanford, a move that also enhanced the governor's position among the state's Republican factions for a presidential bid in 1816.[3] Sanford entered the Senate on March 4, and for the first time in seven years he held only one government office. His term bridged two presidencies: the last two years of the Madison administration and the first two years of President James Monroe's term, from March 1817 to March 1821. On the national level, Sanford was a Democratic-Republican who had favored the declaration of war in 1812. His votes in the Senate in the late 1810s often reflected a republicanism that had shifted away from that of many Jeffersonians who were skeptical about moves toward a national currency and saw agriculture as the prime source of the nation's wealth.[4] Sanford had come to accept the importance of commerce and a national bank in developing the country (a conviction that influenced how he invested his money). In the Senate, he gained respect for how he conceptualized issues, framing what he called "the merits of the question" and contrasting "opinions" while listing the "reasons" behind each of them. He insisted on marshalling facts, especially numbers, or statistics as they were usually called, and then proposing what he considered "sound policy."[5]

Sanford backed many of the directives in the annual message President Madison had sent to Congress in 1815, late in his second term. They called for military pensions, a standing army of ten thousand men, and a viable navy. The president asked Congress to pay attention to economic issues. He urged the reconstitution of a national bank. It would sell government securities in order to raise funds for its operations, provide for a national currency, and extend credit, helping to quench Americans' thirst for loans in a growing economy and, thereby, avoiding the fiscal disasters that had plagued the conduct of the recent war. He asked for passage of a protective tariff that would continue to provide revenue, help the manufacturing sector, and enhance the Republic's security by reducing the country's dependence on foreign suppliers. The president also suggested ideas to spur economic development by asking for improvements in transportation infrastructure and efforts to boost commerce and manufactures, all aimed to protect America's independence in a postwar world.[6] While he engaged in furthering the president's major proposals, Sanford also took stands on administrative reforms. He pursued ways to improve the "present system" of collecting import duties, the primary source of revenue for the federal government.[7] Given his collaborative work with the customs system when federal attorney, he understood the need. He proposed other improvements in public administration: one resolution even required the Department of State to publish the documents created at the constitutional convention in 1788,[8] and Sanford often moved to require the immediate printing of documents for the senators' use.[9] In another proposal to ensure the recording and availability of public information, Sanford submitted a bill that would require the attorney general to compile a report for the Senate that detailed the cases pending in the United States Supreme Court—and in the federal district and circuit courts.[10] A prolific keeper of personal account books, Sanford brought the same mindset to his insistence on accurate and timely public record keeping.

In his second year in the Senate, Sanford turned to the president's priorities, engaging early in the process that led to a charter for a new national bank. The First Bank of the United States had been established in 1791, in part to address the country's perennial shortage of specie, that is, gold and silver coins. The bank was largely a result of Secretary of the Treasury Hamilton's perseverance and persuasive skill: it would hold the federal government's deposits and issue banknotes redeemable for specie. Backers of the proposal assumed that noteholders would constantly reassess the value of their notes in their financial transactions and exchange them for coins—hard currency—when their value began to fall; in response, the national bank would reduce the number of banknotes it issued, restoring the notes' value and forestalling a rise in inflation. The balancing and rebalancing mostly worked.[11] In 1811, however, a bill to re-charter the bank failed in a close vote in Congress, leading to changes in the country's financial patterns. During the next five years, states chartered 175 banks, adding substantially to the number of existing banks. Since the federal government issued only coins, the state-chartered banks printed their own money. It was backed with specie, without a central bank threatening to suspend the convertibility of the paper. Lending was the moneymaking enterprise of these state-chartered banks. As one historian has observed, the banks broadened their clientele: they serviced the needs of "mechanics and farmers as well as governments and merchants" with easy-to-get loans in the form of banknotes, or credit, with long repayment terms.[12]

In late March 1816, the Senate began to address legislation proposed to reconstitute a national bank. Sanford possessed expertise for these debates. He understood the banking system of depositors and borrowers of capital, and of specie and paper currency. He was a former director of the Bank of New York, a bank that favored lending to state-chartered private corporations; in the prewar years it had been dominated by fellow Republicans. While in the Senate, he was also serving on the board of the Mechanics' Bank of New York. These strong state banks gave Sanford a financial education that he used to full advantage during discussions of particular amendments to the bill that called for the incorporation of a central bank. The debates over amendments provide insight into Sanford's thinking as a legislator eager to discipline the financial markets. The senator's positions on numerous banking issues, however, placed him in seeming opposition to the president. The bill that became "An act to incorporate the subscribers to the bank of the United States" had passed in the House of Representatives in mid-March. It chartered the bank with a capital of $35 million: one-fifth of the bank's stock would be purchased by the federal government and the remainder by the public. Of the twenty-five-member bank board, five would be appointed by the president to represent the government's investment.

In the Senate debate over an early amendment, Sanford maintained that the proposed bank was "intended to be a specie bank" and that "every proposition tending more certainly to make it more so, was worthy of favorable consideration." He further argued that the specie requirement in the bill for the initial capitalization of the bank should be raised: "Without amendments to regulate the paper issues of the bank, this would be a mere paper bank, like those which already exist." Sanford's view to highly restrain the central bank's ability to issue its own paper currency—the government issued only coins—was not widely shared and the amendment was withdrawn by its sponsor. During the next meeting of the Senate, Sanford again made a bid to force a more restrictive posture onto the bank's lending habits by supporting an amendment, later defeated, that would require the corporation to pay its bills and notes on demand; in most circumstances, that meant with specie.[13] A few days later, Sanford voted to postpone the bank bill until December and found himself again on the losing side. When the vote was called, he was among only six senators who favored the amendment to postpone, while twenty-nine opposed it. The next day, Sanford again sought to curb the authority of the bank: the amendment offered would have given Congress the right to "abolish the corporation" if it refused to honor its bills and notes in gold and silver within a specified timeframe. If the deadline passed, Congress could decide whether the bank's actions were "injurious to the United States," and it could dissolve the bank. The amendment lost.[14]

When he supported the amendment that required the redemption of bills and notes with specie, Sanford was also concerned about the proliferation of banks and their inflated notes. Additionally, his skepticism about the incorporation led him to take positions to protect the proposed central bank from overextending lending activities that could risk the bank's collapse. When Nicholas Biddle became bank president in 1823, he saw the same risks and took action to make the central bank return the excessive number of paper notes taken in from state banks for redemption in specie, as a way of limiting the smaller banks' prolific loan-making and reducing the possibility of inflation.[15] On April 3, after the amended bill for incorporation was read for a third time, Sanford, like Federalist Rufus King, the other senator from New York, voted against it. They were among twelve senators to reject the bill, while twenty-two favored it. Sanford had plenty of company in his region's tally. Although a majority of congressmen from New York State favored the bank, a majority of the combined votes in the House and Senate from New England and the four middle states were cast against incorporation. Support for the bank came primarily from southern and western states, where farmers saw it as one more source of credit. A few days after the Senate vote, President Madison signed the legislation for the Second Bank of the United States, as it came to be called.[16]

During the following three regular sessions of Congress, the Senate's leadership continued to recognize Sanford's knowledge of banking. At the start of the Sixteenth Congress in 1819, he was appointed to the Committee on Finance, a committee that in earlier Congresses was often called the "committee on financial and an [*sic*] uniform national currency,"[17] a phrase that conveyed a goal of the previous administration. Sanford was soon chair and served on the finance committee until the end of his term in the Senate.[18] In late 1819, the chairman reported an amendment to the 1816 bank bill that addressed administrative issues at the bank and punishments assigned to crimes committed by bank officers and other employees. It responded to a request from President Monroe and the directors of the Second Bank to gain legal authority to relieve the president and the cashier of the bank of the time-consuming tasks of signing and countersigning the bank's bills and notes. The draft amendment proposed that the work be done by "an Agent and a Register" appointed by the bank's directors. In a lengthy closing paragraph, the bank's officers and employees were warned to maintain the integrity of the bank by avoiding fraudulent activities. Applicable penalties were outlined: imprisonment for up to three years and "standing in a pillory, not more than three times, in open day, in some public place. . . ." The bill that passed the Senate in February 1821 dropped the punishment of standing in a pillory.[19]

Establishing the Second Bank of the United States was part of a trend toward a greater acknowledgment of the infrastructure needs of economic development and moneymaking in the postwar Republic. Over the next few years, while agriculture continued to employ the vast majority of the population and international trade began to rebound, internal commerce expanded, too, especially in the North. Exchanges among traders and shopkeepers came to be understood as wealth-creating, where "not only both parties always gained but the society did as well."[20] In representing the interests of New York State and the nation, Sanford paid attention to these affairs, and gained respect for it. He served on the Committee on Commerce and Manufactures during each session of the Fifteenth and Sixteenth Congresses, from December 1817 to March 1821, and was chair until the last congressional session, when he led only the finance committee.[21]

With peacetime, the country's growing commercialization led to increased demands for new or repaired roads, canals, and bridges. Even before his committee appointments, Sanford had often presented appeals concerning transportation to the Senate on behalf of individual constituents and interest groups. Early in 1817, he read a petition, or memorial, from New York State's canal commissioners, "praying the aid of Congress in the construction of canals and locks, between the navigable waters of Hudson river and Lake Erie. . . ." The request for federal funding was referred to a committee and, like previous attempts to get public money for what became the Erie Canal project, it failed. Five years before, in a bill signed by Governor Tompkins, the state legislature had authorized canal commissioners to borrow funds to provide for planning the canal—that authorization was repealed in 1814, when the war was going badly. After the defeat of the appeal to Congress, the state legislature reversed itself and, in April 1817, approved the infusion of capital that allowed construction of the Erie Canal to begin.[22]

Sanford would have known the positions taken by friends and former colleagues who had sought political advantage by supporting this significant internal improvement. His early mentor and a canal commissioner, DeWitt Clinton, "made the canal his vehicle for building a statewide coalition of Federalists and entrepreneurial Republicans," according to one historian. Clinton had hoped that politicians would unite in support of a canal connecting New York City with the Northwest. Daniel Tompkins, the canal supporter who had favored Sanford for the United States Senate seat and was elected vice president in the fall of 1816, lent his initial prestige in that office to the canal; and in the spring of 1817, Sanford's friend, Martin Van Buren, seeing the project's popularity, moved away from his negative position on the canal in a quest to enhance his political power statewide.[23] Within this context, Senator Sanford concluded that New York State was capable of funding the Erie Canal on its own and that state leaders possessed the commitment to build it. Philosophically, he favored reliance on state authority to plan and fund internal improvement projects that would stimulate economic expansion.

Sanford, who had grown up on a farm, believed that advances in agriculture were as necessary as those in manufacturing and trade to boost the economy. During the postwar years, many farmers began to benefit from canals and road improvements that lowered transportation costs. As a result, they became more market-oriented and purchased new farm implements, such as improved iron plows and scythes, to boost their productivity.[24] In 1819, just as the country's credit crisis unfolded, Sanford had an opportunity to share his enthusiasm for agriculture with Major General Jacob Brown, the commander of the army's northern divisions and hero of the War of 1812 in the Great Lakes region of New York. The major general had sent him a copy of his address to the Agricultural Society of Jefferson County in Watertown, New York. After thanking him for the essay, Sanford wrote: "The present time is distinguished by many noble efforts to improve the condition of our country. These attempts are all good: but among them, I regard the effort which is now made to improve our agriculture, as the greatest and the best. It is an exertion, which must produce great benefits unmixed with any evil or doubtful consequence to our country."[25] As Sanford makes clear, he saw a cultural value in rural life in addition to an economic benefit. Americans had long argued that the independent farmer was the foundation of republicanism. In his letter, the senator pointed to a moral worth in agricultural pursuits—as well as the internal improvements so important for their success.

During the same Fourteenth Congress when he reported on the memorial that requested help in funding the proposed canal, Sanford received multiple petitions appealing for the imposition of protective tariffs on specific goods and industries. After the Revolutionary War, tariff debates had centered on the usefulness of interstate tariffs and federal tariffs to protect small manufacturers from foreign competition. When the Constitution forbade the imposition of tariffs by the individual states, the debate shifted to deciding which federal tariffs to use to fund the central government. Manufacturers' preference for protective tariffs meant that consumers would pay higher prices for specific foreign goods; Secretary Hamilton's proposed revenue tariffs, levied on nearly all imports, could utilize a lower rate and still generate substantial funds for the government. Congress had already passed revenue tariffs, which averaged the relatively low rate of 8 percent.[26] As a former federal attorney responsible for customs violations, Sanford would have worked closely with the New York City customs collector when he brought cases against suspected violators into the district court—in so doing, he would become deeply knowledgeable about tariffs. In response to President Madison's request, Congress raised import duties in April 1816. With some qualifications, the bill stipulated that only goods that could not be produced domestically would escape the tariff. Sanford voted against amendments that sought reductions in duties. For example, he voted with the majority in rejecting a bid to reduce the duty on woolen manufactures from the 25 percent proposed in the bill, to 20 percent. He also opposed the request to reduce the duty on salt. The bill that passed Congress, known as the Tariff of 1816, set import duties on targeted goods at 25 percent, on average. The legislation served to help insulate new factories in the Northeast and mid-Atlantic regions from foreign competition but often left consumers with higher prices.[27]

In early May 1816, after the close of the first session of the Fourteenth Congress, the senator left Washington to begin the 225-mile journey home. He would travel by stagecoach on rutted roads, passing through Baltimore and on to Philadelphia. There, he may have taken the stage and steamboat route to lower Manhattan, a thirteen-hour trip. At home, he found his wife, Mary Esther. Since their marriage in 1813,[28] she had raised their daughter and three stepchildren largely on her own. Mary Esther had managed the servants and household money matters as well. Now she was ready to give birth to their second child, Henry.

But complications following the delivery led to her death on May 19, leaving Sanford to grieve for a wife for the second time in five years. Three days later, the *New-York Herald* reported that he led the funeral procession for Mary Esther with "friends and acquaintances . . . from his house at 27 Pine Street."[29] No Sanford family presence was noted—perhaps they lived too far away. Within six months, the senator would return to Washington,[30] again separating his private from his public life.

The election of James Monroe in the fall of 1816 signaled a continuation of Madison's policy of protection toward domestic industries, a policy that the senator had supported throughout his term. During the fifteen years that followed the end of the War of 1812, Congress received more petitions that addressed the tariff than any other topic. No wonder, in appreciating the need for better quantitative information upon which to base decisions concerning the economy, Sanford would request the printing of 500 copies of Adam Seybert's *Statistical Annals of the United States, 1789–1818* for use by members of the government and other purchasers. And, again representing the Committee of Commerce and Manufactures, he supported a bill to authorize the purchase of Representative Timothy Pitkin's *Commercial Statistics*.[31] Seybert was a well-known physician and scientist who had begun to collect statistical data (really, numerical data in today's terms) after his election to the House in 1809. Published in 1818, his *Statistical Annals* included data on the American population, trade and commerce, navigation, the military, and the revenues and expenditures of the federal government. The work was widely acclaimed in the United States and Europe. An act of Congress authorized the payment of $4,673.87 to Seybert for the 500 copies of the *Annals* Sanford had requested, together with Pitkin's *Commercial Statistics*.[32]

By 1819, tariff policy had again surged as a national issue. An excess of credit and land speculation at home, coupled with a reduction in European demand for American agricultural products, among other factors, led the national bank to impose severe restrictions on borrowers. Most banks called in loans. Borrowers unable to pay up lost their investments, homes, and farms. The Panic of 1819 brought near financial collapse on a national scale and the first depression in the United States.[33] To remedy the economic ills, calls for increased protection against foreign competition swelled.

To aid senators in developing policies on tariffs, the Committee on Commerce and Manufactures heeded requests from senators for "complete and accurate statistical accounts of the foreign commerce of the United States" by assembling a report using trade data. Presented to the Senate by Sanford in late December 1819, the report reflected the chairman's usual attention to clarity and reliable evidence. It was based on numerical data given to Congress annually by the Treasury. Summarized in the report, the information covered the total dollar value by year for exports from August 1789 through September 1818, although import data was reported only for the years 1795 through most of 1801. The report also described the role of customs collectors and the means by which goods were valued and their assessments submitted to the Treasury; additionally, it identified the distortions and exaggerations often imbedded in the numbers reported.[34] Unlike exports, the import statistics reflected only a fraction of total imports since only the values of items subject to duties—not all imports—were included, according to the report's commentary. For example, the numbers reported excluded copper, undressed furs, and plaster of Paris, items that entered the country in large quantities duty-free. In addition, Sanford emphasized the need to itemize imports that were also available domestically, since those items would "come into competition here." Examples included "manufactures of cotton," woolens, and iron.[35] Concluding on a highly skeptical note, Sanford's commentary on imports argued that their total value for "most of the last thirty years," that is, 1789 to 1819, was "unknown" and the comparisons made over the years between exports and imports were "uncertain and delusive."[36] It was a broad critique of the government's data gathering.

A third section of the report was devoted to "navigation," the details about shipping, a topic addressed by Seybert in his *Statistical Annals*. This section began with the statement that "So far as that navigation is ours, it is to us, a source of riches and power. So far as it belongs to other nations, its benefits are theirs."[37] This clear assertion by Sanford of the country's national interest and the goal of dominance in international shipping was followed by detailed descriptions of topics such as vessel tonnage, the country of origin of ships, and the numbers of seamen employed. Commentary pointed to the lack of information on the "kinds or quantities of the articles . . ." shipped and other matters.[38] Confronting the documented weaknesses in the data-collection processes that generated information on the exports, imports, and navigation of the United States, the chairman concluded that "No general system for statistical accounts of our foreign commerce has ever been established by law." To resolve the problem, his committee's recommendations became the basis for new data requirements outlined in the bill that Sanford presented to the Senate. It required that the secretary of the treasury deliver "statistical accounts of the commerce of the United States with foreign countries" to Congress every December. The bill would go into effect on September 30, 1820.[39] Among the bill's provisions were that the accounts "state all goods, wares, and merchandise, exported . . . , imported . . . , and all navigation employed in the foreign trade of the United States . . . "; that export statistics show the "production or manufacture of the United States, and their values, and the exports of articles of . . . foreign countries, and their values"; and that the "navigation employed in the foreign trade" be described. In addition, the "kinds and quantities of all imported articles free from duty" were required, and the "collectors shall keep accounts . . . of the imports subject to duties ad valorem. . . ." President Monroe signed Sanford's bill into law in February 1820.[40] Seybert's work with statistical data by category had had an impact on how legislators thought about the kinds of information needed for policymaking, with Sanford the most aggressive enthusiast for the new approach.

The directives in the data collection and reporting law took time to implement. However, comparative tariff schedules published in 1833, after Sanford had retired from the Senate, show that the definitions of goods used in the subsequent tariff update, later called the Tariff of 1824, were far more specific than those used in the Tariff of 1816. The document includes detailed descriptions of subcategories of articles such as glass, "manufactures of wool" and hemp, and books. A listing of "Articles Free of Duty" followed the tables: they were among the "statistical" elements required under the new law. In 1816, the enactment of the duty on imported foreign books had so disturbed Thomas Jefferson that he protested against it as a reflection of the "parochial and unenlightened thinking" widespread in the Republic, as one historian has put it.[41]

Throughout the Sixteenth Congress, Sanford continued to receive petitions urging the passage of protective tariffs. A week after he submitted the bill on ways to improve the statistics collected on foreign commerce, he presented a memorial to the Senate from the American Society of the City of New York urging legislators to take steps to foster the "encouragement of domestic manufactures." At about the same time, the senator and eleven other congressmen were lobbied by agents from the American Society for the Encouragement of Domestic Manufactures, a well-organized protectionist association that extended beyond New York. Its members aimed to petition and lobby "wavering legislators" in what they defined as efforts to reverse the economic stagnation that followed the Panic of 1819.[42] The campaign targeted the tariff bill introduced in the House by Henry Baldwin of Pennsylvania in March 1820. The bill had elicited the backing of protectionist societies, petitioners, and lobbying agents. It passed in the House, but a close vote in the Senate postponed it, meaning that it died. Sanford, still chair of the Committee on Commerce and Manufactures during the first congressional session, supported the protectionist bill and opposed its postponement. In his article on the making of tariff policy, historian Daniel Peart concluded that the 1820 tariff bill "demonstrated that legislators were susceptible to influences other than party and section."[43] In his vote four years earlier for the Tariff of 1816, Republican Sanford had shown that he had already become a moderate protectionist. Unlike many others, his vote in 1820 didn't depend on the persuasion of lobbyists.

While presidents Madison and Monroe shared support for protective tariffs, their views on national defense differed in emphasis. When James Monroe assumed office in 1817, the War of 1812 had ended; the new president looked to diplomacy, as much as to military preparedness, to further enhance the peace. Based on his experience defending the captains and crews of navy vessels at the prize court during the war, Sanford would have appreciated the issues involved in an agreement signed by the United States and Britain to gradually reduce naval arms on the Great Lakes. Other negotiations with Britain followed.[44] To minimize the loss of ships and cargoes, facilitate navigation, and provide the planning for strengthening land defenses, Congress often funded surveys of the country's coasts. As the chair of the Committee on Naval Affairs in December 1818, Sanford reported a resolution that asked the president to authorize surveys of particular "capes and shoals" along the coast of North Carolina. The maps would support decision making, such as determining the locations of the lighthouses used by commercial ships and of defenses along the Carolina coastline.[45] Once again, Sanford succeeded in making the case for obtaining the reliable data that the executive branch required.

Chapter 7

Senate Politics and Reform, 1815–1821

In areas where Sanford had sat on committees, often as chairman—finance, commerce and manufactures, and naval affairs—the senator could feel satisfied that he had established a record for bringing administrative reforms and an expansionist economic outlook to his work. During the same Senate term, however, proposals to reform other practices and laws had come to the fore; most important were contentious matters of human property and freedom, involving slaves and slavery. Other issues were addressed as well. Raising the pay of congressmen—unchanged since first set in 1789—was proposed and finally resolved. A resolution to institute popular voting for presidential electors in all states by constitutional amendment came to the floor, and senators debated how to rid the federal judiciary of incompetent judges. In a case of patronage, Sanford faced a personal dilemma: how to decide between adherence to principle and nepotism when asked by a relative to support his request for a postmaster's position. Given this agenda, the debate and resolutions dealing with slavery consumed the most time and were the most divisive.

Early in 1819, the Missouri Territory requested Congress to pass enabling legislation so it could become a state. For Sanford, his long acquaintance with African Americans, his legal studies, and his political experience would go far to create the context for his votes dealing with this divisive issue. The senator's father and stepfather had been slaveholders in their rural community on Long Island. Stepfather Deacon Hedges had no doubt followed the slavery debates in the state legislature, even though his terms did not exactly coincide with the passage of New York's Gradual Emancipation Law of 1799. The law required the registration of all slave births that had occurred in New York State after July 4, 1799; a public document was needed to certify birthdates, since male slaves were to be emancipated at age twenty-eight and female slaves at age twenty-five. The deacon failed to comply with the law until 1805, the year before he began his last term in the assembly. In a first step, Hedges gave the Southampton town clerk the first names of his slaves' three youngest children to enter into the *Town Record*.[1] In 1817, urged on by Governor Tompkins, state legislators finally turned their attention to further emancipation: all slaves who had come under the 1799 act would be free as of July 4, 1827. Even then, slaves not covered by the earlier law would remain in bondage. Unlike his father and his stepfather, Sanford never owned slaves. As a young man, according to the 1810 federal census, he employed two free blacks in his New York City household.[2]

Like many other whites, Sanford could treat a black man as worthy of his support but experience unease when called upon to decide the trustworthiness of black men in a group. Early in his law practice, Sanford worked on at least one case that involved a free African American. In January 1803, he intervened on behalf of a "free black of Easthampton [Long Island]." London, who became his client, had been jailed in the city and required a habeas corpus appeal. Sanford procured the man's bail and release—commenting in his receipt book that his fee covered "defending him if he should be indicted."[3] Toward the end of the War of 1812, the issue of trusting a group of black men arose when the state legislature supported a bill authorizing two regiments of African American soldiers. Martin Van Buren voted for the 1814 bill, showing his willingness to entrust groups of African Americans with arms. As we have seen, Sanford was among the three Republicans who opposed the measure. In this instance, creating a group of armed black men was problematic; yet, seven years later, he would fight to enfranchise black men in support of a democratic principle.

In the U.S. Senate, Sanford's positions on slavery issues largely mirrored those of other northern Republicans. When seen in the context of his colleagues, his views and voting record on particular bills shed light on the Senate as a whole in the late 1810s. An essay in a Cleveland newspaper listed Sanford among ten leaders of the Senate who were valued by their contemporaries in 1819. These men, the author declared, were "The most distinguished members at that time." In comparing voting records on slavery issues from 1817 to 1821, I have used this list to serve as a grouping against which I identify Sanford's positions relative to his peers.[4] In 1817, for example, Sanford had joined with some like-minded northern senators in voting to prevent harsher treatment of slaves from becoming law; he also opposed the imposition of inordinately lengthy jail terms on slaves who broke the law. A *Senate Journal* entry entitled "Fugitive Slaves" indicated that a bill dealing with "persons escaping from the service of their masters" would go forward, with the support of states-rights Republicans. Among the interest group analyzed here, senators who favored the bill included James Barbour from Virginia, Nathaniel Macon from North Carolina, and William Smith from South Carolina. But the bill was defeated, with help from both of the New York senators, Sanford and Rufus King. The bill would have raised penalties on a reprehended runaway slave—a judge would have been bound to commit the "negro or negroes, mulatto, or other person or persons of color, to the public jail" for an indeterminate number of months.[5]

Sanford also opposed slavery's expansion. The following year, he presented a petition he had received from the New York [Manumission] Society. The petition urged action on getting slaveholders to free (manumit) their slaves and provide protection for those slaves who had been, or might be, freed in the future. The senator moved that the memorial be referred to the committee appointed to study the transport of "persons of color" for sale, that is, the internal slave trade. He specified that the committee should identify the changes to existing laws that were necessary to "prevent the importation of slaves into the United States." The United States, like Great Britain, had outlawed the Atlantic slave trade in 1807. However, a decade after the prohibition on the importation of slaves took effect in1808, its enforcement had lapsed. Sanford appealed to the committee to strengthen the legislation enforcing the law.[6]

Within a few months, Sanford brought these positions to the debates over slavery as a lever to balance sectional political power in the Senate—between the number of slave-state senators and the number of free-state senators. Triggered by the call of the Missouri Territory to join the Union, debate in the House led one of New York's representatives, Bucktail Republican James Tallmadge, to propose an amendment to the statehood bill that would prohibit the importation of slaves into Missouri. A younger brother of the federal judge at the prize court in Sanford's time there, Congressman Tallmadge had lobbied to hasten the pace of emancipation of slaves in New York State in 1817. Now, in February 1819, he proposed that children born to slaves after Missouri became a state be freed at age twenty-five. Like the bill that had passed in New York in 1817, the already enslaved would remain slaves. In the Senate, Rufus King urged his fellow Federalists to support the amendment. Before Congress adjourned in March, the House narrowly approved it, but the Senate, given a near solid voting block of southern Republicans, overwhelmingly defeated it. The loss prevented even a moderate emancipation plan from going forward for Missouri, but the defeat of the amendment served its political purpose: to preserve the balance between slave senators and free-state senators within the halls of the Senate.[7] Soon after Congress reconvened in the fall and Congressman Henry Clay of Kentucky was reelected Speaker of the House, debate raged again over the extension of slavery. Grasping the opportunity, President Monroe, Clay, and Republicans in the Senate forged an agreement with Massachusetts congressmen to support the request from the state of Maine to separate from Massachusetts. Maintaining a sectional balance of power was a concern held by many. It was Clay, however, who began to discuss linking statehood for Missouri with that of Maine.[8]

In this milieu of rancorous debate and numerous amendments to bills, Sanford crafted an update on events from Washington, which he sent to Martin Van Buren, then serving in the New York State Senate. Dated February 3, 1820, his letter summarized the issues at stake in what he called "The Missouri question." These included the admission of Maine and Missouri as states, the "prohibition of slavery in the proposed State of Missouri," and the "question concerning the toleration or prohibition of slavery in the regions which lie between the present territories of Missouri and Arkansas, and the Pacific ocean."[9] The proposal to tie the practice of slavery in one state to its prohibition in most of the western territories was already in circulation. The area at stake excluded the Missouri Territory but covered that part of the Louisiana Purchase north of the northern boundary of the Arkansas Territory and west, until it met the Spanish Territory. Noting in his letter that "These particular questions are all entangled with each other," Sanford assessed the leanings of each house of Congress on the extension of slavery into Missouri: "A considerable majority of the Senate is opposed to any restriction [on slavery] upon Missouri. It is known that the House of Representatives is nearly divided upon this question; and though it is supposed, that a small majority of that House is in favor of the restriction, yet, as the majority, if any, is very small, the fate of the question is still doubtful." Sanford concluded that "These questions are so momentous and produce so much agitation and anxiety on all sides, that they absorb the attention of all; and not much business of public importance will be done in Congress until they shall be decided."[10]

In order to break the legislative logjam over Missouri statehood, Senator Jesse Thomas of Illinois had proposed that Missouri be admitted to the Union as a slave state, and that slavery be prohibited in the area defined as the Louisiana Purchase north of 36° 30' north latitude, the latitude of Missouri's southern border. The first motion, on February 17, challenged the Thomas amendment: it would have further restricted slavery. Sanford supported it. So did fellow Democratic-Republican Mahlon Dickerson from New Jersey. They were joined by Federalists Rufus King and Harrison Gray Otis from Massachusetts. In the main, the amendment's opponents were southern slaveholders who wanted slavery issues decided by the states, not the federal government. They included Barbour, Richard M. Johnson from Kentucky, William R. King from Alabama, Macon, William Pinckney from Maryland, and Smith, all Republicans of a range of persuasions. Barbour, Macon, and Smith had also voted in 1817 to further extend the prison terms for captured fugitive slaves. A second vote of the day let the political settlement stand by a large margin: the tally was thirty-four to ten.[11]

Following the reporting of the amended bill to the House, the Senate finalized its work, passing the statehood compromise bill, twenty-four to twenty. Sanford, along with other antislavery northern senators, voted against the bargain. Two weeks after Sanford had sent his letter to Van Buren, the Senate enacted the bill that became known as the Missouri Compromise. On the following day, the bill's title was expanded to read: "An act for the admission of the State of Maine into the Union, and to enable the people of the Missouri Territory to form a constitution and State government, and for the admission of such State into the Union, on an equal footing with the original States; and to prohibit slavery in certain Territories."[12]

In his analysis of the voting pattern of the congressmen that resulted in the settlement, historian Daniel Walker Howe defined three, perhaps four, clusters of voters. The groupings help place Sanford's positions relative to those of his colleagues, and the categories map well to the senators around Sanford identified in the Cleveland newspaper article as "distinguished." First, a large majority of northerners (eighteen of twenty-two) insisted on a policy of gradual emancipation of the slaves in the future state of Missouri. This antislavery view translated into a vote against the compromise and included Sanford, Dickerson, Rufus King, and Otis. A second group of northerners (composed of four senators) came to support the amended bill: they voted for the bill in the belief that only the concession to allow for the admission of Missouri as a slave state into the Union would garner the votes required for passage. A third cluster (twenty) from the South supported the amended bill. Howe concludes that it was "remarkable how many southern Congressmen felt willing, in 1820, to concede a ban on slavery in the greater part of the territories." Southerners Barbour, Johnson, William King, and Pinkney belonged to this group. Finally, there were extreme proslavery senators among Republicans in the South; among the men I have identified, two voted against the bill: Macon and Smith. In so doing, they registered their opposition to any restrictions on slavery in any territory. While the amended bill squeezed through the Senate, the House passed it handily, with an outsized majority, 134 to 42.[13]

The Missouri Compromise had political as well as moral consequences. According to Howe, southern leaders achieved their central demand: the "preservation of the principle that there could be no emancipation against the wishes of a local white majority." A second impact was the "new principle" that territories would be allowed to join the Union only in pairs, in order to maintain the balance of the states by section.[14] Other results included the division of the Republican Party according to section and the surging power of the Senate. Contemporaries also recognized the influence of Henry Clay on the compromise, while President Monroe acknowledged the "patriotic devotion" of northerners who voted for the compromise in order to maintain the Union. As we have seen, Sanford was not among them. The president signed the final bill on March 6.[15]

Not long thereafter, delegates to Missouri's constitutional convention drafted a document that legalized slavery and forbade "free negroes and mulattoes from coming to and settling in this State."[16] Rancorous debate ensued in Congress over the final approval of the admission of Missouri into the Union. Many northerners objected to the proposed constitution. From the Senate floor on November 23, 1820, Sanford read resolutions he had received from New York's state legislature into the record. The resolutions "instructed" the state's two senators and "requested" the state's representatives "to oppose the admission, as a state, into the Union, [of] any territory not comprised within the original boundaries of the United States, without making the prohibition of slavery therein an indispensable condition of admission." The New York legislators also informed the congressional delegation that Missouri's ban on freedom of entry into the proposed new state by free African Americans who were citizens of their home states was unconstitutional.[17] Like other state legislators in the North, they maintained that the prohibition ran counter to the "privileges and immunities" clause in the federal Constitution. Starting with the case of Missouri, Congress left the conflicting interpretations of the applicability of the clause unresolved, that is, whether the clause applied to all free

African Americans or, as Missouri interpreted it, only to those free blacks who were accorded citizenship in their home states.[18]

In late February 1821, the Senate voted twenty-eight to fourteen to admit Missouri into the Union as a slave state. The ten senators of interest here lined up on the same side as they had the year before in the vote that became the Missouri Compromise. Sanford aligned himself with his state legislature's instructions; like him, the southern Republicans Macon and Smith, although proslavery, voted against Missouri statehood but for a different reason. The two states-rights southerners were convinced that the Senate lacked legitimate authority to even review Missouri's constitution.[19] The work of compromise was over.

While no other challenge during his first term created what Sanford had called the "agitation and anxiety" that slavery aroused in Congress, he addressed other issues that came before the Senate during the Fourteenth Congress. One was a proposed pay raise for congressmen, to which many in the electorate objected. Sanford voted against the bill. He had already weathered the storm of criticism about the multiple offices he once held and excessive fees he may have charged, accusations that swirled about him after he entered state politics in 1808. Perhaps because of these experiences with accusations of greed, he stood against the pay raise, which was signed into law by President Madison.[20] For Sanford, the raise would have mattered little since he continued to receive substantial outside income from his law practice. For example, while on business in Albany in 1816, he received information pertinent to his client of longstanding, the trustees of the Town of Huntington, Long Island: nearby Islip town had petitioned a state legislator who, as Sanford wrote in his letter to a Huntington trustee, would "hold the Petition in his hands" until Huntington had a chance to respond to it. Islip had appealed the legislature to grant it ownership of certain disputed barrier islands along its Atlantic shore. Huntington's decision to hire Sanford, as the town had for the past ten years or so, was no doubt based on the attorney's knowledge of property law and his legislative connections.[21] Many in Congress did not have such outside work, making the prospect of a pay raise very appealing.

The pay issue had a history of controversy, in part because of the particular public service imperatives associated with George Washington's generation. In 1816, legislators earned a per diem of six dollars while Congress was in session, the rate set by the First Congress in 1789. This rate barely covered personal expenses, let alone those of a family. The annual salary of $1,500 in the Compensation Act that had passed in March nearly doubled the pay. In defense of the raise, supporters argued that increases in the cost of living had led some incumbents to leave Congress, and the raise would help attract talent to legislative service. The arguments failed to convince the public of the need. The uproar among voters was further stirred by an aggressive press.[22] In the North, especially, citizens from a broad spectrum of backgrounds expressed rage that the new salary would apply to incumbents and come from voters' tax dollars.

Respect for an aristocratic ethos of honor and service had declined for decades among many of the growing middling groups in society, and thinking about politics had begun to shift to a proud support by voters for democratic values. The change showed, for example, in the growing use of the label "Democratic-Republican" to replace Republican. Given the popular response to the act, the compensation law was repealed early in 1817, following the fall election, where three-quarters of the representatives in the House from New York State were defeated by disaffected voters.[23] Sanford was spared—he had been elected by the state legislature, not the voters, and his Senate term had only recently begun.

Other matters, the selection of presidential electors, the process for removing incompetent federal judicial appointees from office, and the use of patronage had also drawn Sanford's attention during his first term. In 1816, senators proposed to expand democracy by amending the Constitution to require that all states adopt a form of popular voting for selecting the electors who chose the president and vice president of the United States. At the time, the states were equally divided between those where electors were selected by a popular vote and those where state legislators decided who the electors would be. Rufus King, like Sanford, supported the resolution. It would challenge New York's practice of the selection of electors by the legislature. The Senate, however, defeated the resolution when it failed to reach a two-thirds majority required of both houses of Congress to initiate amending the Constitution.[24] Two years later, Sanford proposed popular voting by district as the means to move the selection of presidential electors from state legislatures to the voters. Responding to instructions he had received from the Bucktail-dominated New York State legislature, he offered an amendment to the Constitution, like the one that had already passed the North Carolina legislature. It would divide the states into districts, and "persons qualified to vote for representatives" to the House would also be qualified to vote in the selection of electors. The proposal met with little support in the Senate and languished. In January 1820, however, two-thirds of the Senate, including Sanford, supported a similar resolution. When sent to the House, the amendment appears to have been tabled. These efforts to expand direct democracy proved hard to achieve. New York State did not adopt popular voting for presidential electors by district until 1828, a decade after Sanford and the state legislature sought the reform through a federal constitutional amendment. In 1832, the state legislature approved the choice of electors by direct, statewide popular vote—the process in effect today.[25]

Controversy also swirled around the issue of competency in the federal judiciary. In April 1816, a House committee asked the Senate to permit Nathan Sanford to come before it to testify in the inquiry into the "official conduct" of Judge Matthias B. Tallmadge of the District Court of New York. Among the charges of absenteeism made against Tallmadge was his failure to hold court in the new Northern District of New York to which he had been appointed by Congress two years before. The failure of Tallmadge to appear at his court was widely explained by the judge's ill health.[26] The decision to call Sanford to testify was not surprising, as the former federal attorney and the judge had collaborated at court in New York City for a decade, and the senator was well informed about the division of the court district. Months earlier, Sanford had implicitly acknowledged the problem: he had supported a bill that became law ensuring that judicial proceedings would not be affected by lapses in the scheduling of court sessions. In the case of Tallmadge, the sessions were to take place in upstate New York. One location scheduled for the court was Canandaigua, about 400 miles from New York City, among the Iroquois Indians. With Tallmadge's absences, the court in the Southern District finally assumed the cases. In March, Sanford went further in his effort to enforce judicial competency: he proposed a constitutional amendment that addressed the hold federal judges had on their offices. It would require the president's support and agreement from Congress that the "public good will be promoted by removal. . . ." The resolution failed in the Senate.[27]

The court issue was a longstanding one, a source of acrimony in the 1790s, when many Democratic-Republicans accused the Federalists in power of using judicial appointments to promote their political views. While Republicans preferred the election rather than the appointment of federal judges, President Jefferson in 1802, in recognizing the value of a judiciary independent of the executive and legislative branches of government, relinquished his support for the election of federal judges. He turned to the remedy of removal for bad behavior by supporting a constitutional amendment that would allow the president to remove a federal judge after he had addressed a majority of the members of Congress. The proposal languished. Five years later, Jefferson again proposed a constitutional amendment. It aimed to hold federal judges accountable to the nation, although they would still be appointed.[28] The amendment failed, like Sanford's motion of 1816, when the House, perhaps preoccupied with weightier matters, postponed its investigation into the "alleged misconduct" of Judge Tallmadge, a Republican who went on to nominally serve as the first judge in the Northern District until a few months before his death in 1819.[29]

All along in his political career, the senator had engaged in occasional communications with his extended family and constituents on the South Fork of Long Island. In February 1816, residents of East Hampton, led by the physician Dr. Abel Huntington[30] and Major Jeremiah Miller, signed a petition addressed to their senator asking for a post office. Sanford presented the petition to the Senate, where it was referred to a committee. Like the removal of judges, federal patronage had its roots in the 1790s, when the government significantly expanded its network of post offices, as well as post roads that reached from state to state. Towns and villages also recognized the need for improved long-distance communications: their investors, merchants, tradesmen, and farmers had come to rely on the commercial information contained in newspapers and other print sources delivered by post.[31] In the case of East Hampton residents, moreover, the economic reasons for petitioning for postal service were nearby: the town included most of Sag Harbor, a federal port of entry and a center for the booming whaling industry.

In addition to the petition, Sanford had received letters from the retired Major Miller, the relative who had served as a commander in the defense of Sag Harbor during the War of 1812 and now sought the appointment as postmaster. In his reply, the senator described the next steps for the petition that had been forwarded to the committee: "It will . . . rest in this state until nearly the close of the session, when a Bill will probably pass both houses embracing all the changes of Post Offices and Post Roads. . . ." A few weeks later, Sanford sent a surprising response to Miller's letters. He had learned that "It now appears that Doctor Huntington is recommended by a meeting of the people of the town [for the position]. In these circumstances and after reflection I have determined to recommend nobody and not to interfere in the selection of a Post Master, in any manner whatever." In the end, Miller received the commission, while his family contact, the senator, remained uninvolved, refusing to acquiesce in the appeal for patronage. Miller would join one of the roughly 3,300 post offices distributed throughout the country by

1816. At the time, the service accounted for close to 70 percent of the civilian jobs in the federal government.[32]

In these immediate postwar years, Sanford spent a good portion of his time away from home. Arduous trips between New York and Washington, and bouts of ill health, would presumably prove exhausting to the senator, then in his late thirties. When he lost his second wife in May 1816, again from the aftermath of childbirth, feelings of sadness must have overwhelmed him and his family. He was the head of a large household that still resided at 25 Pine Street in New York City. The 1820 federal census shows that the household included himself; five children, ages four to fifteen; two women, one a "free white" and the other a "free colored," who no doubt performed the duties of childcare and housekeeping; and a third servant, a "free colored" man.[33] The senator alone became responsible for managing this household of nine. Again, he would be away from home: he left for Washington to serve his last session in the Senate in the winter of 1821.

Less a visionary than a conscientious legislator, Sanford defined the role of the central government as one of monitoring and regulating, rather than initiating broad new programs. With that mindset, he left a mixed record in the Senate. He argued over amendments to the bank bill in an effort to shape the central bank in a more conservative direction. While he supported the protective tariff and naval defenses, he was satisfied that the Erie Canal received state help rather than a federal subsidy. Sanford voted against the pay raise for congressional incumbents, perhaps anticipating a public outcry. Yet he was a reformer who fought for principles. During debates to curtail slavery, he twice objected to compromises with proslavery positions. He was willing to amend the Constitution to give more power to voters through the direct election of presidential electors, and to facilitate the removal of federal judges for reasons of conduct. He questioned the use of patronage, refusing to intervene to obtain a postmaster's position for a cousin. On this record, Sanford felt prepared to run in the state legislature for a second term in the Senate.

Chapter 8

“Here there is but one estate—the people,” 1821

At the end of his Senate term, Sanford’s contesting constituencies in the New York State legislature became embroiled in two major issues: the upcoming vote to decide the next United States senator, and the calling of a constitutional convention to reform state government institutions and practices. Powerful groups and personalities were in play. Sanford wanted to keep his seat in the Senate, but in their caucus, Bucktail Republicans backed his friend, state senator Martin Van Buren. Federalists and followers of Governor DeWitt Clinton, who saw Van Buren’s strong party control as a source of oppression, supported Sanford.[1] Against Bucktail opposition, incumbent Sanford lost his bid for a second term in February 1821. But as a politician who had witnessed many of the social and economic changes that had recast New York City and the state, he would remain engaged in the turbulent politics of the era.

For some time, the city had been growing more rapidly than any other in the country. Already the leading seaport, with greater than 25 percent of total coastal tonnage by 1810, New York’s supply of capital soon exceeded that of banks in Philadelphia, Boston, or Baltimore. In 1817, with the formation of a Board of Brokers, New York became the center for the securities market. Like the city’s, the state’s population had grown, from about 340 thousand residents in 1790 to well over 1.3 million by 1820. But wealth did not spread evenly. For many white laborers, small farmers, and tradesmen, the social value of their work and opportunities to become independent proprietors had diminished. The drift seemed to threaten white male heads of households who had achieved a middling status and value in the public culture.[2] From revolutionary times, many Americans had believed that republicanism itself required the ownership and broad distribution of real property. Land ensured a household's independence and lessened the risk that farmers, in particular, would tumble down the economic and social ladder to become wage earners. To avoid a dependency on large farmers or manufacturers for employment, many families moved to western New York State to start anew, adding to other arrivals, often from New England. While the city, Long Island, and areas up the Hudson Valley had constituted over 85 percent of the state's population in 1790, by 1830 over 60 percent of the population was living in the new counties to the west and the north of that region.[3]

Free blacks also grew in number in the early years of the Republic, clustered largely in northern cities and towns. In 1820 New York City, they counted for 8.8 percent of the population and tended to hold low-paying jobs. Like white men, they would become enmeshed in the politics of suffrage reform. Of all the states, New York's freehold property requirements for voting were among the most stringent. In 1790, about 45 percent of white men were excluded from the franchise. Propertied men of color could vote, but they were few in number, and they faced an additional hurdle after 1811 when Republicans in the state legislature sponsored a bill that required free blacks to present a certificate of manumission at the polls. In part, the law aimed to reduce the number of qualified blacks who had voted for Federalist candidates during the Revolution and thereafter. By 1820, turmoil swirled around the issue of access to the ballot: political participation proved to be the primary factor in calls for revisions to the state constitution. As one historian has put it, in New York, "electoral politics . . . was the dynamic fulcrum between . . . an ancient linkage of property and rights and the now rising expectations of democracy."[4]

The Bucktail-dominated state legislature saw a constitutional convention as a means to address these grievances. It began to debate its scope in January 1820. During August, meetings held at Tammany Hall resulted in the decision to hold the convention as soon as possible, in an effort to more effectively undermine the political career of newly reelected DeWitt Clinton as governor. His alliance with Federalists—committed to a society based on deference—had alarmed Republicans dedicated to Jeffersonian ideals. Led by Van Buren, the Bucktails succeeded in harnessing pressures to revise the 1777 constitution to their liking. In the spring of 1821, a popular vote to convene a convention won handily.[5]

Delegate selection began in early summer 1821. The June 12 issue of the *New-York Spectator* published the "Independent Republican ticket," billed as a selection of men from among those who accepted the "patriotic offer of an independent ticket, without reference to party politics." Sanford appeared on this list of mostly Clintonian Republicans, vying for one of eleven places in the County of New-York delegation, the largest.[6] As reported in the *New-York Evening Post* a week or so later, he also ran on the Bucktail ticket, apparently giving little heed to his acceptance of nonpartisanship. The slate won; of the eleven Bucktails on the list published in the *Post*, Sanford received the most votes.[7] Unlike Sanford in his county, newly elected senator Van Buren had little chance of winning election as a delegate to the convention from solidly Federalist Albany, where he lived, or from his home county. But he managed to join the slate of Republicans in the County of Otsego and won a seat.[8]

The convention opened on August 28 in the assembly chamber in Albany and set about the task of organizing its work. Daniel Tompkins, the former governor and a resident of Staten Island, who had been reelected in 1820 to a second term as vice president of the United States, was chosen president. The agenda was also decided; each topic would be represented by a select committee of seven members appointed by the president. President Tompkins appointed his colleague, Nathan Sanford, chair of the suffrage committee.[9] Although he attended every session from August 28 to the closing day on November 10, and participated in every

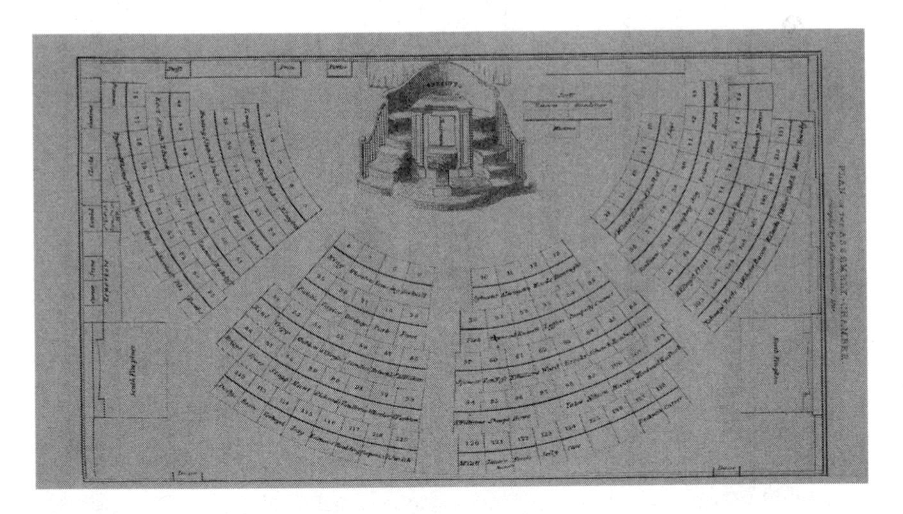

Figure 8.1. *Plan of the Assembly-Chamber Occupied by the Convention*, 1821. Courtesy of the New York State Library. Sanford occupied seat number five in the front row on the aisle.

vote on the floor of the convention, Sanford rarely engaged in debate, a consequence of his lung disease. The two reporters who recorded and published the "Proceedings and Debates of the Convention of 1821" noted that when he did speak, they couldn't hear him. They commented at one point, "we were unable to hear," and on another occasion, they wrote that "Mr. Sanford spoke in explanation, but inaudible."[10] The delegates, no doubt, had trouble hearing him as well. The condition that had long affected his ability to speak at length in public did not prevent the retired senator from taking stands during the proceedings and influencing the constitutional issues that now, after his Senate experience, meant the most to him: the state of the judiciary; a prohibition of slavery; a bill of rights, specifically involving libel and guarantees of freedom of the press; and, above all, the expansion of the suffrage.

The convention addressed reform of the legislative and executive arms of state government first. Although Sanford did not participate in these debates on government organization, he voted for the Bucktail-led proposals. Among the decisions that strengthened the power of the legislature was the elimination of the Council of Revision, an entity that included the chancellor and supreme court justices. The Council could veto legislation and had been widely accused of abusing its authority under the Constitution of 1777. The Council of Appointment was eliminated as well, having been transformed over the decades into a vehicle for patronage, controlling roughly 15,000 state offices. The governor's term was reduced from three years to two, in a partisan move by Bucktails to require Clinton to run for reelection a year earlier. The office, however, gained the appointment power for judges, although appointments would require the senate's consent.[11]

With the judiciary still dominated by Federalists, Sanford's interests were less in designing a new blueprint for the courts than in defining the political process to be used in developing such a plan. In the amendment he offered to the judiciary committee's proposal, he envisioned that "The legislature shall have power to modify, alter or abolish any court of law or equity, to establish new courts of justice, and to transfer the functions, or jurisdiction of one court to any other court. . . ." Sanford went on to list certain restrictions that he favored for the judiciary. They included the requirement that judges in the higher courts could hold office only "until they shall attain the age of sixty years,"[12] a limitation that was already in the constitution of 1777. Later in the debate, the former federal attorney informed the delegates that he had "submitted a plan . . . on the subject of the judiciary." It supported keeping both the court of chancery and the supreme court, with some modifications in their responsibilities. But he continued to argue that through its democratic process, the legislature, not the constitutional convention, should reorganize the courts. He made his point succinctly: "The great question upon which we differ, is, how much will be done upon this subject in the constitution, and how much shall be left to the legislature."[13] The judiciary committee's report had placed nearly all responsibility for judicial change with the convention. In his challenge to the committee's proposal, Sanford maintained that judicial revisions placed in the constitution "would probably become inadequate to the exigencies of the state in twenty years from this time; and . . . the legislature would then be destitute of power to make the alteration which the public good might require." He went on to say, however, that the "court of the last resort" should be "established by the constitution." He noted that this idea was imbedded in the United States Constitution and that he felt no "distrust" of the legislature in its ability to carry out these responsibilities.[14] Delegate Kent, still chancellor, expressed the opposing conservative view that it would be "unsafe to commit such unqualified powers concerning the judiciary to the discretion of a legislative body."[15] Sanford wanted the electorate's representatives to displace some of the power of judges, thus bypassing the lengthy and complex process of amending the constitution.

Unlike suffrage requirements, which most delegates agreed should be difficult to change and therefore belonged in constitutional law, the convention split on judicial issues. Sanford reasserted his views during the continuing debate. He reasoned that most changes to the judiciary should be legislated by statute, and reiterated his position that courts had to respond to evolving conditions in society. In addressing his opponents who wanted the convention to decide most judicial reforms, thus placing them in the constitution, Sanford cautioned that "we shall do for future times that which can much better be done by future legislatures."[16] When his amendment came up for a vote, Sanford proposed that the convention act first on the committee's report, which it did. Long into that debate, Martin Van Buren offered a resolution that supported a significant role for the Bucktail-dominated legislature. His position reflected much of Sanford's thinking.[17]

In early November, Sanford was appointed to a committee of three to organize all of the amendments to the constitution that had been passed by the convention. The committee decided to meet in a nearby house on State Street. Having completed the task, Chairman Sanford presented the committee's report to the convention, although the secretary read it. The first sentence of Article Five on the judiciary included language

Sanford had proposed during the debate when he invoked the legislature and the public good: "Sec. V. The state shall be divided, by law, into a convenient number of districts, not less than four, nor exceeding eight, subject to alteration, by the legislature, from time to time, as the public good may require."[18] Among the responsibilities of the district, or circuit, judges were the trying of supreme court civil cases and presiding over certain cases that had previously been tried at the court of chancery. These changes aimed at reducing the heavy caseload—and the power—of the older courts. In 1823, when the new constitution took effect and Sanford had been appointed chancellor, following James Kent, his reduced authority would allow him only to hear appeals in equity suits and decide cases that involved parties from more than one of the circuits (or districts), or parties from one circuit and from outside of the state.[19]

Over the course of the nearly twelve weeks that the convention was in session, issues left unresolved returned to the floor. On October 19, James Tallmadge, who had fought to ameliorate the conditions of slavery in New York State in 1817 and during the Missouri statehood controversies in Congress in 1819, amplified upon his resolution to put the ban on slavery into the state constitution. He pointed out that according to current law, children born to slaves in New York State would continue in bondage until after 1827, the date set by the legislature for slavery to end. Chancellor Kent opposed outlawing slavery in the constitution, maintaining "the law should remain as it is." While Sanford was quiet on the issue, he voted for the resolution to ban slavery through the constitution, but it lost.[20] With his vote, Sanford expressed the sentiment that the end of slavery was one of the fundamental principles that should be encased in the state's constitution, not in statutory law. Trial for libel was another.

On the following day, the convention took up the question of trials for libel, a topic that was part of the report from the committee on the bill of rights. While declaring that "Every citizen may freely speak, write, and publish his sentiments," the committee had proposed, as part of the constitution, that in libel cases, "the truth [of sentiments expressed] may be given in evidence" at the trial if the "matter charged as libelous, was published with good motives, and for justifiable ends." The approach was grounded in a libel bill passed by the legislature in 1805. The committee's report followed that law in stating that the jury was responsible for determining fact and law but the judge alone would decide whether the motive was a good one or not. Sanford countered the proposal on the issue of motive. His amendment proposed that the jury determine motive. If a defendant acted with "good motives," he would be acquitted;[21] if motives were bad, the accused would be found guilty.

Declaring that "freedom of the press is the best security of public liberty," Sanford voiced his wish in his amendment to "confide this great trust of protecting the freedom of the press, and deciding upon its abuses, to the juries of the state."[22] Later in the debate on libel, Sanford also questioned the political process to be used to effect change, the same issue he had raised during the controversies over reforms in the judiciary and the abolition of slavery. He warned that "it [was] . . . of great importance that the freedom of speech and of the press should be secured by the constitution" and added that "The liberty of the press in this state, now depends upon the pleasure of the legislature."[23] The Sanford amendment changed that. It passed overwhelmingly, ninety-seven to eight. Chancellor Kent voted against it. As one historian has noted, the amendment "vastly increased the power of juries and decreased that of the bench,"[24] where Federalists continued to wield substantial power.

No issue in the convention, however, not judicial reform, slavery, or freedom of the press, motivated Sanford's intellectual and political leadership as much as that of reform of "The Elective Franchise." At the Saturday, September 1 session, President Tompkins had announced that Sanford would chair the committee "On the right of suffrage." In making his appointment, Tompkins showed that he trusted the senator and respected the knowledge and experience he had gained from his many years in appointive and electoral offices. The fellow Republicans had known each other for twenty years as members of the bar: they had received their licenses to practice before the state's supreme court on the same day. In 1805, Justice Tompkins wrote the decision in the Fox Case, basing his opinion on appellant lawyer Sanford's arguments. Both politicians had supported the leadership of Martin Van Buren as it emerged during the years of war and factional conflict. But there is no evidence indicating whether Tompkins had anticipated Sanford's support for black suffrage without a property requirement when he appointed him chair of the committee.

Tompkins also named the six other members of the suffrage committee. James Fairlie, the clerk of the supreme court, had been elected to the convention, like Sanford, on both the Bucktail and Clintonian tickets; he also represented the County of New York.[25] General Stephen Van Rensselaer, a graduate of Harvard University and a Federalist, had served in the state legislature and as lieutenant governor; he later became a congressman. At the convention, he represented the County of Albany.[26] The remaining four committee members identified with Van Buren's Bucktails. State senator Peter R. Livingston was from Dutchess County. John Cramer, a graduate of Union College, practiced law near Albany, and had served in the assembly.[27] A lawyer and former assemblyman and state senator, Colonel Samuel Young, like Cramer, represented the County of Saratoga. John Z. Ross, a physician, came from Genesee County in western New York. As delegates signed into the convention, they were asked to record their profession, one of many categories of information listed in the logbook. In the register, Nathan Sanford, Stephen Van Rensselaer, Peter Livingston, and John Cramer jotted down "Agriculture" under the heading "Profession or Occupation."[28] While in Sanford's case, his agricultural land and his farm rental incomes would be modest, the lawyer-politician could easily also self-identify as a farmer, given the values he grew up with and the higher social status that he understood was conveyed by land ownership.

Of the topics assigned to ten committees, the convention spent more of its time on suffrage than on any other. In the main, the committee focused on reforming the voting requirements for adult men. The Constitution of 1777 had given suffrage rights to freeholders and life-leaseholders whose assessed value in real property reached at least £100 (understood to equate to about $250 at the time): these taxpayers could vote for governor, lieutenant governor, senators, and assemblymen. Lesser freeholders and tenants renting much less land gained only the right to vote for assemblymen. After 1788 and the ratification of the United States Constitution, both tiers of enfranchisement continued to vote for congressmen. A small number of free blacks qualified under these terms.[29]

At the end of the convention in 1821, a strong majority of delegates voted to broaden the franchise for white men twenty-one years of age who met residency requirements and other criteria: the vote shifted the linkage of suffrage and real property to a franchise valid for all government officers, based on having paid a tax or, if exempt, on having served in a militia of the state, or, if exempt, having performed service in a fire company. With a longer residency, adult white men could vote if they performed work on the roads or paid an assessment in lieu of labor. Free blacks, however, were required to meet the same longer residency and possess a freehold valued at $250 "above all debts and incumbrances [*sic*]" on which they had paid their property tax.[30] With these requirements, New York joined other states in rolling back the enfranchisement of black men. Connecticut had withdrawn the suffrage from black men in 1818, and Rhode Island would do the same in 1822. It went largely unsaid at the convention that women, many white men, Native Americans, slaves, and free black men who didn't meet the required freehold threshold could not vote. Through his chairmanship of the committee and strong presence at the convention early in the suffrage debate, Sanford played a significant role in defining the theoretical underpinnings of universal manhood suffrage in New York State. Conscious of the need for a moral righting of past wrongs, as his votes in the committee of the whole illustrate, he continued to support the inclusion of blacks in the suffrage on an equal footing with whites, even after he had been defeated within his select committee on the issue of racial preference for white men.

On Wednesday, September 12, the convention began to deal with suffrage. President Tompkins opened the session, and a memorial from "free people of colour, of the city of New-York" was read. It asked the delegates, in a confirmation of the "declaration of independence, and constitution of this state," to take action to prevent "future legislatures from imposing restrictions upon them in relation to the right of suffrage."[31] The appeal was tabled, and committee member John Cramer[32] proceeded to read the suffrage report that proposed seven amendments to the constitution and carried the full title, "right of suffrage, and the qualifications of persons to be elected." The report began with the words "Every white male citizen" and ended with an oath required of legislators and all officers to uphold, among other commitments, "the constitution of the United States."[33] In his committee, Chairman Sanford had voted against the majority of members who favored restricting the suffrage to white men; he opposed the recommendation on race that appeared in the report. After the reading, Sanford moved that the report be sent out to be printed for the delegates. He no doubt hoped that debate on the floor would result in greater congruence with his own views on race. In the matter of the disposition of the memorial from "free people of colour" that had been read earlier, there was no resolution, although speakers referred to it during subsequent debates.

A week later, on September 19, Sanford took the floor and delivered an explication of the "principle of the scheme," or plan, supported by a majority of the suffrage committee. He defined the committee's task this way: "The question before us is the right of suffrage—who shall, or who shall not, have the right to vote." He pointed out that the voting tiers in current state law derived from ". . . British precedents. In England, they have their three estates, which must always have their separate interests represented." The King, House of Lords, and the House of Commons were

Figure 8.2. Portrait of Peter Williams. Unidentified artist, circa 1810–1815. Oil on canvas, 25 inches x 20.25 inches. Object #X.173. Courtesy of the New-York Historical Society. Williams would no doubt have supported universal manhood suffrage.

the governing bodies that represented the monarchy, the aristocracy, and commoners, in sharp contrast to the United States. As an institutional reformer, Sanford aimed to make government more responsive to citizens by expanding the suffrage. He found his voice in a call to republican ideals as he understood them:

> Here there is but one estate—the people. To me, the only qualifications seems [*sic*] to be, the virtue and morality of the people. . . . The principle . . . is, that those who bear the burthens of the state, should choose those that rule it. There is no privilege given to property, as such; but those who contribute to the public support, we consider as entitled to a share in the election of rulers.[34]

Sanford and his committee had identified suffrage requirements they saw as elements in the "public support" of the "state." They were the contributions of tax payments on real or personal property, "so that the odious distinctions of property" (in the form of land) could end, or "work on the high roads," or "actual service" in the militia. He expanded on the issue of tax payments: "we have considered personal service, in some cases, equivalent to a tax on personal property, as in work on the high roads."[35] Here, the committee offered options for the franchise without an explicit tax payment.

Then Sanford addressed "restrictions" to the right of suffrage. First, "The voter must be a citizen." Second, "The service required must be performed within the year, on the principle that taxation is annual, and election annual." A third restriction described residency requirements.[36] Unlike the report from his committee, which Sanford must have opposed in committee, he never used the term "white" or mentioned race on the floor of the convention.

In an evaluation of the requirements, Sanford affirmed that the committee proposed to extend suffrage "almost as far as the male population of the state." He went on to address the concerns of "respectable citizens" who argued that a broad expansion in the number of male voters would threaten property rights; he marshalled many arguments to dispute this traditional claim, mainly from large landowners. Other laws and the administration of justice in the state, he maintained, would not change with an expansion of suffrage. Moreover, "Every gentleman is aware that the scheme now proposed, is derived from the law calling this Convention." Sanford expanded on the fact that broad male suffrage requirements had already been used statewide in the vote to approve the convention: ". . . In the constitution of this body, we have the first fruits of the operation of the principle of extensive suffrage—and will any one say that this example is not one evincing the discretion with which our people exercise this right?" Finally, he highlighted additional proof that dropping the property requirement would not be disruptive to the polity: experiences in other states and in "our town meetings" in New York, where elections represented the "highest proof of the virtue and intelligence of our people," served as evidence.[37] One source of Sanford's understanding of town government was his family. When a youngster, Sanford's father was a justice of the peace in the Town of Southampton, and his mother's family had held local offices in the adjacent Town of East Hampton. The curious son had held onto those memories of civic engagement. Sanford closed by saying that the "scheme" was proposed by a majority of the committee and "founded in just and rational principles."[38]

Sanford's view of property was also based on his recognition of economic changes that had taken place in the state by the early nineteenth century. The increasing investment in movable assets (as distinct from real property) that accompanied commercial expansion had influenced his position. He understood the weakness in equating voter independence with landed assets, exclusive of other kinds of assets. At the convention, he fought against the implications drawn by delegates who believed that the growing number of manufacturing jobs, for example, would attract the nearly landless worker who would impact politics negatively if he could vote and thereby challenge the social order. In a defense of propertied political power, these delegates argued that a shift of votes to New York City would reduce the influence of voters from rural areas.[39] They demanded voter qualifications that would keep a disproportionate amount of political power north and west of the city.

Sanford expressed his deepest convictions in short but cogent speeches, constrained by his inability to speak at length. He argued for the primacy of the legislature in reorganizing the court system through statutory law, believing that the people's representatives, in their deliberations, would compromise to support the "public good." Individual rights, however, required placement in the constitution and were "principles." As such, he fought for a ban on slavery in the state, libel law that upheld freedom of the press, and the individual's right to vote. In the delicate balance between individual rights and social order, Sanford exposed the false arguments for order and prioritized rights. The stage was set for a continuing debate.

Chapter 9

The Suffrage Debate, 1821

In his speech to the convention on September 19, Sanford presented a framework for suffrage reform focused on the theme that in the United States, "there is but one estate—the people." Already delegates understood that the idea conflicted with the suffrage committee's report that included issues of race and property. Sanford was followed in the debate by John Ross, who at thirty-six was the youngest member of the committee. He spoke at length about the "reasons" behind the report's recommendation to extend the suffrage to "white men only." The physician maintained that, unlike white men, black men "are seldom, if ever, required to share in the common burthens or defence [*sic*] of the state" and therefore should be excluded from the right of suffrage. He continued: "they are a peculiar people, incapable, in my judgment, of exercising that privilege [of the vote] with any sort of discretion, prudence, or independence." Ross raised the issue of the memorial that had been read the week before. He linked it to the assumption that African Americans would not be independent-minded in voting and warned that "The petition presented in their behalf . . . in all probability has been instigated by gentlemen of a different colour [that is, whites], who expect to control their votes."[1] No doubt Dr. Ross had manipulating Federalists in mind.

Other committee members expressed independent views on the majority's proposed service options for gaining the franchise: work on the roads and military service. General Van Rensselaer, known as the Great Patroon, had been appointed by Governor Tompkins in 1812 to command the New York militia in the Niagara campaign.[2] He joined a minority on the committee in opposing the inclusion of the militia as a qualification since, he said, it would enfranchise a "wandering population, men who are no where to be found when the enemy, or the tax gatherer, comes." However, the general would include the "farmers and farmers' sons" who served in the militias and offered language that would enfranchise both groups as taxpayers. His proposal stipulated that the male citizen who had been "assessed and paid" a "tax, together with the sons of citizens qualified aforesaid," would qualify for the vote if the sons met age and residency requirements.[3] Van Rensselaer assumed that the tax would be on the farmers' land. Committee member and former officer in the Revolutionary War James Fairlie also opposed the inclusion of militia service. Fairlie objected to roadwork as well, implying that the services were an insufficient contribution for the privilege of suffrage.[4]

During the first two days of debate, challenges made by others to specific voting requirements were overwhelmed by the intense wrangling of certain delegates. These delegates called for answering Sanford's question, "who shall, or who shall not, have the right to vote," in terms of race. Dr. Ross had spoken early for the "white men only" clause, followed by Colonel Young, who moved to add the "limitation of white" to Van Rensselaer's proposal.[5] Later, Peter Livingston spoke at length, explaining his justifications for the committee's restriction on black male suffrage. He commented sarcastically on the memorial sent to the convention by free people of color in New York City: "Out of about fifty petitioners, more than twenty could not even write their names—and those petitioners were doubtless of the most respectable of the colour." Like Ross, Livingston raised the concern about a voter's independence, concluding that "Such persons must always be subject to the influence of the designing."[6] On September 20, former congressman General Erastus Root added to the opinions expressed on the petition. He claimed that New York City blacks followed their employers in their voting habits, and he commented with disdain on what to call African Americans: "*negroes*; or in the polite language of the day, . . . *coloured people*." Here, Root implied that the phrase "coloured people" had been used by blacks to convey their respectability, an idea considered outrageous by most whites.[7]

Of the seven members on the suffrage committee, John Cramer and Nathan Sanford, while eloquent in demanding that real property be separated from the right to vote, failed to speak directly to the committee of the whole in defense of the inclusion of black men in the suffrage. They were joined by Van Rensselaer and Fairlie in keeping their views, but not their votes, on race to themselves. Condemnations of the exclusion of African Americans heard on the floor were left primarily to a few

Federalists.[8] At the close of debate, the vote was called on the "question of striking out the word *white*." Somewhat surprisingly, the delegates voted sixty-three to fifty-nine in favor of deleting the term. Members of the suffrage committee, however, voted four to three in favor of keeping the language, presumably the same way they had voted in the select committee. The exclusionary majority was made up of Ross, Young, Livingston, and Fairlie. In the minority, desiring a franchise that would "embrace almost the whole male population of the state," as Sanford had said in his opening remarks, were Sanford, Cramer, and Van Rensselaer.[9]

The close vote on whether to include African Americans in the suffrage report's franchise proposals was part of a larger issue, according to David N. Gellman and David Quigley in their volume *Jim Crow New York*: "opponents of black suffrage understood that granting African Americans the rights they demanded would mark a fundamental alteration in the meaning of citizenship for everyone in New York." As citizens in the state, connected to a certain place and its government, free blacks would gain the central right of suffrage, become obligated to protect and defend their country, and be expected to pay taxes.[10] The report that addressed "Every white male citizen" had shown that the franchise would overlap with a particular definition of citizenship. Delegates cast their votes understanding this connection. Among the delegates not on the committee who voted with Sanford to drop the term *white* were James Tallmadge, Martin Van Buren, and James Kent. President Tompkins was not present, having excused himself at the start of the session.[11]

During the days that followed the vote on race on September 20, delegates took issue with the suffrage report on other topics, mainly property. One proposed amendment would require ownership of a minimum $250 freehold as a qualification for state senatorial suffrage. Kent joined the exchange. Railing against the "report before us," he objected to the proposal that would "annihilate, at one stroke, all those property distinctions [in the qualification of voters for governor, lieutenant governor, senators, and assemblymen] and to bow before the idol of universal suffrage." The chancellor lauded the "agricultural interest: It is the foundation of national wealth and power." He aimed, he intoned, "to preserve our senate as the representative of the landed interest."[12] No sharper words could have divided Kent from Sanford.

First to launch a withering critique of the conservatives who sought to continue the linkage of property with the suffrage and perpetuate a two-tier voting system was Peter Livingston from the suffrage committee. Like many Democratic-Republicans since 1789, he cited the positive impact of events that had taken place in France during the Revolution: "Where the interest of one individual [nobleman] has been sacrificed, the interests of thousands have been promoted."[13] In criticizing England, Livingston maintained that "men of wealth" in the kingdom conferred the "right of representation on the few, to the exclusion of the many."[14] In this thinking, Livingston's racial distinctions did not interfere.

Adding to the notion that a suffrage based on legal privilege or wealth had no place in a democracy, Daniel Tompkins offered a defense of the militiamen who had fought in the War of 1812. He asked, "Who filled the ranks of your armies? Not the priesthood—not the men of wealth—not the speculators: the former were preaching sedition, and the latter decrying the credit of the government, to fatten on its spoil." He went on to decry the ordinary soldier's lack of the vote. Then, in a sudden turn to racist rhetoric, Tompkins accused the convention of withdrawing its support for the white "patriot soldier" while delegates dithered away on questioning the impact on social order of allowing militiamen to vote. He charged that the convention was not attuned to the sacrifices of white militiamen but that it was "very sensitive . . . on the question of excluding the blacks—a class confessedly degraded, ignorant and vicious. . . ."[15] The governor's racist outburst, like his absences from the convention was, in part, the consequence of years of "financial privation and heavy drinking" that began around 1815.[16]

John Cramer was the last member of Sanford's committee to engage in the suffrage debate. Having presented the committee's report at the start of the proceedings, he now launched an informed attack on the defenders of property and ended his critique with a plea to "grant universal suffrage, for after all, it is upon the virtue and intelligence of the people that the stability of your government must rest."[17]

On September 25, on the sixth day of the suffrage debate, opponents of the freehold requirement had their way. Van Buren rose to address the convention. In a lengthy speech, he argued for a broader eligibility for the suffrage and pointed out that thousands of freeholders with land valued at less than $250 would continue to lack the vote under the latest proposed amendment, which he opposed.[18] At the close of debate, Colonel Young added that the Constitution of the United States did not provide that "either the electors, or elected, should be freeholders." On that note, since the "usual hour of adjournment" was approaching, the vote to require a freehold for the state senate was called: it lost one hundred to nineteen. No one on the suffrage committee supported the amendment, although Federalist Stephen Van Rensselaer, the largest landowner in the state, was absent, his name not appearing in the tally of the vote. Neither did that of James Kent. Perhaps both Federalists from the County of Albany foresaw its defeat. Like the suffrage committee members, Tompkins, the president of the convention, voted against the freehold requirement.[19]

Having largely disposed of the issue of separate qualifications to vote for state senators, subsequent debate turned to consideration of the breadth of options men would have in order to qualify to vote for the offices of governor, lieutenant governor, senator, and assemblyman. The convention began by reevaluating the service options in the report. An amendment to strike militia service was overwhelmingly defeated. But the proposal to drop work on the public roads passed: opponents of road labor as an enabler of the franchise met growing concerns that it would result in nearly universal manhood suffrage. Of the seven members of the suffrage committee, only Fairlie and Van Rensselaer voted to strike the highway option.[20] The other members, including Sanford, viewed the work as a way to cast a wider net for voter eligibility.

On Friday, September 28, the discussion that had favored suffrage expansion veered in a different direction: a proposed amendment would confirm the suffrage for men currently entitled to vote and, with certain conditions, extend it to those who had resided in the state for three years and for one year in the town where they voted. The idea of reducing voter qualifications to mere residency requirements made many delegates uneasy, as such an amendment would have a broad inclusionary impact. One delegate cautioned about its "injustice and danger." But the amendment passed in a close vote, sixty-three to fifty-five. In their continuing opposition to near universal male suffrage, suffrage committee members Fairlie and Van Rensselaer objected.[21]

Martin Van Buren also declared that he was "against the amendment, and against universal suffrage." He warned that the delegates were "hazarding every thing by going to such lengths in the amendments—the people would never sanction them."[22] Van Buren's practical concern for the future ratification of the new constitution led him to dampen expectations that it would contain language that supported universal suffrage. The Bucktail leader faced a dilemma—the need to deliver a significant expansion in male suffrage in order to grow his following in future years while avoiding suffrage qualifications that would alienate many voters.

By the following day, the new language for male suffrage included only age and residency as basic requirements. In response to a feeling among delegates that race and service options for the suffrage required reconsideration, a resolution that proposed constituting a new select committee to replace the Sanford committee reached the floor. A committee of thirteen members to reevaluate the suffrage report, along with the amendments "made thereto in committee of the whole," was proposed. The committee would work to redraft the suffrage section to integrate it into the constitution. It was also explicitly charged with reporting "their [*sic*] *opinion upon* the expediency of excluding people of colour from the right of suffrage." The resolution passed. Samuel Young was appointed to the new select committee and became chair.[23] An avid defender of a white-men-only restriction, he was the only holdover from the Sanford committee appointed to the committee of thirteen.

The new committee's report, made on October 4, included two sets of options for white men. Among the requirements for the first choice was one year's residency in the state and taxes paid; for the second choice, a three-year residency and work on the highways were required. Neither option included service in the militia. "Male citizens, other than white" were required to have resided in the state for three years and own a $250 "freehold estate" upon which the taxes had been paid. Debate, amendments, and votes followed.[24] An amendment to strike the requirement for work on the public roads as part of an option came to the floor two days later but was defeated, eighty-six to fourteen. This time, Sanford joined the small minority that included Fairlie and Van Rensselaer in voting to drop work on the highways as a qualifier for suffrage: the option was limited in this version of the amendment to white men with three years' residency in the state.[25] This was a change from Sanford's previous position. With this decision on October 6, Sanford supported male suffrage based only on citizenship, age, and a longer residency—for whites. In his thinking at this point, tax payments, roadwork, and militia service did not apply.[26]

The most impactful—and spiteful—portion of the new committee's report, however, was the proviso that excluded free black men from voting unless they possessed a $250 freehold and had paid their property tax. The proviso passed, seventy-two to thirty-one. Among the members of the disbanded Sanford committee, Fairlie, Ross, and Young voted for the proviso. It would disenfranchise nearly all African American men who currently had the suffrage. Nathan Sanford and Stephen Van Rensselaer were among the minority that opposed the imposition of the freehold qualification on African Americans. No vote was recorded for Cramer or Livingston. For the first time, Martin Van Buren voted for black exclusion in his support of the amendment.[27] He believed that white voters in the state would reject a constitution that offered suffrage to blacks without a property requirement. Two days later, on October 8, a similar amendment on the proviso won a strong majority. Votes from members of the old Sanford committee remained unchanged, except that Cramer and Livingston showed up to vote for it. Van Buren again supported the freehold requirement for blacks arguing, patronizingly, that it was an "inducement to industry. . . ." Chancellor Kent and other Federalists, in contrast to the Bucktail leader, voted against requiring a freehold for blacks[28] even though, earlier in the debate, Kent had reasoned that blacks were "in some respects a degraded portion of the community. . . ." Nevertheless, he continued, he was "unwilling to see them disfranchised. . . ."[29]

Before the last vote of the day was called, however, the tone in the chamber became heated. Delegates were asked to decide on the entire suffrage section, including the proviso. Colonel Young from the committee of thirteen stepped forward and, again, advanced race-based remarks. The colonel suggested that he would force a motion to the floor that excluded all blacks from the vote if the convention failed to carry the "compromise" put forward in the second suffrage report. He stated that he considered the "proviso as the result of compromise" and went on to issue a threat to his colleagues, informing them that "if this proviso was rejected, he should move to insert the word *white* in the report and exclude them [the blacks] altogether."[30] Hearing this, Sanford sensed where the convention was headed on race and chartered his course. Having worked with Young on the suffrage committee, he knew the colonel's efforts to deny giving the vote to African Americans first-hand. Unlike in previous votes in which the lawyer-politician had consistently opposed black exclusion, this time he compromised his traditional Republican principles of equal rights and universal manhood suffrage: he consented, reluctantly, to the $250 freehold requirement for African Americans that restricted their right to civic participation. He also joined the majority of delegates, seventy-four to thirty-eight, in approving the entire suffrage section. Among the Sanford committee members, Fairlie and Van Rensselaer opposed the language in the section.[31]

Returning to suffrage issues two weeks later, the convention began its review of the "Elective Franchise." Again, resolutions challenged specific qualifying options in the proposed article on suffrage. Delegates defeated a motion to strike work on the highways as a qualifying factor for suffrage, eighty-one to twenty-nine. A proposal by James Fairlie passed: it created a suffrage option for men who had been exempted from the militia because they served as firemen. A final attempt to eliminate militia duty as an enabler lost, eighty-four to twenty-one. In these votes, the members of the first suffrage committee were consistent, voting as they always had, with Sanford reverting to his longtime support for labor on the highways as an option to qualify for the vote.[32] On Monday, the convention began to finalize the suffrage section of the constitution. Efforts to adjust the language that preceded the proviso largely failed, but a motion to provide a "substitute" for the proviso passed by a wide margin. It clarified the language in the paragraph and restated the requirements: they included a three-year residency for African Americans and possession of a $250 freehold for at least one year.[33]

On Saturday, November 10, the convention voted ninety-eight to nine in favor of the revised constitution. Six of the seven members of the Sanford committee joined the majority—Stephen Van Rensselaer either did not vote or was absent. At the close of the convention, Sanford offered a resolution thanking his friend, and convention chair, Daniel Tompkins, "for his able, faithful, and impartial discharge of the duties of that station." It carried unanimously.[34] In January 1822, New York State voters ratified the constitution, 74,732 to 41,402. In 1826, a constitutional amendment passed by popular vote reduced the requirements for white male suffrage to citizenship and meeting the criteria for age and residency. These categories were the same as those favored by Sanford in his vote at the convention five years earlier.[35]

The suffrage debate among the delegates ended in a compromise on the contentious issues of race and property and lost sight of Sanford's initial framework for reform centered on "the people." Requirements based on taxes, roadwork, military service, residency, and age, as well as a conservative push to tie the vote for state senator to property ownership, drew impassioned argument: at the conclusion, only black male suffrage suffered. Until an October 8 vote, Sanford had been among a minority of delegates defending racial inclusion. Then he changed his position and supported the compromise that required African American voters to own a $250 freehold. He feared, like others, that current white voters would fail to ratify the constitution, with its substantial expansion of the suffrage, if they were going to be treated as equals to blacks.

In his articulation of the principles behind the rights he valued and defended, the retired United States senator who so influenced the convention of 1821 also left a lasting impact on New York State constitutional law. His knowledge of the classics and feel for modern history, his formal legal training, and his enthusiasm for ideas shaped his arguments for reform: universal male suffrage free of real property requirements, a judiciary responsive to changes in society, a constitutional ban on slavery, and freedoms of speech and of the press.

A generation later, while the nation postponed the decision to achieve freedom from slavery, Frederick Douglass took note of Sanford's voice. The escaped slave and leader in the abolitionist movement expressed his appreciation for the senator's efforts to restore and expand black suffrage. In his address to the Colored National Convention held in Rochester, New York, in 1853, Douglass declared that "By birth, we [Freed Colored people] are American Citizens . . . [and, he added, as Nathan Sanford had proclaimed,] 'Here there is but one estate—*the people* . . . [and] those who bear the burthens of the state should choose those that rule it.' "[36] Recognized by Douglass, American historians have let Sanford's contributions to democratic rights go unnoticed.[37] Alexander Keyssar is an exception. In *The Right to Vote*, the author began his second chapter, "Democracy Ascendant," with an epigraph taken from Sanford's speech at the convention: "The course of things in this country is for the extension, and not the restriction of popular rights."[38]

Chapter 10

Chancellor, 1823–1826

When forty-two-year-old Sanford signed New York's constitutional convention roll in late August 1821 as "widower,"[1] he had already lost his first wife, Eliza Van Horne, and outlived Mary Esther Isaacs, his second wife, by five years. Home was shared with his five children in his New York City townhouse at 27 Pine Street. With his election to the legislature in 1808, work had often kept Sanford away from home. By the close of the convention, he had boarded in Albany for more than two months, an additional source of stress. Given his work schedule, it is unlikely that he ever involved himself significantly in the rearing or tutoring of his children. He would cover more than 150 miles during the trip back home from the convention, time enough to contemplate the new era in his life that was about to begin.

Despite being back in private life without a public office—for the first time in twenty years—Sanford made sure that he kept in contact with his network of former colleagues and political allies. In January 1822, he received posts from two United States senators, Rufus King and his old friend, Martin Van Buren. King had been a delegate from Queens County to the constitutional convention. In the Senate and at the convention, the two politicians had often voted alike. In 1817, King had denounced slavery, emerging as leader of a Federalist faction whose members had backed Bucktails in recent state legislative elections.[2] In separate mailings to Sanford, King and Van Buren sent documents that pertained to the convention; one reported the results of the recent popular vote that ratified the new state constitution. In his acknowledgment, Sanford thanked both senators and added that "there is no doubt that a great majority of those citizens who have not voted would have given their suffrages for the

new constitution, if they had gone to the polls," a reference to the persistent problem of voter turnout. He also enclosed a recent anti-constitution pamphlet, the "only formal dissertation, which has issued from the press, against the new constitution." Sanford dismissed its contents as "a tissue of miserable nonsense . . . proof that nothing better can be agreed in opposition."[3] Over the next several months, the former federal senator rekindled other relationships and associated with members of the political, cultural, and educational elites of his day. In August, he received an appeal from former congressional colleagues to join a subscription to benefit the retired judge, Tapping Reeve, his teacher at the Litchfield School of Law. The letter asked for a donation "from each of the judge's pupils" to help resolve Reeve's financial difficulties.[4] The congressmen included a copy of their initial circular letter distributed in early May. It had received a swift response from John Calhoun, a Yale graduate who had studied at Litchfield, following Sanford by only a few years. The secretary of war informed the group that he had already joined the subscription and added that "No period of my life . . . has been spent more advantageously to myself [than that at the law school]."[5]

Two months later, Sanford would meet senior public officials at the second anniversary meeting of the American Academy of Languages and Belles Lettres held at City Hall in New York. As reported in the July 10, 1822, issue of the *Baltimore Patriot and Mercantile Advertiser*, the academy's objective was the "general improvement of the English language." Its involvement with scholars from many countries had resulted in some success in achieving "uniformity" in the "meaning . . . and orthography of words," the paper reported. A voluntary association aiming to improve the general culture, the academy was headed by a notable board of directors. At the meeting, the Honorable John Quincy Adams, secretary of state, was elected president and Joseph Story, an associate justice of the United States Supreme Court, was elected first vice president. Sanford was chosen one of nine counselors, a group that also included Henry Clay, the recent Speaker of the House of Representatives, already entertaining a run for the presidency. Among the others were a college president, a bishop, the chief justice of North Carolina, and the governor of Louisiana. The reporter estimated that the academy's funds from subscriptions totaled about $10,000. In spite of its financial prowess, the academy was short-lived, although for Sanford the political contacts he made may have helped his career.

Other honors came his way. On August 5, 1823, only days after he became chancellor of the State of New York, the trustees of Columbia

College granted Sanford an honorary doctor of laws degree. Commencement was held at Columbia's campus on Park Place, a location a few blocks north of Trinity Church and west of Broadway in the lower part of Manhattan. It began with five orations, followed by the bestowal of twenty-nine bachelors and nine masters of art degrees to young men. Two doctors of divinity and four doctors of laws degrees were also presented. Recently retired chief justice of the supreme court of the state and loyal Clintonian Ambrose Spencer received his LLD first. He was followed by Sanford, John Savage, the newly appointed chief justice of the supreme court who replaced Spencer, and Edward Livingston, a lawyer.[6] Livingston had served as mayor of New York from 1801 to 1803 and as federal attorney for the District of New York until 1803, when Sanford replaced him. Livingston then moved to New Orleans, which became his base for launching a successful second political career. Deservedly, Sanford found himself in illustrious company. Of the recipients of the honorary law degrees, all were Republicans, and three had been appointed to the bench. Sanford's parchment stated that the "honorable man, Nathan Sanford" was "From the offices of the Chancellor" and explained that the conference of the degree was "because of his learning in the doctrine and studies of the liberal arts." Another reason may have been that many of Sanford's contemporaries had viewed his tenure as federal attorney as bringing a period of stability to the office, after the scandal of embezzlement surrounding Livingston's departure. Sanford's degree was signed "Clement C. Moore, clerk."[7] Moore, a longtime trustee of Columbia College, was the author of *A Visit from St. Nicholas*, later known as *'Twas the Night Before Christmas*. He first read the poem to his children on Christmas Eve 1822. Moore was a distant cousin of Sanford.[8]

Politicians had also been busy engaging Sanford's future. In a move attributable to Martin Van Buren's influence, Joseph Yates, the newly elected governor and a Bucktail Republican, nominated Sanford to become chancellor, a judicial post that dealt with commercial disputes, wills, and trusteeships for the property of orphans and widows. During the period after the close of the constitutional convention in the fall of 1821 and his unanimous confirmation by the Bucktail-controlled senate in January 1823,[9] Sanford had been considered for federal appointments as well. In May 1822, he received a letter from Colonel Henry Rutgers that informed him that President Monroe was no doubt engaged in recruiting men to become ambassadors to the South American republics and "to other Powers or States. . . ." Rutgers went on to laud Sanford as a "Stateman [*sic*] and Politician" and encouraged him to look favorably upon such opportunities.[10] A year later, President Monroe weighed the possibility of appointing Sanford to the post of minister to France.[11] The proposal had been circulating in the president's political circle. In a postscript attached to a letter from Monroe's secretary of the treasury, William H. Crawford, the Georgian informed Senator Van Buren of his conversations concerning Sanford. The postscript did not refer to the ambassadorship explicitly. However, Crawford, who had preceded Albert Gallatin as ambassador to France, mentioned that he had recently seen the outgoing minister. But in the note, Secretary Crawford told Van Buren that he had stopped expressing preferences about applicants for positions and had explained to President Monroe that he thought the "appointment of Mr. Sanford would be as acceptable . . . as that of any other person. . . ."[12]

In any event, a public figure nearly fluent in French, but a widower with at least four of his children at home, service abroad would have presented challenges to Sanford. Crawford's noncommittal comment to the president confirmed that the senator would not garner strong support for the post. In the body of the letter, the secretary also conveyed his view on another matter: the directions certain states were leaning in regard to his bid for the presidency.[13] Since Van Buren had already backed Crawford's candidacy to succeed Monroe, the information the senator acquired from the letter about the breadth of Crawford's support would be helpful to him as the leader of the strongest group of Republicans.

Confirmed by the state senate as chancellor, Sanford assumed the office on August 1, 1823, having already moved his family to Albany. He had often boarded in Albany as a young legislator, so he knew the city well. Settled by the Dutch on a bluff above the Hudson River, and the state capital since 1797, Albany counted nearly 16,000 inhabitants when the Sanfords arrived.[14] Sanford was listed in the 1823 edition of the *Albany Directory* as "chancellor," living at Park Place.[15] His townhouse faced the large tree-dotted Green near the center of government. State Hall, called the Capitol, was located there. Built in 1799, State Hall housed the offices of the state government. Nearby, Congress Hall, also on Park Place, was Albany's major hotel. In addition to hosting travelers, the hotel served as the informal headquarters for legislators and lawyers. By 1800, the city had become a transportation hub, boasting stage lines and turnpikes. Passengers would take a ferry across the Hudson from the capital's bustling west bank and then go by roadway south to New York City. In the 1810s, steamboats following set schedules ran on the river. Traveling from Albany to New York, Sanford would make the trip in about twenty-four hours, enjoying the varied scenery in the Catskill Mountains as he passed through.[16] Locating in New York State's capital, close to his new workplace, benefited the chancellor's political prospects, and eased the task of providing for his children and his household. Thirteen-year-old Eliza, his younger daughter, always prided herself on writing to her brother, Edward, a student at Union College, in French. She often addressed him as "Mon cher frère." Writing from Albany in June 1823, she gleefully explained that "Father succeeded in getting a French governess [for us]. . . ." [17]

The court of chancery Sanford entered was restricted by the new constitution, even though its workload had been growing during the war and thereafter. In 1814, a vice-chancellor for New York City and a court reporter had been appointed to expand the court's administrative staff. By 1823 the new constitution had reduced the civil court's jurisdiction to hearing equity appeals, cases that involved parties located in more than one of New York's judicial districts, and suits that crossed state lines.[18] Nonetheless, as he had in the past when entering a new organization, Sanford worked early in his tenure to secure documents. He insisted that published judicial opinions and law reports be carefully preserved. On August 11, he addressed a letter to New York City's common council requesting an office for the use of the assistant register of the court in order to ensure the "Safe keeping of public Papers in a Building."[19] Sanford appointed state senator Samuel M. Hopkins, a Federalist congressman in 1813, as court reporter at the chancery.[20]

Sanford soon became embroiled in cases that included disputes over the enforcement of contracts and the regulation of steamboats subject to both state and federal law. In late winter 1824, Navy Lieutenant William A. Weaver filed a suit against three New York City merchants in chancery court in Albany. At court, complainant Weaver described how he had agreed to use his ship to protect the merchants' vessel and its cargo, mainly flour, during a voyage to Lima, Peru, three years earlier (Weaver's diversion of a navy vessel for private use was itself illegal). The lieutenant would board the merchant ship and "represent her as a store ship," carrying supplies for the navy. For his efforts, Weaver was to receive one-fifth of the profits that might accrue from the deal.[21] He charged that the merchants did not fulfill their obligations under the agreement. The decree that ended the case appeared in the *Albany Argus* on March 23 and was reprinted a few days later by Hezekiah Niles in his *Weekly Register*, the country's first news magazine. In his decision, Chancellor Sanford was dismissive of the contract and the suit. After a lengthy exposition, he

Figure 10.1. Portrait of Nathan Sanford. An 1880 copy of the circa 1825–1830 original. Court of Appeals Collection. Courtesy of the Historical Society of the New York Courts.

declared that ". . . the strain of this transaction rests not on the laws of this country. This contract being illegal, its execution cannot be enforced; and the suit is dismissed, with costs."[22]

The case aroused widespread public interest, focusing a spotlight on Sanford and the court. Niles reprinted letters to the editors and columns about the case taken from newspapers in other cities and towns—the *New-York Gazette*, the *New-York Evening Post*, and the *National Intelligencer*. They argued for one party or the other in the suit, some of them attacking Sanford. While Weaver, in a letter to the editor, protested that "the term 'bribe' does not apply [to me]," Sanford was accused of siding with the merchants. On May 1, the navy suspended Lieutenant Weaver, pending the return of its ship.[23] From Sanford's position, the scrutiny of the contentious case communicated opinions about him and the court, which for many more years would be criticized for vesting too much authority in a single person.[24]

The dispute over the activities of a young naval officer was a narrowly bounded case, unlike those that involved steamboats, where suits often had broad ramifications. The case brought by the Albany-based North River Steamboat Company to the court of chancery in 1824 had its origins in the state legislature many years earlier and in courts. The North River Company had descended from the partnership between politician, investor, and former chancellor, Robert R. Livingston,[25] and inventor Robert Fulton, who had built the *North River* (later called *Clermont*) in 1807. It was the first commercially viable steamboat to operate on the Hudson River. In a move to stimulate economic growth and reward technological innovation, the New York State legislature granted Livingston a monopoly over steamboat commerce on state waters.[26] Often challenged by competitors, the monopoly survived in the court of chancery under James Kent in a case brought by North River's licensee, Aaron Ogden, against Thomas Gibbons. It claimed exclusive navigation rights for North River in New York's waterways and along the Jersey shore. In his decision, Kent supported an injunction against Gibbons's competing steamboats, thereby ensuring the continuation of the monopoly, by concluding that the acts of the New York legislature did not conflict with United States laws. In 1820, Gibbons appealed the judgment to the court of errors of New York, where he lost again.[27]

In response to his failed suit, Gibbons took his case to the United States Supreme Court, where the federal court held jurisdiction since New York's boundary included coastal waters between two states, New York and New Jersey. The landmark case, *Gibbons v. Ogden*, clarified that the Constitution gave Congress ultimate authority to regulate commerce among the states. Chief Justice John Marshall delivered the decision on March 2, 1824, a ruling refined to allow for state regulation, enforceable until a conflict between state and federal law emerged; at that point, state law would yield to federal law. In this decision, the North River Company and Ogden lost the monopoly over steamboat transportation and commerce with New Jersey.[28] *Gibbons v. Ogden* also annulled the "decree of the Chancellor," James Kent.[29]

In June, the ever-aggressive and resolute competitor North River filed a complaint in chancery court seeking, again, to protect its right of "exclusive" navigation with steamboats in state waters. The plaintiff's attorney resorted to arguing for state over federal power: "It is upon State rights we stand; and State rights are State liberty." Chancellor Sanford disagreed. He decided for the defendant, John R. Livingston, the owner of the steamboat that had engaged in commerce during a landing in New Jersey, and a distant cousin of Robert R. Livingston. The vessel had departed from Jersey City and stopped in New York City, a "way landing" en route to Albany, one writer slyly noted.[30] The route touched two states and was deemed legal under the recent Supreme Court decision. Sanford's determination may have been the reference point for Horatio Stafford's quip in his pocket guide to travelers printed in September 1824 about the new Troy Steam-Boat Company: its two boats would be "plying *direct*, between Troy and New-York, *by the way of 'Jersey City,'* a perfectly ridiculous farce, even if played 'according to law.' "[31] During these years Sanford never had a steamboat named after him, but others did. Companies honored the judges who had promoted their commercial interests in cases dealing with water transportation. North River operated the *Chancellor Livingston* and the *James Kent*, and on March 15, 1825, the *Chief Justice Marshall*, a steamboat owned by the new Hudson River Line, began her maiden voyage from New York City to Albany and on to Troy.[32]

As Sanford's political and judicial activities became known within government and among the public in the early 1820s, he acquired a degree of stature in New York State. He had participated in the expansion of democracy at the constitutional convention of 1821 by contributing to judicial reform and by providing a rationale for universal manhood suffrage. Among the concrete details of appeals at the court of chancery, he broadened notions about how the law could help expand commerce. Although he had his critics as chancellor, even James Kent could not diminish his Republican support. Sanford had followed Kent, who had entered involuntary retirement on August 1, 1823, at age sixty.

Kent resented his forced retirement and Sanford for having become his successor. Moss Kent, a former state legislator and congressman, unlike his brother, James, had shown respect for Sanford as chancellor, at least in the Weaver decree: "In this case he appears to possess the mantle of his Predecessor [James Kent]," Moss Kent wrote in a letter to his brother. Years later, writing in his *Necrologies*, the retired chancellor took a shot at Sanford's career moves during this period. Kent attacked the former senator for campaigning through the use of "Intrigues"[33] in seeking two positions—that of chancellor, and two and a half years later, the office of United States senator for a second term. Written in the 1840s but not published, this critique of Sanford as a person, and as a lawyer-politician, gave voice to the former chancellor's lingering dislike of his successor at the chancery.

Chapter 11

Candidate and Senator, 1824–1831

While Sanford was chancellor, a few of Martin Van Buren's followers among the divided Bucktails floated his name as a candidate for governor. In April 1824, they aimed to replace Joseph Yates, the governor who had recommended two anti-Bucktail candidates for the state supreme court, and been widely ridiculed for it in the Republican press. For the gubernatorial post, the group felt out Sanford, characterized by one student of the period as "wealthy and marmoreal!" They were also thinking ahead to the presidential election of 1824: these supporters had seen in Sanford someone who might bring New York's followers of Henry Clay into their partisan circle. As Speaker of the House, Clay was their favored nominee for the presidency. Cautious about the circumstances of the entreaty, Sanford requested an endorsement for governor from the entire legislature, mainly from other Bucktail Republicans. In reality, this was a way for him to reject the nomination, suspecting that his support was not widespread—and he was right: Van Buren's increasingly well-organized and rising group among the Bucktails, named the "Albany Regency" by Van Buren enemies, went on to nominate Samuel Young,[1] the delegate to the constitutional convention who had threatened to exclude African Americans from the suffrage. In September, the new People's Party, which embraced a more popular democracy than the opposition Bucktails, nominated former governor DeWitt Clinton, who won handily in the November election, defeating Young.[2]

In the national politics of the early 1820s—a time when Republicans had begun to splinter—presidential hopefuls began campaigning for the next election almost immediately after the reelection of President Monroe. The still influential political brokers Thomas Jefferson and James Madison favored Secretary of the Treasury Crawford as the president's successor. The secretary stood for keeping power in the states and for minimal federal government spending, that is, the Old Republicanism. In February 1824, as was still customary in the nominating process, a small Republican congressional caucus organized and led by Van Buren, the enforcer of party-like discipline, met and selected Crawford as their nominee.[3]

This hotly contested election drew other politicians. Tennessee senator General Andrew Jackson, who ran as a seeming outsider, led in the Electoral College tally but lost when the outcome was decided in the House of Representatives. Two other candidates were regional; Kentuckian Henry Clay had help from the West, and Secretary of State John Quincy Adams, from Massachusetts, received support in New England and other parts of the Northeast.[4] By October, Clay had come to realize that he needed a running mate from outside his region to broaden his appeal. His followers had already targeted New York State: they recruited Nathan Sanford, who knew politicians sympathetic to Clay's positions in the state legislature and the U.S. Senate. As the vice presidential candidate, Clay's backers thought the chancellor could influence Republican state legislators to vote a significant share of New York's thirty-six electoral votes for their man.[5] John Calhoun also joined the fray. A Republican nationalist, Secretary of War Calhoun had defended internal improvements, the Second Bank of the United States, and the Tariff of 1816.[6]

By November 6, Hezekiah Niles would report that Calhoun had won the election for vice president, thereby becoming "president of the Senate . . . ," which the publisher considered the "most dignified station in any legislative body in the world." Niles was not surprised that Calhoun had defeated Sanford and Clay, who had also appeared on the vice-presidential ballot. Niles had described Calhoun as the candidate who "the people have . . . regarded as the proper person. . . ." Confirmation of this news came on February 9, 1825, when the House, following the electoral tally, announced Calhoun as vice president with 182 votes. Sanford received a total of thirty votes, losing overwhelmingly in his own state—with seven electoral votes to Calhoun's twenty-nine. Both candidates received seven votes from Kentucky; in Ohio, Sanford garnered sixteen votes to zero for Calhoun.[7]

Meanwhile, defeated in the vice-presidential race, Clay had faced presidential balloting at the Capitol in Albany. New York was one of only six states of twenty-four where the legislature still chose electors, having squashed numerous attempts to legislate popular voting for the presidency.[8] There, Crawford's supporter, Van Buren, managed to persuade enough New York electors to drop Clay, who then failed to rank among the top three candidates. The contest, among Jackson, Adams, and Crawford, was forced into the House of Representatives since no candidate had won a majority in the Electoral College. On February 9, Congressman Stephen Van Rensselaer, the sole Federalist to serve on Sanford's suffrage committee at the constitutional convention, cast the deciding electoral vote for Adams.[9]

In the fall of 1825, a decision by the new president would create an opening for Sanford to return to the United States Senate: Adams offered the position of minister to Britain to Senator Rufus King from New York. The nomination of a Federalist outraged Old Republicans, but King vacated his seat in the Senate, and Sanford would win the election in the state legislature "by a nearly unanimous vote." He was backed by the Regency as well as followers of DeWitt Clinton.[10] On January 24, 1826, he resigned from the court of chancery, a week after he had submitted a report to the New York State Assembly on the "judiciary system."[11] Hezekiah Niles took the opportunity to satirize the politics behind the election of Sanford by the state legislature:

> All parties appear to be well pleased with this selection. . . . Mr. Sanford, ejected from the Senate by the 'republican' party in 1821, is now sent to it on the nomination of the same party . . . notwithstanding these changes of opinion as to the gentlemen, the great probability is that their opinions . . . either on the policy of the United States or of the state of New York, have not undergone any change at all.[12]

When he became president in March 1825, Harvard graduate John Quincy Adams had already served in the United States Senate, and possessed a long and accomplished diplomatic career, particularly during his years as secretary of state under President Monroe. In his address to Congress on December 6, Adams lauded past improvements in transportation and communication. He praised the General Survey Act of 1824 that had authorized the Army Corps of Engineers to clear rivers and dredge harbors, and urged expansion of the act. The president endorsed even more improvements to the economy's infrastructure and public education, and he applauded free trade and a stronger navy to protect commerce. A naval academy and astronomical observatory were proposed.[13] However, President Adams and his followers faced strong opposition in their efforts to implement the ambitious program. With few internal improvements made by 1828, the Adams administration had failed to strengthen the federal government; expenditures actually fell during the 1820s. By the '30s, they were lower than those made by state and local governments combined.[14]

Problems in foreign affairs and Indian policy, like commercial improvements, plagued Adams's presidency too—perhaps even more so. In 1826 and '27, events in these areas contributed to the administration's loss of the Senate and the House. It was a defeat for Adams's nonpartisan politics, one based on government by consensus where the men who served in government were assumed to require keen intelligence.[15] Adams's critics were more like Sanford, who had maintained at the state constitutional convention that the "people" were at the center of electoral politics. He gave the example of towns, where elections expressed the "virtue and intelligence of our people."[16] The opposition to President Adams was led by Van Buren, who had been "forging a new politics that worked from the grass roots up, based on patronage, organization, and partisan loyalty."[17] Van Buren's feat in the state legislature to drop Clay had been enabled, in part, by this mid-1820s transformation in much of New York's politics: Bucktail Republicans allied with Van Buren and his Regency organization, "standing for minimalism in state government," while the opposition to them emerged from a "shifting coalition of former Clintonians, Federalists, and the occasional Bucktail. . . ," as one historian has put it. The group became known as the Adams Republicans, the faction behind President Adams that challenged Van Buren's Regency. By 1828, the political scene had changed again when the Bucktails began to be called Democrats, followers of Andrew Jackson, who had won a plurality of the popular vote in the presidential election of 1824.[18]

From 1826 until his retirement from the Senate in 1831, these developments defined the context for Sanford's political allegiances, and set in motion the means by which he would be used by factional leaders to achieve their goals. A mere two months after he took his seat, Regency leaders were evaluating, once again, the senator's prospects in a run for governor, challenging their opponent, incumbent DeWitt Clinton. From Albany on April 2, General Erastus Root, a member of the assembly and the candidate for lieutenant governor who had been defeated by Clinton's People's Party nominee two years earlier, addressed a letter to Van Buren. In the letter, Root described the work of the "Tammany Hall committee" in recruiting candidates to stand for the November election and concluded that "Sanford is the most likely to succeed. He would secure a portion of the Adams men." He added that ". . . altho [*sic*] an Adams man, he would be more civil to us than [DeWitt] Clinton."[19] As the senator's political allegiances had shifted away from Tammany Hall in the years 1826 and 1827, he had become "an Adams man" in the eyes of some Bucktails. Even the president took note of the relationship. In a reference he made in his diary to the period before the spring of 1828, the president declared that "Mr[.] Sanford was formerly a cool political friend of mine . . ."[20] in a relationship built on mutual respect.

In his letter, a concerned Root went on to outline an internal improvement proposal that could win votes for Governor Clinton. Illustrating some of the minutia of state politics, Root complained to Van Buren that opposition to the project from Saratoga County's Samuel Young and other Bucktails had inadvertently boosted Clinton's popularity. The road would run through the southern part of New York and was expected to open the area in the south to economic development in the same way that the new Erie Canal had helped the north. Root noted that "The conduct of Young & other bucktails in regard to our state road will secure to Clinton a majority [of votes] in the southern tier of counties." He also showed his exasperation toward President Adams and Governor Clinton: "We are in a d—l [devil] of a pickle!—a federal pres t. [president] & a fed l [federal] gov r [governor]."[21] Root was referring to Adams as a former Federalist and to DeWitt Clinton, who had run for president in 1812 as a Federalist.

While in recess after the close of the first session of the Nineteenth Congress, Sanford dealt once again with these appeals to run for governor. In September 1826, he wrote from Albany to a delegate to the upcoming Republican convention to be held in Herkimer. In his letter, the senator protested that he had learned of intentions to nominate him. Sanford reminded his supporter that he had announced his decision not to run in the July 6 issue of the *Albany Argus*, the Regency newspaper. He repeated that he would not be a candidate, although he was "deeply grateful for every proof of the favour of my personal and political friends."[22] In November, Clinton won reelection.

In the cold of February 1826, Sanford traveled from the state capital to Washington to join the first session of the Nineteenth Congress, a few weeks after it had convened. His seat had been vacant since March 1825. The trip covered nearly 375 miles, which Sanford traveled by ferry, steamboat, stage, and carriage. His family remained in Albany. He knew the nation's capital from his first term in the Senate that had begun in 1815, after the close of the War of 1812, and he would find many aspects of the material environment unchanged. Washington remained a rural place where cows grazed in open fields and hogs scavenged the refuse dropped along roadways. Sanford would have noticed that the wings of the Capitol, housing the Senate and the House of Representatives, had been rebuilt after the damage inflicted on them by the British in 1814. The wings were now joined together by a central section topped with a copper-covered wooden dome. Still lacking large businesses, year-round residents were mainly government employees, shopkeepers, laborers, a few boardinghouse proprietors, and many indigents. Native Americans often visited the city, meeting with government officials to express grievances.[23] Congressmen had already created a community of transients around Capitol Hill, finding lodging close to their workplace in order to avoid the rutted roads. The brick boardinghouses were three stories high; lodgers ate together and found tailors, grocers, bookstores, an oyster house, and a liquor store nearby. At the Capitol, the Senate housed a semicircular auditorium furnished with desks: the legislators' places of work. In addition, Congress had its own library and post office.[24] Similar to his first term in the Senate, Sanford would participate little in debates, as he continued to wrestle with the lung problems that prevented him from speaking audibly in large groups. In Washington, he would meet up with Van Buren, the senator from New York who had been elected in 1821 to replace him.

During this second term, which straddled the presidencies of John Quincy Adams and his 1828 successor, Andrew Jackson, Sanford's primary interests were government organization, the maintenance of records and the dissemination of public information (both areas of past concern), foreign affairs, commerce and transportation, and the nation's currency. In his First Annual Message to Congress, President Adams had proposed the creation of an interior department, an idea that Sanford supported. Understanding the need for additional resources for the executive branch, the senator made clear that he also favored the expansion of the attorney general's office into a Department of Justice.[25] In December 1826, Sanford introduced a bill that would require the public reporting of Supreme Court decisions. The bill stipulated that a reporter be hired at an annual salary of $1,000 to record decisions, and then have them printed (within six months) and delivered to the secretary of state for distribution. Another instance of Sanford's concern for public documents addressed the Senate's journal: while representing a select committee appointed in March 1828 to review its status, Sanford moved that the entire Journal of Executive Proceedings of the Senate be printed and published under the direction of the secretary of the Senate.[26] These were additional efforts to institutionalize administrative practices essential for the republic's orderly expansion, and both motions were approved.

Early in his term, John Calhoun, the president of the Senate, appointed Sanford to the Committee on Foreign Relations. Vice President Calhoun had come to oppose many of President Adams's policies. To diminish the president's standing, Calhoun seeded many of the standing committees with presidential critics. Starting late in 1826, Sanford was among them.[27] He became chair on December 11, 1826, but served only during that session, although he was reappointed annually as a committee member throughout his term.[28] On the floor of the Senate, Sanford offered narrowly focused proposals and made procedural points. During the debate over a treaty with the United Mexican States (formed in 1823), he proposed a resolution to delete the term "inhabitants" and replace it with "citizens." In another instance, he reminded the Senate that the conventions of London signed in September 1827 constituted a treaty. The conventions had dealt with adjustments to the boundary settlement—between the United States and the British dominions in America—that had been stipulated in the Treaty of Ghent. Sanford insisted that the conventions required the "advice and consent of the Senate." Also on February 17, 1829, the *Senate Journal* recorded that Sanford moved that the Committee on Foreign Relations "be discharged" from its work in evaluating the appointment of the "king of the Netherlands, umpire" to help resolve another boundary dispute: the controversy between Great Britain and the United States over the shared northeast boundary. The Senate agreed.[29]

Plagued by personal conflicts among the secretaries and partisan disputes in the Congress, even Henry Clay, the forceful secretary of state, made little headway in foreign affairs under Adams. The environment appears to have also affected the work of the Committee on Foreign Relations, with Sanford showing frustration with the lack of results. In February 1827, as chairman, he presented a report to the Senate on memorials the committee had received from "merchants and traders" in Portsmouth, New York, Philadelphia, and Baltimore. They had "lost property by the depredations of the French subsequent to the year 1806." Having served as federal attorney for the District of New York, the senator possessed first-hand knowledge of these types of seizures at sea and the subsequent claims for damages from the owners of ships and cargoes. As prosecutor, he had initiated the legal proceedings that resulted in the prize cases that proliferated in federal court during the Napoleonic Wars and the War of 1812, the years when the North Atlantic trade boomed, and when many merchant ships and their cargoes were destroyed. Without the administration having achieved any major resolutions of claims brought by American citizens against the seizures of their property at sea, Sanford ended his report to the senators by asking that the committee no longer be required to review such petitions.[30]

Around this time, in 1826 and 1827, Sanford shed his reputation as a supporter of President Adams due, in part, to the administration's ineffectiveness in foreign relations. In his diary, the president confirmed that his once friendly relationship with Sanford had deteriorated. He wrote on May 27, 1828: "in the lapse of time [he] has estranged himself from me, and during the recent session of the Senate [from December 3, 1827 to May 26, 1828] has avoided visiting me almost entirely."[31] In drawing away from Adams, the ever-political Sanford had begun to perceive the hand of Martin Van Buren in architecting the coming defeat of the president in his bid for reelection in the fall of 1828.

In regard to the persistent issue of spoliation claims advanced by American sea merchants against European countries, settlements would meet with greater success after 1828, under President Jackson's aggressive tactics, than they had under Adams. From his position on the Committee on Foreign Relations, Sanford encouraged the work of Jackson's appointed envoys. In May 1830, for example, he reported a settlement between the King of Denmark and the United States regarding American shipping losses. The Danish seizures had taken place between 1808 and 1811. The Senate consented to the convention, and the agreement resulted in Denmark paying the United States an indemnity of $650,000.[32]

In late 1829, the first year of the Jackson administration, Sanford joined the Commerce Committee, in addition to sitting on the Committee on Foreign Affairs. Four years before, the Commerce Committee had been separated from the Committee on Commerce and Manufacturing, the same committee the senator had chaired during his first term. In creating two committees, some senators had reasoned that members of the joint committee, who had backed manufacturers' interests, had consistently favored protective tariffs while advocates for commerce had supported free trade.[33] The split was seen by its supporters as a means to enable senators to dedicate more time to discussing a range of issues raised by the expanding economy. For example, the Commerce Committee could now concentrate on responding to memorials and make proposals to improve internal navigation, such as deepening waterways, improving harbors, and reviewing the activities of customs collectors. Sanford's interest in transportation as a means for boosting commerce had been known before his committee appointment and was partially responsible for it. In the summer of 1827, a New York newspaper had reported that Senator Sanford had surveyed the progress of work on the Delaware and Hudson Canal, a waterway built to link the Delaware and Hudson Rivers. The purpose of the canal was to create a supply line for large amounts of coal and lumber to reach New York City markets. From the vantage point of a new aqueduct on the route, the senator and company officials had observed a canal boat passing through the locks, having safely traveled forty miles of the one hundred-mile length of the waterway.[34]

While tariff policy did not come under the Commerce Committee, Sanford would present the Senate with petitions he had received from his constituents who raised the issue. In February 1829, he read a memorial from the Chamber of Commerce of New York City. It complained about the "injurious effects of the tariff system, as established by the law of the last session, on the commerce of the United States." The petitioners were referring to the tariff bill signed by President Adams in May 1828. The bill had passed the Senate twenty-six to twenty-one, an outcome Sanford had predicted three months earlier in a response to his friend, Assemblyman Nathaniel P. Tallmadge. Sanford wrote that "a small majority in each house [is] in favor of additional duties." Sanford and Van Buren had joined that majority,[35] but for different reasons. A moderate on protectionism, Sanford's vote had mirrored Adams's belief that federal tariffs benefited national economic development. Moreover, Sanford had backed tariffs before, during his first term. He had voted for the tariffs of 1816 and 1820 and was consistent in his policy view. But the political context differed in 1828, with the rise of Martin Van Buren to national politics and the emergence of a disciplined Democratic Party. Van Buren viewed the tariff bill as a political tool: he had encouraged his followers to adjust the stipulations in the bill to favor the regions of the country that Jackson needed to carry in the coming election. The strategy worked, and the tariff was soon named the Tariff of Abominations by opponents of Jackson and Van Buren.[36] With his stand, Sanford experienced that opposition—from his New York merchant constituency, as the memorial shows. His vote had helped New York's largely pro-tariff manufacturing interests.

In addition to his proposals to improve the administration of government, and the issues he promoted in foreign affairs and commerce, Sanford spearheaded efforts during the Jackson administration to address problems that stemmed from the lack of uniformity in the values of the nation's coinage. During the 1780s, under the Articles of Confederation, Congress had adopted the dollar as the single unit of account, a uniform measure of value for all coins in all the states, and in 1787, the Constitution prohibited the states from coining money. Only the federal government could mint precious-metal coins, regulate their value, and offer them as legal tender for paying debts. Paper money, however, would be issued by an independent national bank (not by state banks). Under the Constitution, the value of all paper currency was tied to specie. Despite the prohibition on states printing money, they went ahead, chartering banks that offered their own notes.[37] In 1792, the U.S. Mint had defined the dollar as worth the equivalent of "24.75 grains of pure gold." In spite of the standard, variations in the valuation of coins persisted into Sanford's time. Foreign coins, such as English shillings, circulated widely and carried different valuations; businesses assigned different values to foreign coins regardless of their precious-metal content. And gold and silver coinage was often adulterated with base metals.[38]

The mounting variability in the nation's coins in circulation alarmed Sanford. The senator had addressed issues involving currency during his first term in the Senate: a hard money advocate during the debate over the chartering of the Second Bank of the United States in 1816, he had maintained that the level of specie reserves proposed to back the bank's stock offering to raise capital for its operations was too low. As a result, the bank would risk becoming a "mere paper bank."[39] Sanford voted against issuing the charter. In another example of his tenacity in furthering currency regulation, he had advised the Senate to require its finance committee to evaluate the extent to which the law that aimed to regulate foreign coins had been implemented. He followed up in November 1818, proposing that the committee look into the "expediency"—that is, enforceability—of the April 29, 1816, law that dealt with the "currency of certain foreign coins within the United States."[40] The Senate seems to have tabled the proposal. The following year, Sanford's amendment to the 1816 bank bill that dealt with criminal offenses passed; it required that the penalties for fraud when committed by employees of the national bank be enforced.

With president-elect Jackson, a critic of paper money who believed that only gold and silver should circulate as currency, Sanford reasserted himself into the pursuit of currency reform. He targeted the need to reevaluate the accuracy of the values assigned to the nation's coins. On December 24, 1828, he submitted a resolution to the Senate that required the secretary of the treasury to ascertain and state the values of gold and silver "in true relative value." The resolution passed; it required the secretary to report back to the Senate during the next session. A year and a half later, just within the deadline set, the secretary of the treasury complied with the resolution. His report described the "proportional values of gold and silver" and included a plan to force the conformance of gold coin to its "true relative value" of silver coin. To further the dissemination of this public information, the Senate ordered 1,000 copies of the report printed.[41]

A year later, in the first annual message he sent to Congress, in December 1829, President Jackson criticized the Second Bank of the United States for failing to establish a "uniform and sound currency." Jackson supported the goal of a common currency, understanding it as a means to promote national cohesion. Taking on the president's admonition, Sanford again pointed to the continuing problems with coins; in the Senate, he moved the appointment of a select committee on coins. This committee would define problems with the coins circulating throughout the country and propose amendments to current laws to resolve them. A select committee of five was designated, including Sanford; Mahlon Dickerson, the New Jersey Democratic-Republican who had cast an antislavery vote with Sanford during the Missouri debate in 1820; and Edward Livingston, the recipient with Sanford of an LLD from Columbia College in 1822.[42]

On January 11, 1830, Chairman Sanford presented the committee's report and submitted a bill that supported its findings. Passed to a second reading, the bill used dollars and cents to establish the system of measure for valuing each type of coin and defined how each type could be used as legal tender. These were ambitious goals. "Copper coins of the United States" could be used to pay "debts and demands not exceeding ten cents"; silver coins, each valued at less than a dollar depending upon their silver content, were allowed to be used for value up to ten dollars. For the time being, rules governing the usage of the more expensive gold coin as legal tender were not addressed. However, both gold and silver coins would have to be withdrawn as legal tender if a coin weighed less than ninety-six percent of its assigned standard weight, a stipulation that addressed the problem of degradation in the metallic purity of coins. Finally, the bill made the use of foreign coins illegal. The bill required a staged implementation: enforcement of the rule for copper coinage, and the full weight criterion for gold and silver, would begin upon passage of the bill; the use of foreign coins would be illegal beginning July 3, 1831, a year and a half away; and on July 3, 1833, the regulated use of silver coin would be enforced. In its lengthy enforcement deadlines, the bill recognized the difficulties in affecting permanent change in a chaotic system of coinage.[43]

When Hezekiah Niles wrote a short article on the committee's report a week later, he summed it up as "interesting." Implying that most banks in the United States held specie that would fail according to the criteria set in the bill, Niles concluded that "There are very few whole dollars in any of them [that is, the banks]."[44] The select committee was reappointed in December 1830, after the president had once more criticized the national bank in his annual message. Sanford served as chair, and only he and Dickerson continued as members from the first committee. Again, Sanford delivered the committee's report and bill. Both dealt with the amount of gold that the government would require for a range of gold coins used as legal tender. The coins were also identified according to their corresponding dollar value. Niles wrote in his *Register* that the point of the bill was to raise the value of gold relative to silver in order to meet the European standard. Then, he continued, the United States coins would remain "desirable" as currency. The Senate passed the bill in January 1831, a few weeks before Sanford left office.[45]

In contrast to his leadership role in the reform of coinage policy, Sanford largely stood on the sidelines while debate raged over the Indian Removal Bill that rose to the top of President Jackson's legislative agenda in the winter of 1829–30. By the 1820s, most Native Americans in the Old Southwest had managed to remain on their ancestral lands, unlike those in other states. Their continued presence had been upheld by federal treaties. Yet calls from white settlers for dispossessing Indians of their lands had been mounting. Responding to these demands, state politicians in Georgia fought especially hard for the removal of the Cherokees from their land within the state's boundaries. In his annual message to Congress in December 1829, President Jackson essentially supported Georgia's position: he announced that the federal government would refrain from defending Indian lands if a state government had extended its jurisdiction over them. He thereby put the tribes at risk of violent confrontations and set the stage for an intense and lengthy debate about Indian rights.[46]

Criticism of Jackson's position came swiftly, from within the Senate and from without. On January 4, 1830, Sanford presented a petition from a "meeting of the citizens of the city of New York." They appealed for the "protection of the United States for its Indians against injustice and oppression. . . ." On February 22, the day after the chair of the Senate Committee on Indian Affairs introduced the bill on removal, Sanford read a memorial from the "Indian board for the emigration, preservation and improvement of the aborigines of America, in New York." It took a different tack from the citizens group. The Indian board supported removal, implying that it would save lives and ensure survival of the tribes. The memorial asked "for the removal of the Indians within the several states, to such places as put them within the exclusive control of the federal government." The position mirrored that of President John Quincy Adams at the end of his term; he had come to believe that removal was the preferable alternative to options that risked the use of force by state governments.[47] Both petitions from the New Yorkers appealed to the federal government to protect Native Americans. The bill on the table that responded to the president's call for removal in his annual message provided for "an exchange of lands with the Indians residing in any of the States, or Territories, and for their removal west of the Mississippi." Given the explosive nature of the topic among Americans, the Senate ordered 6,000 copies printed.[48] Weeks of debate ensued. The bill's most persistent critic, Theodore Frelinghuysen, senator from New Jersey, proposed amendments that included giving Indians discretion in relocating "until they shall choose to remove." Sanford's amendment to the bill included a similar phrase: "Indians shall choose to remove." But the Senate defeated both amendments that carried the stipulation.[49] By the close of debate on April 26, Sanford, unable to get his way, joined the Jacksonian majority in voting for removal. The bill passed, twenty-eight to nineteen, in spite of opposition from other northern senators.[50]

Sanford's affirmative vote on Indian removal reflected his reluctance to extend moral imperatives or legal arguments to resolve conflicts involving indigenous peoples. In his support for removal, he denied Native Americans' tribal rights. Similarly, at the constitutional convention of 1821 in New York State, he supported the final proviso to the suffrage reform bill, a political compromise that restricted access to the franchise for African American men, curtailing their right to vote. No doubt submitting to political pragmatism, and a belief that he had achieved a degree of justice for the oppressed in both cases, Sanford showed himself to be a reluctant reformer.

Chapter 12

Retirement, 1831–1838

In the middle of his term, on the day after the close of his third session in Congress, Senator Sanford married twenty-seven-year-old Mary Buchanan. The May 27, 1828 date marked twelve years after he had become a widower for the second time. The marriage ceremony took place in Baltimore at Saint Paul's Protestant Episcopal Church, located in a parish formed in 1692.[1] Of Sanford's family, only his eldest son, Edward, attended. Still uncertain about the date of the wedding in late April, Sanford had informed Edward from Washington that "Miss Buchanan wished that you should attend." By mid-May, the date had been set, and the senator arranged to meet his son at the sumptuous Barnum's Hotel in Baltimore on the 26th, the day before the wedding.[2] Many invitations had been sent, including to relatives on the bride's side of the family in Washington. Mary Buchanan's mother had died young, and her father had remarried. Caroline Johnson Buchanan, the sister of Louisa Johnson Adams, President John Quincy Adams's wife, became Mary's stepmother. In 1819, eighteen-year-old Mary had been hosted in Washington by her aunt and uncle.[3] But the president and Louisa could not attend her wedding, held on a Tuesday. In a reference to their invitation, her uncle inscribed a matter-of-fact entry in one of his diaries:

> . . . [t]his evening Mr Nathan Sanford, a Senator from New York, was married to Miss Mary Buchanan at Baltimore; a match first projected when she passed the winter with us in 1819—so that Mr Sanford has kept his peace nine years. My wife and I were invited to the wedding, but could not conveniently attend.[4]

Buchanan's family, like Senator Sanford's, had deep American roots: his were rural and town-based, while hers were urban and state-based; his father was a justice of the peace, her grandfather was chief justice of the Pennsylvania Supreme Court. Grandfather Thomas McKean had signed the Declaration of Independence and served as a Republican governor of Pennsylvania.[5] Respect and feeling for heritage perhaps counted in linking the couple; and for Sanford, the marriage was also a means to mount and climb the ladder of social status. Mary was twenty-four years her husband's junior.

Mrs. Sanford often accompanied her husband to Washington during the three years that remained in his Senate term. She visited her Adams relatives there, and would journey to see her sister and other family members in Baltimore,[6] forty miles away. She met government officials while engaging in Washington's social life, activities that mixed leisure with politics. Mary also visited and conversed with other wives over tea and at receptions. By spring 1829, she had become acquainted with Margaret Bayard Smith, whose letters and notebooks on "Washington affairs" were published after her death. Smith noted that "Mrs. Sanford and I interchanged several visits and she passed an evening with us. . . ." The much older Mrs. Smith went on to add dismissively that "she did not interest me." The Sanfords no doubt made the social rounds of parties as well.[7] While journeying back and forth between Albany and Washington, they spent time in New York City, perhaps to check up on the senator's rental properties there. In a letter from Washington in March 1829 to Edward in New York, Sanford asked his son to reserve a room for him and Mary at Mrs. Wilkinson's boarding house. He mentioned that they had had a pleasant stay there in November. In the meantime, the couple was in Philadelphia, paying a visit to another of Mary's aunts, Letitia Buchanan.[8]

In Albany, during spring 1831, the Sanfords, as parents, engaged with an active household: Mary had become the stepmother of two children still at home, and in December, she gave birth to a son, Robert. Edward, Charles, and Eliza, Nathan's three oldest children by his first wife, Eliza Van Horne, were grown and had left the household. His eldest, twenty-six-year-old Edward, a graduate of Union College, had long questioned his chosen profession, the law. In 1828, he had written his father that he hated it. The senator responded to his disillusioned son: "You say that you hate the law, but you do not suggest anything else which you would prefer." He continued with fatherly advice for Edward:

> If you ever attain fortune or distinction it must be by your own exertions; and whether you ever attain either of these advantages

> or not, you must live by your own labor and industry. To earn your bread by some honest and respectable pursuit must be the first object of your attention. You now are or ought to be competent to judge of life and its pursuits for yourself. Desiring nothing but your welfare, I wish only that you may succeed in the pursuit which you may select; but some occupation of productive business you must have.[9]

Ending on a note of empathy for his son, Sanford wrote that "for bad as the profession [of law] is for beginners like yourself, I could not then perceive, nor do I now see, anything better to recommend to you."[10] Edward continued to pursue law as his profession, although he also engaged in other occupations later in life. By the time his father had retired to Albany with Mary in 1831, Sanford's second son, Charles, appears to have been boarding with a farm family in Flushing and learning the business.[11] Sanford's daughter, Eliza, now twenty-one, had married an Albany merchant, John Le Breton, in March 1826. Senator Sanford's trip home from Washington for the occasion may have been plagued by the chilly and rainy weather of upstate New York in early spring. The Le Bretons had two daughters, Sanford's first grandchildren.

At home in the townhouse on Park Place in Albany in 1831 were Sanford's children by his second wife, Mary Esther Isaacs: they were seventeen-year-old Mary and her younger brother Henry, Sanford's third son. Henry would die the following year at age sixteen while a student at Union College. He may have succumbed to cholera during the epidemic that reached its height in the area in 1832. The household also included three "Free Colored Persons"; the women were, no doubt, housekeepers and the man was, perhaps, a servant in charge of the stables, the carriages, and the maintenance of the townhouse.[12] Daughter Mary supervised the household in her parents' absence—and had a loving relationship with her father. She wrote Edward that she played chess with him.[13]

During late 1830 and early 1831, Sanford's declining political influence in New York State had reached its nadir. In September 1830, the senator received one vote for governor at the Republicans' convention in Herkimer, where his name had been placed on an informal ballot. Sidestepping Sanford five months later, the state legislature elected William L. Marcy, an associate justice on the New York Supreme Court and a leader of the Albany Regency, to succeed the senator. At the time, followers of Martin Van Buren may have recalled privately that in 1826 they had understood that Sanford's formal political career would end at the close of his second term in the Senate.[14] Retired at fifty-four years of age, Sanford kept up with politics nonetheless, and devoted time to building his law library. Invited by political associates to an anniversary dinner sponsored by the Tammany Society, he penned a public letter in April 1831 declining the invitation: his reason was "sickness in my family," a reference, perhaps, to his son Henry's illness.[15]

Sanford followed congressional proceedings in some detail. At the urging of President Jackson, senators had begun to consider the renewal of the charter for the Bank of the United States. Sanford wrote to the new senator from New York to request his help in broadening his knowledge of America's "political economy." In his letter, the retired Sanford referred to the "multitude of speeches, essays and pamphlets" that the "question" of charter renewal would trigger, and he asked Senator Marcy to send him the titles of relevant readings so that he could "procure books or pamphlets, here or in the City of New York." In closing, Sanford listed the other topics that interested him. They reflected an understanding of the term "political economy," his longstanding concerns about banking that dated from his vote against the 1816 bank bill, and his more recent efforts to reform the nation's coinage: "The discussions which I most desire to see are those which treat banking, paper money and currency, as questions of political economy affecting all the interests of the country."[16]

An avid collector of books, Sanford's personal law library is documented in a copy of the May 1839 auction catalog printed after his death. His collection of 1,300 volumes included colonial legal tomes, such as William Blackstone's *Commentaries*, and modern studies of the law—Kent's *Commentaries*, for example. The public documents consisted mainly of collections of British colonial, United States, and New York State laws. Reports included congressional committee publications but, more frequently, records of court decisions, such as the twenty-volume collection of *Johnson's Reports* and the single volume *Hopkin's Reports*.[17] State papers included congressional journals, debates, and statutes, while other holdings covered such topics as annuities, legacies, bankruptcy, and mortgages—in single volumes. The library rivaled other private law libraries of the time. The auction also offered Sanford's two mahogany bookcases and a lawyer's writing desk.[18] Sanford may have found inspiration to form his own large library when he studied at the Litchfield School of Law in 1798, in a room lined with law books belonging to his teacher, Judge Tapping Reeve. He subsequently became an astute user and builder of libraries. Early in his second term he was one of three senators appointed to a select committee tasked by the Senate to develop a library. Six years later, the project came to fruition when the law library became part of the Library of Congress.[19]

In Albany, the Sanfords were active in the city's cultural and social life. A newly built theater had opened in 1825, and five years later, the second Saint Mary's Church was established. Protestants as well as Catholics contributed to the church building fund: Stephen Van Rensselaer donated $100; Nathan Sanford and Martin Van Buren each gave $50.[20] But most of the Sanfords' socializing appears to have revolved around their own drawing-room gatherings, with some of the records about them illuminating, indeed.

The invitations that Mrs. Sanford had printed for her soirées left a space to fill in the invitee's name. On January 9, 1830, she requested the "pleasure of Mr. Rathbone's company" at seven o'clock—on two dates, both Thursday evenings, a third having been crossed out. The invitation was addressed to the Eagle Tavern, where Rathbone, a wholesale grocer with political aspirations, appears to have been boarding.[21] Sanford and his wife hosted these parties for political acquaintances—dancing followed dinner. At one gathering, his eighteen-year-old daughter, Mary, was "seated between Mr Speaker [Charles L.] Livingston [from the state assembly] and Mr [Nathaniel P.] Tallmadge of the [state] Senate." In the same letter to Edward in New York, Mary went on to describe the goings-on at yet another party:

> We have had two dinners and a soiree, the latter of which was highly amusing. The people are invited as usual for seven o'clock, and accordingly at a few minutes after, a week ago yesterday, all the Yahoos of the members [of the legislature] arrived, and seated themselves around the rooms, with their feet crossed, a red bandanna handkerchief spread upon their laps, and two kinds of cake one upon each knee, together with a cup of coffee as sausy [*sic*] as you please, and we could hardly persuade them to give their seats to the ladies. One of them remarked that he wished they would give him a glass of beer instead of whiskey punch, as he much preferred it. Another said that he would take some of that stuff what shook, and a variety of other equally queer speeches were made much to the amusement of the whole company.
>
> There were but 2 ladies here owing to the night's being so severely cold.[22]

Perhaps Mary had exercised youthful exaggeration in her description of the Republican guests, yet it is surely plausible that good manners and civility were not always on display at such gatherings. For her own life, this daughter of Nathan Sanford made certain that she chose a gentleman for a husband: on June 4, 1833, Mary married Peter Gansevoort, a descendant of a Dutch patrician family. Gansevoort had graduated from Princeton, and, like his father-in-law, had studied at the Litchfield School of Law. Many years Mary's senior, he had served on Governor DeWitt Clinton's military staff as his judge advocate general from 1819 to 1821. Later, he became a follower of Martin Van Buren and part of his Regency. In 1832, he was elected to the state senate. The couple honeymooned at Niagara Falls, 300 miles northwest of Albany, and then traveled on to Montreal.[23]

Mary's husband also had business interests. Gansevoort had been appointed a director of the Bank of New York in 1832, the same year that the extended family's commercial buildings on their home lot in Albany were destroyed by fire. By the mid-1830s, involvements in the rebuilding project and speculative land investments left Gansevoort deeply in debt. Moreover, his finances became entwined with the Panic of 1837, the credit squeeze that followed President Jackson's refusal to renew the charter of the Second Bank of the United States in 1836. As happened to bankers in New York City, large merchants, and brokers, Gansevoort's credit had been overextended and his mortgage loans were called.[24] The efforts to resolve the financial difficulties coincided with the years when Mary bore five children, suffered declining health, and would be left with fewer visitors from her side of the family in Albany, her father and stepmother having moved to Flushing in 1835.[25]

Throughout his career, the upwardly mobile Sanford had supported his growing family in an increasingly refined lifestyle, carefully managing his personal investments. He had sold his securities prior to the move to Albany in 1823, no doubt using a portion of the proceeds to purchase the townhouse on Park Place,[26] and he continued to implement his plan to add to his already significant accumulation of urban and rural properties. Beginning with the inheritance of his father's farm in Bridgehampton, the lawyer-politician had purchased and then rented a variety of holdings: common lands in Montauk, the Pine Street buildings in Manhattan, and the Grace Church lots that faced the Hudson River. In August 1825, Sanford traveled to the city to petition New York's Common Council for "Water grants" to use with his Grace Church lots so they could be developed. He appeared before the council again in 1827, in regard to his having neglected to fill in a "Lot with good earth. . . ."[27]

Sanford managed his expanding rural properties with the same care he applied to his urban investments—particularly, the farms and land he had begun to acquire in Flushing in 1817. He added to his purchases there in 1822, buying several farms that fronted what became the main avenue in that town.[28] Having returned home to the city from a visit to Flushing the following year, Sanford, now the nominee to become chancellor, addressed a letter to a member of the state senate from Queens. He had been approached, Sanford wrote to John A. King, a son of Rufus King, by "some of the good people there" proposing to construct a road across Flushing meadows "at their own expense and then, to give the whole to the public, as a free road. From the legislature . . . they want nothing but the permission of the State to establish a bridge over the creek, which is navigable by boat." Sanford was clearly advocating for the project, adding that "Long Island farmers will enjoy a great advantage" by saving time "in their communication with . . . New York."[29]

Always dedicated to promoting agriculture, Sanford had selected wisely when, in the late 1810s, he began to invest in farms in an area with productive soil close to New York City. After all, he would have heard about President George Washington's interest in soil quality and his visit to the Prince Nursery, a business started in Flushing in 1737. On October 10, 1789, the president wrote in his diary that he "set off about 9 Oclock in my Barge [from New York City] to visit Mr. Prince's fruit Gardens & shrubberies at Flushing on Long Island."[30] He left the nursery carrying cuttings. By 1823, the town had grown, and a steamboat line had begun to run round trips, twice daily, to the city.[31]

Not all new road proposals through the town pleased Sanford. In January 1829, the second-term senator learned that interested parties were considering the construction of a road from Huntington to New York City—intended as a "public improvement." However, the route, Sanford pointed out by return mail to his correspondent, "would be through my farm at Flushing." In an attempt to rise above his own self-interest, Sanford maintained that route selection should be made "with a single view to the public good. I am an interested individual; but they who propose to take my property for their own use, are also interested. . . ." He went on to stress that he preferred an "amicable arrangement," but if that proved unsuccessful, "impartial Commissioners" should be retained. In a rare expression of feeling about his surroundings, Sanford revealed his intent to construct a mansion on the property for use during his retirement: "On that farm I have selected a favorite spot for building a house for my own residence; and with that view, I have already made expensive improvements."[32]

Sanford needed to amass considerable funds in order to cover his property "improvements" and construct his mansion. He had already put the Bridgehampton farm up for sale by public auction, and his receipt book indicates that he had continued to accumulate other cash at around this time.[33] In 1830, he won a lawsuit that paid him over $1,300. Over the years, Sanford had extended private mortgages and bonds, receiving income in return: in 1831, he acknowledged receipt of $5,300, the principal and interest owed to him from a "bond and mortgage"; in 1834, he received $1,000; and in 1835, more than $3,500. He also continued to earn from his rental properties, urban as well as rural. Although he had undertaken these financial activities in order to fund his large building project, they had clearly aroused anxieties. In an entry on November 10, 1830, less than a month before the start of his last session in the senate, he recorded that he had "Deposited in the Mechanic's and Farmer's Bank, a sealed trunk, containing my most valuable private papers." His fears, perhaps of their theft, dissipated, and he retrieved the trunk a few months later.[34]

After his retirement from the Senate, Sanford and his wife lived year-round in Albany for only four years. In 1835, with four-year-old Robert, nicknamed Bobby,[35] in tow, they left the state capital. They retired to Flushing, a Dutch and English settlement dating from the middle of the seventeenth century. In the 1830s, the village counted over 2,000 inhabitants and about 140 dwellings. Saint George's Episcopal Church; two Methodist churches, segregated by race; and two Quaker Meetings offered a degree of religious diversity—and toleration. The town had already attracted residents of means who had built elegant mansions. The Sanfords would enjoy the view to the west that reached the "palisades of the Hudson" from the "elevated site" of Flushing, which was quickly becoming a "village of palaces," as one commentator enthused.[36] With their Mansion House, the Sanfords joined this elite group on an estate that occupied a portion of Nathan's largest holding in Flushing—an area known as Eagle Nest Neck. It consisted of 130 acres of land, partly salt meadows and woodland; a small parcel called "long meadows" was nearby.[37]

Nathan and Mary may have stayed for a short time in one of their farmhouses before moving into their three-story, Greek Revival–style mansion with "park-like grounds" when it was finished in late spring 1835.[38] The property boasted "doors of solid mahogany, and floors, walls and pillars of polished marble." The marble had been costly—and it was white.[39] Sanford's mansion was judged "one of the most superb edifices [in] our country."[40] Another contemporary wrote that it was "among the most sumptuous and elegant in the state . . ." and, like other observers, the historian pegged the cost at nearly $100,000.[41] A house where Mary and her husband could entertain in grand style, the mansion symbolized wealth, social status, and an education in gentility. Here, the senator could identify with the rentier gentry, living on an estate located about three miles from water access to Long Island Sound to the north, a spot reminiscent of Bridgehampton's agricultural and maritime setting where he had grown up. Moreover, Flushing was near New York, the bustling city of the lawyer-politician's early professional and family life.

Whether the project's true costs were unanticipated or Sanford never fulfilled his financing plan is unclear. What is certain is that he

Figure 12.1. Sanford Hall, Flushing, New York. Built in 1835 by Nathan Sanford. Wood engraving, *Frank Leslie's Illustrated Newspaper*, November 14, 1857. Author's collection. The fence was added after 1845 when the mansion became an institution for the mentally ill.

soon fell deeply in debt. In April 1836, he mortgaged a fifty-three-acre farm to William and Benjamin Wright in order to secure his payment on a bond that had come due: Sanford owed the Wrights $7,000. In May, he mortgaged two more farms and the "fresh meadow" nearby, again, to secure a bond held by another member of the Wright family—Gilbert Wright.[42] By mid-June, mounting debt owed to the Mechanics' Bank in New York—where he had once sat on the board of directors—soon overwhelmed him. Edward, now a Commissioner of the City, helped sort out his father's finances. At his office, Sanford and Mary would sign documents mortgaging the properties at 27 and 29 Pine Street in lower Manhattan. The collateral included the "warehouses and buildings" on the lots that backed up to Wall Street,[43] property Sanford had owned since 1800.

By the early 1830s, his emerging financial concerns and exhaustion from extensive travels from Albany to New York City and Flushing to oversee his properties accentuated Sanford's disagreeable temperament. His outbursts led daughter Mary to share the family's household tension with Edward. She would write her brother that Father "has been as cross as a bear to poor Mother during his stay in town [Albany] altho pretty good to me."[44] When Sanford became even more irritable, with the return of painful inflammations in his lungs in the fall of 1837, Mary traveled to Flushing to help her stepmother care for him. Hoping that a warm climate would restore his strength, Sanford's physician and his family convinced him to spend time in Cuba. His passport application profiled the sixty-year-old Sanford, who would travel with a servant, "both native born," according to the passport. At five feet, seven inches, tall with "dark gray" hair, Sanford's "pale" complexion framed an "aquiline" nose.[45] His trip took about two weeks, and he remained in Cuba for about four months, but he was never free of his financial burdens. He received at least one letter from his longtime lawyer, who had entrusted it to Mr. Garcia, a messenger who got the letter to San Marcos, where Sanford had traveled from Havana under a doctor's care. It informed the senator that the Grace Church properties had been rented for $2,800 plus taxes for the coming year. His lawyer noted that he didn't negotiate hard because he found it uncomely for a landlord (Sanford) to place himself even "more in the power of a peasant-tenant."[46]

While in Cuba, Sanford worked hard to improve his health. He was, presumably, using the remedies his doctor had ordered for curing his particular illness, which appears to have been chronic pulmonary disease.

The condition would have obstructed airflow from his lungs and interfered with his breathing. Sanford's treatment was similar to the remedies proposed for tuberculosis in the early nineteenth century, including a healthy diet and vigorous exercise, such as horseback riding. In a letter to his wife, besides criticizing his physician for urging him to seek a "mild climate" and telling Mary that "my health is no better," the retired senator elaborated on how he felt—and his exercise regime:

> . . . my affliction of the throat is still the same thing, fixed obstinate and unchanged. My pulse is a little quicker than it was last fall and summer . . . I have lately had some disposition to night sweats. I ride on horseback from one to two or three hours every day.[47]

Nothing Sanford tried seemed to help, and the strenuous horseback riding probably aggravated his illness. Six months after he returned from Cuba, he died. Sanford passed away at his mansion on October 17, 1838, having succumbed to the lung condition he had suffered for over thirty years. He died intestate, survived by his wife, four children, and four grandchildren.[48] That Sanford left no will is evidence of his unrealistic assessment of the health problems he had once ably managed. Building on his success, he acquired an arrogance that permitted him, as he approached age sixty, to believe his death lay in the distant future. He may also have feared uncovering and facing the extent of his financial liabilities.

A week after his father's death, Edward, identified in legal papers as the "administrator of the goods, chattels and credits," assigned two appraisers to inventory his father's personal property, as was the practice at the time. The inventory offers another glimpse of Nathan and Mary Sanford's lifestyle and values. First listed were books: a single volume of *Johnson's Reports* was appraised for thirty cents—it was also in the collection offered later at the auction of Sanford's law library; Milton's *Paradise Lost* was valued at twenty-five cents. The total assessed value of the library, including the law books, reached $773. "Brussel carpets," an upright piano Fort, and one silver pitcher appraised at thirty-six dollars were listed. Fine wines were plentiful in his personal property: the fifty-eight bottles of "very superior old Maderia [*sic*] wine" included some, the oldest, assessed at more than two dollars apiece. A few months later, the wine was sold locally for $400. Edward noted in a letter to his sister that "this is more than we could get at auction in the city, especially in times like these," a reference to the depression that followed the Panic of 1837. Bay Carriage Horses were also recorded, appraised at ninety-six dollars for the pair.[49] A month or so later, Edward organized an estate sale. As advertised, the "public vendue" offered the farm's animals, equipment, and produce. It would be held at the Mansion House on November 19 and cover "valuable Household Furniture, Cattle, Stock, Farming Utensils, Farm Produce, &c. Fodder, Grain and Vegetables." The stock included horses, cows, and oxen.[50]

Edward's initiative in taking an inventory and holding a sale did not sit well with some members of the family and creditors. They were surprised that he had facilitated the Pine Street buildings' mortgage and had assumed an administrator's responsibilities for his father's estate.[51] In November, Peter Gansevoort, his wife, Mary, and Charles Sanford challenged Edward in the court of chancery; the three members of the Wright family in Flushing joined the suit in an amendment. Edward, Widow Sanford, her son, Robert, and Nathan Sanford's two grandchildren in Albany were subpoenaed to answer the complaint that the plaintiffs had been kept ignorant of the scope of Sanford's borrowings. Deliberations took place at the chancellor's house in Saratoga Springs, not far from the capital, Mary Sanford Gansevoort's home. A master of the court was appointed to conduct an inventory of properties that included their encumbrances, to make an accounting of the estate, and to report the findings. During the proceedings, in January 1839, Edward Sanford acknowledged that his father had executed "several bonds and mortgages" in order to "secure the payment of the sums of money . . . mentioned and stated in the said bill of complaint."[52] Despite the lawsuit, Nathan's older children, Edward, Charles, and Mary, appear to have remained on friendly terms. In a letter to Mary, Edward closed by writing, "Love to Gan, and the children, Your brotr," and to Charles, when he wrote to ask that his younger brother put aside "apples and vegetables" for their "Mother." He signed the note, "Your affectionate brother, Edward."[53]

In the fall, one of the commissioners appointed to appraise Sanford's New York City and Flushing properties submitted a report to his colleagues that assessed the "whole value" of the senator's holdings of real property at $164,775.[54] The Mansion House, already being referred to as "Sanford's Folly," was not included. Chancellor Reuben Walworth issued his Final Decree nearly four years later.[55] In this decree, the court required that the house and twenty acres of surrounding land be sold at public auction and the mortgages let by the Wrights were to be paid.[56] Excluding his personal property, and setting aside encumbrances to his real estate, Sanford's assets by 1830 had been worth close to $2.5 million in today's dollars—a handsome sum.

~

Throughout his career, Nathan Sanford, the often reluctant reformer, steadfastly sought influence through politics and government service, while he participated in the idealism of republicanism and the opportunistic culture of his day. He worked tenaciously to enhance services provided by the central government for the citizenry, primarily in the areas of administration, the national banking system, the acquisition of statistical data, and coinage; he also engaged with the complex and divisive issues of expanding democracy. He was forced by his times to debate and take positions on slavery, the popular election of presidential electors, libel and freedom of the press, universal manhood suffrage, restrictions on the African American voter, and Indian removal.

For thirty years, Sanford's lung disease constrained his career, limiting his ability to project eloquence and strength. Not perceived as a major threat in his political roles, Sanford's particular public presence enabled him to thrive among the factional leaders of the period. In his 1828 letter to his son, he called out the "advantages" of "fortune" and "distinction": the father achieved both rewards for his ambitions. But in being away from home for considerable lengths of time, Sanford suffered costs, too—to his family and his health.

Whatever his flaws, his sometimes suspect wealth, and his "Folly," many of Sanford's near-contemporaries judged him favorably. In an obituary that appeared in *The New York Post*, a reporter offered this assessment: "He was a man of worth and talent, of a cultivated mind, and possessed of that firmness of character which is so necessary in public life."[57] A few years later, lawyer-historian Benjamin F. Thompson wrote that Nathan Sanford "loved the science of law. . . . He was a finished scholar . . . as familiar with the French language as his own. . . . The Latin poets were his delight. . . ." Thompson added, however, that as a politician, "he was naturally secret[ive] and taciturn; and . . . few men had less of what may be properly termed 'small talk.' "[58] A half-century after the settlement of his estate, reporters from the *Brooklyn Eagle* collected memories from "those who knew him." These acquaintances portrayed yet other aspects of the chancellor's demeanor: he was a "tall, dignified man, smooth shaven and of genial disposition. He dressed in the long high buttoned, pigeon tailed coats, with high rolling collars, so much the style among statesmen of a former generation."[59] This image is a remarkable contrast to the description of Sanford in his 1837 passport application, after he had aged: an old man with gray hair and a pale complexion.

For Sanford, a mix of adherence to principle and unbounded personal ambition had played out over his lifetime. It was a combination anticipated in a note sent by President John Adams to his son John Quincy in 1804. The elder Adams wrote: "I take it for granted that public Virtue is no longer to rule: but Ambition is to govern the Country. . . ."[60] Ambition helped set the course of Sanford's political trajectory, where he accomplished much. In his last years, it came to govern his life.

Abbreviations

CU	Rare Books & Manuscript Library, Columbia University, New York, NY
EHL	East Hampton Free Library, East Hampton, NY
LC	Library of Congress, Washington, DC
NARA	National Archives and Records Administration, National Archives Building, Washington, DC
NYHS	Manuscript Department, New-York Historical Society, New York, NY
NYPL	Manuscripts and Archives Division, New York Public Library, New York, NY
NYSL	Manuscripts and Special Collections, New York State Library, Albany, NY
SCSC	Suffolk County Surrogate's Court, Riverhead, NY

Collections and Document Imprints: Shortened Titles

AGP-NYHS: Albert Gallatin Papers.

Carter and Stone, eds., *Reports*: Nathaniel H. Carter and William L. Stone, eds. *Reports of the Proceedings and Debates of the Convention of 1821, Assembled for the Purpose of Amending the Constitution of the State of New-York.* Albany: E. and E. Hosford, 1821. http://purl.nysed.gov/nysl/2158481.

DWCP-CU: DeWitt Clinton Papers

EAI-NYSL: Early American Imprints, Series II (1801–1819), Shaw-Shoemaker

Final Decree-NYS Archives: Chancellor's Enrolled Decrees and Papers after 1800

GLC-NYPL: Gansevoort-Lansing Collection

Lampi Collection: *Lampi Collection of American Electoral Returns, 1788–1825.* American Antiquarian Society, 2007. A New Nation Votes. elections.lib.tufts.edu/terms

LIC-EHL: Long Island Collection

Lloyd, *Trials*: Thomas Lloyd. *Trials of William S. Smith and Samuel G. Ogden: For Misdemeanours, Had in the Circuit Court of the United States for the New-York District, in July 1806*. New York: I. Riley, 1807. https://archive.org/details/trialswilliamss00circgoog.

MVBP-LC: Martin Van Buren Papers, Manuscript Division

NSP-NYSL: Nathan Sanford Papers, 1799–1834

Receipt Book: Receipt Book, 1802–1835. GLC-NYPL

RG 21-NARA: Prize and Related Records for the War of 1812 of the U.S. District Court for the Southern District of New York, 1812–16, Record Group 21. https://www.fold3.com/search/#cat=247.

RG 59-NARA: General Records of the Department of State; Record Group 59; Appointment Records; Administration of Jefferson, 1801–1809

RTSH: Records of the Town of Southampton, Long Island, N.Y., vols. 2, 3, 4, 6. Sag Harbor, NY: John H. Hunt, 1877–1915

SFP, GLC-NYPL: Sanford Family Papers

U.S. Congressional Documents and Debates, 1774–1875, were accessed on the Internet at *A Century of Lawmaking for a New Nation: U.S. Congressional Documents and Debates, 1774–1875*, http://memory.loc.gov/ammem/amlaw/lawhome.html. Abbreviations used, by collection, are *Annals*-LC (for the *Annals of Congress*), *Congressional Documents*-LC, *Register of Debates*-LC, *Senate Executive Journal*-LC, and *Statutes at Large*-LC.

Notes

Introduction

1. Different branches of the family have used different spellings. Nathan Sanford dropped the first "d" in Sandford, his birth surname, as a young man. I am a second cousin of Nathan Sanford, five generations removed.

2. Chancery was a civil court carried over from the colonial government and dealt with such matters as commercial disputes, wills, and orphans; see James D. Folts, "Courts, State," *Encyclopedia of New York State*, ed. Peter Eisenstadt (Syracuse, NY: Syracuse University Press, 2005), 412.

3. Quoted in Donald M. Roper, "The Elite of the New York Bar as Seen from the Bench: James Kent's Necrologies," *New-York Historical Society Quarterly* 56, no. 3 (July 1972): 229–30. http://nyhistory.org/library/digital-collections. Kent's marginalia, no doubt written soon after Sanford's death in 1838, was not published until Roper's article appeared. In classical times, "demagogue" meant a leader who defended the interests of common people. Kent was chancellor 1814–1823. Roper has published Kent's obituaries of "friends, enemies, and colleagues, numbering over a hundred": ibid., 202.

4. DeAlva Stanwood Alexander, *A Political History of the State of New York*, vol. 1, *1774–1832* (New York: Henry Holt and Co., 1906; reprint, Elibron Classics, 2006), 170.

5. See Harvey Strum, "Property Qualifications and Voting Behavior in New York, 1807–1816," *Journal of the Early Republic* 1 (Winter 1981): 350 (hereafter cited as *JER*), http://jstor.org/stable/3122826.

6. Henry A. Reeves, "The Commerce, Navigation and Fisheries of Suffolk County," in *Bi-Centennial History of Suffolk County* (1885), nA76, https://archive.org/details/historyofsuffolk00titu_0.

7. See Robert A. Ferguson, *Law and Letters in American Culture* (Cambridge, MA: Harvard University Press, 1984), Part I, for a discussion of the value eighteenth-century American lawyers placed on "learned eloquence," the classics, and public service. The quotation here is on page 6.

8. Death Notice, *Washington (DC) Globe*, October 23, 1838, http://newspaperarchive.com.

9. See *New York Times*, October 27, 2014. The 225th anniversary events scheduled from November 2014 to October 2015 to honor the "attorney's office for the Southern District of New York" mainly featured the work of judges. The "Historical Publications" section of the District's website includes downloadable copies of court histories by Charles Merrill Hough (1934; first published in 1923) and by H. Paul Burak (1962). Very few of the district attorneys are named. Nathan Sanford is not identified as a district attorney. See http://nysd.uscourts.gov/events-exhibits.php. Biographical information, including Nathan Sanford's, can be found in *The First 100 Years (1789–1889): The United States Attorneys for the Southern District of New York* (United States Court of Appeals, 2nd Circuit, Historical Committee, 1987). A series of essays organized by state, *Bicentennial Celebration of the United States Attorneys, 1789–1989* [1989], has brief biographies of attorneys, including Sanford, and can be found at https://www.justice.gov/sites/default/files/usao/legacy/2011/11/23/bicn_celebration.pdf.

Chapter 1

1. Charles Henry Pope, *The Pioneers of Massachusetts, a Description List, Drawn from the Records of the Colonies, Towns and Churches, and other Contemporaneous Documents* (Baltimore, MD: Genealogical Publishing, 1900; reprint, 1991), 480. For a discussion of the term "proprietor," see David Goddard, *Colonizing Southampton: The Transformation of a Long Island Community, 1870–1900* (Albany, NY: Excelsior Editions, State University of New York Press, 2011), 32–33.

2. *Records of the Town of Southampton, Long Island, N.Y.*, vol. 2, transcribed by William S. Pelletreau (Sag Harbor, NY: John H. Hunt, 1877), 75. Hereafter cited as *RTSH*.

3. James Truslow Adams, *Memorials of Old Bridgehampton* (Port Washington, NY: Ira J. Friedman, 1962; first edition, 1916), 91. In another work, Adams dates the house from 1686: see James Truslow Adams, *History of the Town of Southampton* (Bridgehampton, NY: Hampton Press, 1918), 84–85. Known as the "Sandford Homestead," the house is located on Bridge Lane in Bridgehampton, NY, and remains in the Sandford family.

4. *RTSH*, vol. 2, 110; see Adams, *Southampton*, 86; Adams, *Bridgehampton*, 91–92.

5. Daniel Sayre to George Clark, April 18, 1711, transcribed by Adams, in *Bridgehampton*, 263, note.

6. *RTSH*, vol. 3 (1878), 176, 199, 208.

7. Will, Thomas Sandford, December 7, 1785, Liber A, 85, Suffolk County Surrogate's Court, Riverhead, NY. Hereafter cited as SCSC. See Goddard, *Colonizing Southampton*, 34–35: Goddard's analysis of the tax assessment roll for 1818 lists the "Sandfords" among the "leading families" of the town and among the "proprietors" based on the sum of the assessments of many Sandford households. The bequest to Nathan included the farmhouse on the corner of Woolley's Lane

and Scuttle Hole Road in Bridgehampton where Nathan was born. The name of the road was changed in the mid-nineteenth century to Cook's Lane; see *RTSH*, vol. 4 (1896), 232.

8. "List, to Governor Tryon, Prepared by Isaac Post and Thomas Sandford 2 October 1778," *Long Island Source Records*, ed. Henry B. Hoff (Baltimore, MD: Genealogical Publishing Co., 1987), 600–601; "A List of Persons in Suffolk County, Long Island, Who Took the Oath of Allegiance and Peaceable Behavior Before Governor Tryon, 1778," contributed by Michael Kearney, *New York Genealogical and Biographical Record* 143, no. 2 (2012), 77.

9. See Christopher Minty, "A List of Persons on Long Island: Biography, Voluntarism, and Suffolk County's 1778 Oath of Allegiance," *Long Island History Journal* 24, no. 2 (2015): 9–11, 13, http://lihj.cc.stonybrook.edu.

10. See Adams, *Southampton*, 312, for the transcription of the August 1775 Articles of Association where Sandford had added "ye Third" to his name. Frederic Gregory Mather, *The Refugees of 1776 from Long Island to Connecticut* (Albany, NY: J. B. Lyon Co., 1913), 548; will, Ezekiel Sandford, June 18, 1789, Liber A, 176, SCSC.

11. See *Heads of Families at the First Census of the United States Taken in the Year 1790, New York* (Washington, DC: Government Printing Office, 1908), 167.

12. Jeannette Rattray, *East Hampton History Including Genealogies of Early Families* (Garden City, NY: Country Life Press, 1953), 205–7. The lengthy proceedings ended in an acquittal in a Hartford, Connecticut, courtroom: see T. H. Breen, *Imagining the Past: East Hampton Histories* (Reading, MA: Addison-Wesley Publishing, 1989), 127–37. A fireplace and the beams of the colonial kitchen, remnants of the circa 1650 Baker Homestead where the initial deliberations took place, survive on Main Street in East Hampton. They are preserved within a much larger structure built around them in 1898.

13. Grover Merle Sanford, *The Sandford/Sanford Families of Long Island* (Baltimore, MD: Gateway Press, 1975), 15–16, 19, 27. See *Heads of Families*, 167; Adams, *Bridgehampton*, 315; Mather, *Refugees*, 393.

14. See *Heads of Families*, 167. The ditching of Sagg Swamp by slaves is cited in Adams, *Bridgehampton*, 114, from anonymous oral sources; the commentary is also quoted in Paul H. Curts, ed., *Bridgehampton's Three Hundred Years* (Bridgehampton, NY: Hampton Press, 1956), 120; *RTSH*, vol. 3, 112–13, 366.

15. Stephen Burroughs, *Memoirs of the Notorious Stephen Burroughs of New Hampshire* (New York: The Dial Press, 1924), 268. For ships to New York, see Adams, *Southampton*, 213. For political offices, see Records of Southampton Town Meetings for 4 April 1786, 2 April 1799, 5 April 1803, 3 April 1804, 1 April 1806, 7 April 1807, in *RTSH*, vol. 3, 312, 356, 365–66, 375, 381; Franklin B. Hough, *New York Civil List from 1777 to 1858* (Albany, NY: Weed, Parsons & Co., 1858), 163–65, 177, 179–80. Hedges served in 1786–89, 1804, and 1806–07.

16. Benjamin F. Thompson, *History of Long Island from its Discovery and Settlement to the Present Time*, 3rd ed., 3 vols., revised by Charles J. Werner (New York: Robert H. Dodd, 1918), 2:95, http://history.pmlib.org/ClassicLIHisDocCollections.

17. See Hough, *Civil List*, 148. Nassau County was not yet formed.

18. Writing in 1910, Henry Hedges estimated the population at 1220 in 1776, using a local census. For the entire town east of Water Mill, the population was 1432. See Henry P. Hedges, "The Story of Bridgehampton, Long Island, 1660–1910," in *Tracing the Past, Writings of Henry P. Hedges, 1817–1911, Relating to the History of the East End*, ed. Tom Twomey (New York: Newmarket Press, 2000), 345; "Federal Census, 1800, Suffolk County, Long Island, New York," *The New York Genealogical and Biographical Record* 56, no. 2 (April 1925): 127–37. For the Shinnecocks, see Adams, *Southampton*, 40; John A. Strong, *"We Are Still Here!": The Algonquian Peoples of Long Island Today* (Interlaken, NY: Empire State Books, 1998), 17–19, 81–84. In comparison, the village of Concord, Massachusetts, founded in 1636, twenty years earlier than Bridgehampton, numbered roughly 1570 people when it led the American Revolution. See Richard W. Wilkie and Jack Tager, *Historical Atlas of Massachusetts* (Amherst: University of Massachusetts Press, 1991), 140. Hudson, New York, the hometown of Martin Van Buren, numbered 1,500 inhabitants by 1786: John L. Brooke, *Columbia Rising: Civil Life on the Upper Hudson from the Revolution to the Age of Jackson* (Chapel Hill: University of North Carolina Press, 2010), 74.

19. Timothy Dwight, *Travels in New England and New York*, ed. Barbara Miller Soloman, 4 vols. (Cambridge, MA: Belknap Press of Harvard University Press, 1969), 1:222. Dwight's chapter, "Journey to Long Island," is conveniently reprinted in *Journeys on Old Long Island: Travelers' Accounts, Contemporary Descriptions, and Residents' Reminiscences, 1744–1893*, ed. Natalie A. Naylor (Interlaken, NY: Empire State Books, 2002). The Bridgehampton reference is on page 94.

20. Solomon, "Introduction," in Dwight, *Travels*, 1: x, xxxiii, xxxvii.

21. See "Map extending from Water Mill to Wainscott—About the year 1800," in William Donaldson Halsey, *Sketches from Local History* (1935; reprint, Southampton, NY: Yankee Peddler Book Co., 1966), n.p.

22. Ann H. Sandford, "Rural Connections: Early Republic Bridgehampton and Its Wider World, 1790–1805," *Long Island Historical Journal* 15 (Fall 2002/Spring 2003): 2–6; Dwight, *Travels*, 3:217–18, 222. Lyman Beecher was the minister in East Hampton from 1799 to 1810.

23. Nathaniel S. Prime defined Bridgehampton as "including Sagg, Mecocks, the Hay Ground and Scuttle Hole" in *A History of Long Island, from Its First Settlement by Europeans, to the Year 1845* (New York: Robert Carter, 1845), 199; see Sandford, "Rural Connections," 2–3.

24. For meeting house and beach travel, see Adams, *Bridgehampton*, 185–86, 190–91.

25. Ibid., 128, 135–38; Mather, *Refugees*, 393.

26. Burroughs, *Memoirs*, 271–72, 279.

27. Ibid., 255, 276–79, 355. The year is derived from an analysis of the seasons referred to in these pages. He remained in Bridgehampton from 1791 to 1794.

28. Hedges, "Bridgehampton," in *Tracing the Past*, 351.

29. See Hedges, "Bi-Centennial of the Bridge-Hampton Presbyterian Church," in ibid., 98; Hedges, "Bridgehampton," in ibid., 351; Adams, *Bridgehampton*, 191–92, 203; "Federal Census, 1800," 133; Breen, *Imagining the Past*, 203. Buell died in 1798.

30. Reverend James Brown had retired in 1775: see Hedges, "Bi-Centennial," in *Tracing the Past*, 97–98.

31. Amy Osborn Bassford, "Clinton Academy," n. d. [c. 1960], 1–4, Long Island Collection, East Hampton Free Library, East Hampton, NY: hereafter cited as LIC-EHL. The academy was certified in 1787 by the New York State Board of Regents.

32. *New York Gazette of the United States*, May 5, 1790, 468, in East Hampton Historical Society Archives, East Hampton; see John Hallam to Caroline Hallam, February 17, 1787, ibid.

33. Bassford, "Clinton Academy," 4.

34. For the family connections, see Sanford, *Sandford/Sanford Families*, 19, 27.

35. Will, Thomas Sandford, December 7, 1785, probated on March 27, 1789, Liber A, 85, SCSC.

36. See Susanna Ashton., "A Corrupt Medium: Stephen Burroughs and the Bridgehampton, New York, Library," *Libraries & Culture, A Journal of Library History* 38, no. 2 (Spring 2003): Appendix, 120. For a version of the original 1793 book list, see Halsey, *Sketches*, 116–17. The library survived into the early nineteenth century. For a discussion of the dissemination of books on manners and the influence of novels, see Richard L. Bushman, *The Refinement of America: Persons, Houses, Cities* (New York: Alfred A. Knopf, 1992), 29–30, 36.

37. The subscription price was £1: see Burroughs, *Memoirs*, 279–80; Halsey, *Sketches*, 115. Numbers of libraries are cited in Cathy N. Davidson, *Revolution and the Word: The Rise of the Novel in America* (New York: Oxford University Press, 1986), 27.

38. For an analysis of the newspaper's contents, see Beatrice Diamond, *An Episode in American Journalism: A History of David Frothingham and His Long Island Herald* (Port Washington, NY: Kennikat Press, 1964), 68–91. Sag Harbor had no newspaper from December 1798 until 1802, when the *Herald*'s publisher, Henry Dering, launched a new paper: see Steven R. Coleman, "Political Journalism in the 1790s: *Frothingham's Long Island Herald*," *Long Island Historical Journal* 4, no. 1 (Fall 1991): 101. In October 1794, a federal post office was established in Bridgehampton: Ernest S. Clowes, *Wayfarings* (Bridgehampton, 1953), 263–64. The Sag Harbor post office dates from 1794: Coleman, "Political Journalism," 97. The Southampton post office dates from 1804: Adams, *Southampton*, 215.

39. Nancy F. Lyon to the author, November 17, 2014, mssa.assist@yale.edu; in comparison, DeWitt Clinton entered Columbia College at age fifteen. See Evan Cornog, *The Birth of Empire: DeWitt Clinton and the American Experience, 1769–1828* (New York: Oxford University Press, 1998), 14–15.

40. Beecher graduated from Yale in 1797. In 1799, he accepted an invitation from the Presbyterian Church in East Hampton to become its minister. See Breen, *Imagining the Past*, 6–7.

41. See Edmund S. Morgan, *American Heroes: Profiles of Men and Women Who Shared Early America* (New York: W. W. Norton, 2009), 177–79, 186–87. Morgan cautions that evidence from student letters, like reminiscences, require their "proper context."

42. Quoted in Robert Stevens, *Perspectives in American History*, eds. Donald Fleming and Bernard Bailyn, vol. 5 (Cambridge, MA: Charles Warren Center for Studies in American History, 1971), 414–15.

43. Sidney I. Pomerantz, *New York: An American City, 1783–1803, A Study of Urban Life* (New York: Columbia University Press, 1938), 397, 397n49.

44. Gordon S. Wood, *Empire of Liberty: A History of the Early Republic, 1789–1815* (New York: Oxford University Press, 2009), 350–53. The quotation is on page 353.

45. Coleman, "Political Journalism," 98–100.

46. Alan Taylor, *William Cooper's Town, Power and Persuasion on the Frontier of the Early American Republic* (New York: Vintage Books, 1996), 263–65.

47. Henry Dering had ceased printing the *Herald* two days earlier because he was concerned about the political atmosphere that had developed in response to the Sedition Act. See Coleman, "Political Journalism," 101.

48. Quoted in Diamond, *Episode*, 50–51. The Republican-leaning *New York Journal* supported Thomas Jefferson and other opponents of the Federalists.

49. Quotations are from the *New York Journal*: see Diamond, *Episode*, 50–51. For a discussion of public entertainment devoid of refinement, see Bushman, *Refinement of America*, 49. Bull Head Tavern was also known as Wick's Tavern, after John Wick who established it around 1710. See Adams, *Bridgehampton*, 95.

50. See Taylor's discussion of "rhetorical violence" in *William Cooper's Town*, 181; see Wood, *Empire of Liberty, 641*, for demonstrations similar to the one in Bridgehampton.

Chapter 2

1. List of Letters, *The Daily Advertiser* (*New York*), February 2, 1798, http://infoweb.newsbank.com. A letter to Sanford remained at a New York post office in 1798, indicating he had resided in the city in 1797. For Sanford's attendance at Litchfield, see Marian C. McKenna, *Tapping Reeve and the Litchfield Law School* (New York: Oceana Publications, 1986), Appendix 5, "Catalogue of Students at Litchfield Law School, 1774–1833," 194. Sanford is cited in the correspondence concerning "Circular Letter," May 4, 1822, in McKenna, *Tapping Reeve*, 201.

2. Stevens, *Perspectives*, 413.

3. See the chart for the year 1794 at Litchfield in ibid., 433.

4. Angela Fernandez, "Copying and Copyright Issues at the Litchfield Law School" (July 14, 2008), Legal Studies Research Paper No. 08-13, University of Toronto. Available at SSRN: http://ssrn.com/abstract=1160023.

5. Mark Boonshaft, "The Litchfield Network: Education, Social Capital, and the Rise and Fall of a Political Dynasty, 1784–1833," *JER* 9 (Winter 2014): 563, 567, 570, 578–80.

6. See *Descendants of Jacob Sebor, 1709–1793, of Middletown, Connecticut*, compiled by Helen Beach (n.p., 1923), 15–16: the booklet is based on interviews. It is probable that Sanford also read for the bar earlier than 1799, perhaps in 1796–97, when Jones, despite his advancing years, was the New York City recorder and a state senator from Queens County. Although Federalist, Jones had associated with New York's Governor George Clinton, a Democratic-Republican, during the ratification of the Constitution in 1788: see Edward Countryman, "From Revolution to Statehood," in *The Empire State, A History of New York*, ed. Milton M. Klein (Ithaca, NY: Cornell University Press, 2001), 250. See also Benjamin F. Thompson, *History of Long Island from Its Discovery and Settlement to the Present Time*, 2nd ed., 2 vols. (New York: Gould, Banks & Co., 1843) 2:542, http://history.pmlib.org/ClassicLIHisDocCollections. Thompson placed Sanford in Jones's office in 1797.

7. License, Nathan Sanford Papers, 1799–1834, Manuscripts and Special Collections, SC14054, Box 1, New York State Library, Albany: hereafter cited as NSP-NYSL; Folts, "Courts," *Encyclopedia of New York State*, 412.

8. Minute Book of the New York State Supreme Court of Judicature, May 1, 1801, Division of Old Records, New York County Clerk, Surrogate's Court, New York.

9. Minute Book of the Court of Chancery, April 2, 1805, ibid.

10. Dixon Ryan Fox, *Yankees and Yorkers* (New York: New York University Press, 1940), 19–21.

11. Deed, Cornelius C. Van Arlen to Nathan Sanford, April 25, 1800, Sanford Family Papers, Gansevoort-Lansing Collection, Manuscripts and Archives Division, Box 286, New York Public Library. Hereafter cited as SFP, GLC-NYPL. The French Church was founded by Huguenots in 1659.

12. *New York Genealogical &Biographical Record* 78, no. 4 (1947): 114; *Commercial Advertiser*, May 11, 1801, p. [3], NY.

13. Wood, *Empire of Liberty*, 520.

14. See notary public commission, NSP-NYSL.

15. The story presented here expands on the summary in Ann Sandford, "Rural Wealth and American Property Law: The Sagaponack and Bridgehampton Connections 1802 and 1805," Bridgehampton Museum's *The Bridge* (Summer 2011): 18–21.

16. See Angela Fernandez, "The Lost Record of *Pierson v. Post*, the Famous Fox Case," *Law and History Review* 27, no. 1 (Spring 2009): 161, 164–65, http://www.jstor.org/stable/27641649, for the identification of John N. Fordham as the

justice of the peace and the place, although not the physical location, of the initial trial in Hugh Gelston's house in Southampton; see William S. Pelletreau, "Main Street Plan, Southampton" (1878), Southampton Historical Museum, Southampton, NY, for the plan that shows house lots and owners' names. Gelston's father, Hugh Gelston Sr., is noted as occupying the corner lot during 1717–75. He was Judge of the court of common pleas of Suffolk County under the British. Upon his death in 1775, he left the house to Hugh Gelston Jr. See Adams, *Bridgehampton*, 127, for a 1776 muster role that lists "Hugh Gelston, Clerk." He may have served at his father's court. Hugh Gelston Jr. married Puah Corwith from Bridgehampton, and in October 1794 he became that hamlet's first postmaster: see Mather, *Refugees*, 355–56; Clowes, *Wayfarings*, 263. For the slave tally by household, see "Federal Census, 1800," 135. For an editor's note that states that Hugh Gelston Jr. died in 1815, see William S. Pelletreau and James A. Early, eds., *RTSH*, vol. 6 (1915), 239. Ages of the litigants were deduced from the cemetery stone transcriptions in Adams, *Bridgehampton*, 319, 334.

17. The reference to the "beach" is from the case record in Bethany Berger, "It's Not About the Fox: The Untold History of *Pierson V. Post*," *Duke Law Journal* 55, no. 6 (April 2006): 1091, 1119.

18. The phrase "dogs and hounds" is quoted from the 1805 record in Angela Fernandez, "*Pierson v. Post*: A Great Debate, James Kent, and the Project of Building a Learned Law for New York State," *Law and Social Inquiry* 34, issue 2 (Spring 2009): 304.

19. The suggestion that the event occurred near Peters Pond in Sagaponack and that Pierson struck the fox with a "rail" was first made by Henry P. Hedges: see *Sag Harbor Express*, October 24, 1895.

20. The description of the 1802 trial is in Fernandez, "The Lost Record," 161–65. For the story of how Fernandez located the record, see ibid., 156–57. See ibid., 158, 163, 169, for the depositions and the expenses in the case.

21. See Adams, *Bridgehampton*, 137–38. On trade, see Burroughs, *Memoirs*, 269–70. The British West Indies were partially reopened to American trade in the 1790s. The Post gravestone in Poxabogue Cemetery, Sagaponack, reads in part, "respectable Magistrate . . . a good Patriot." According to Mather, *Refugees*, 512, Post may not have been a militia officer but the captain of the armed sloop *Revenge*. He may have been distantly related to the branch of the Post family based in Southampton's center. They were "trustee proprietors" in the town after 1818; see Goddard, *Colonizing Southampton*, 40, 140.

22. For indicators of Pierson family prominence, see Goddard's references to their participation in drawing up the deed between Southampton trustees and the Shinnecocks in 1703 and to the presence of wealthy Pierson households on the 1818 tax assessment roll; Goddard, *Colonizing Southampton*, 35, 186.

23. Ann Sandford, "Bridgehampton's 'Accidental' Settling, 1650–1700," unpublished paper delivered at the June 2007 New York State History Conference, Cooperstown, NY. For Captain David Pierson, see Adams, *Bridgehampton*, 75–76, 126–27; Mather, *Refugees*, 505; Berger, "It's Not About the Fox," 1124–25.

David Pierson was well known to the Gelston family: his first wife was Elizabeth (1746–77), the daughter of Deacon Maltby Gelston. See Adams, *Bridgehampton*, 185.

24. See Sanford, *Sandford/Sanford Families* for the family linkage, 14–16.

25. Fernandez, "The Lost Record," 171–73, 176–77. The question of motives behind the aggressiveness of Post and Pierson in both suits has been much discussed. To Pierson, the wild animal was vermin, a predator of chickens, to be eliminated as expeditiously as possible; see ibid., 166. Perhaps there were other motives, particularly relating to the possible social animosity between the two families: see Berger, "It's Not About the Fox," 1090, 1120, 1132–33. On the amount of the recovery, which included court costs, see Angela Fernandez, *Law and Legal Professionalization: Pierson v. Post and the Hunt for the Fox*, forthcoming, Cambridge University Press. In 1806, Post was elected lieutenant in Sag Harbor's first voluntary military company: see Dorothy Ingersoll Zaykowski, *Sag Harbor—The Story of an American Beauty* (Sag Harbor Historical Society, 1991), 60.

26. Fernandez, "*Pierson v. Post*," 303, 322. The quotation is on page 303.

27. Berger, "It's Not About the Fox," 1093–94, 1136–37.

28. Fernandez, "*Pierson v. Post*," 305 and see 301, 303–4 for a discussion of how the "lawyers and judges involved in the [1805] case" used the appeal to engage "Roman and other civil law sources on how to establish possession in wild animals . . . on land that belonged to no one." For a discussion of shared rights to property, see Berger, "It's Not About the Fox," 1094, 1107–18. That the case continues to be cited is described in Fernandez, "The Lost Record," 150n6: cases in oil and gas, and the ownership of a baseball hit into the stands with multiple claimants are examples.

29. Fernandez, "*Pierson v. Post*," 308.

30. Ibid., 330.

31. Ibid., 316.

32. Minute Book of the New York State Supreme Court of Judicature, May 1, 1801, Division of Old Records, New York County Clerk, Surrogate's Court, New York.

33. Fernandez, ibid., 304, 311, 316, 326, 329. Fernandez identifies Sanford as the "stronger of the two" lawyers; prominent Federalist Cadwallader David Colden represented Lodowick Post.

34. Fernandez, "The Lost Record," 149–50; Fernandez, "*Pierson v. Post*," 313, 328. The case is described, with excerpts from the justices of the supreme court and a section for student discussion, in the widely used text by Jesse Dukeminier and James E. Krier, *Property*, 2nd ed. (Boston: Little, Brown and Co., 1988), 15–23.

35. See Goddard, *Colonizing Southampton*, 181–82, 187, 201–2. The quotations from Sanford's opinion are on 202–3.

36. Ibid., 203.

37. Fernandez, "The Lost Record," 176.

Chapter 3

1. See Bruce H. Mann, *Republic of Debtors, Bankruptcy in the Age of American Independence* (Cambridge, MA: Harvard University Press, 2002), 224–25, 330n7, 248: Congress repealed the act in December 1803.

2. Memorandum, Samuel Mitchell to Albert Gallatin, May [26], 1801, Manuscript Department, The New-York Historical Society (hereafter cited as AGP-NYHS). By 1803, bankruptcy cases were largely under the district court's jurisdiction, and the federal attorneys reported to the secretary of the treasury.

3. Recommendation, DeWitt Clinton to Department of State, May 31, 1802; General Records of the Department of State; Record Group 59; Appointment Records; Administration of Jefferson, 1801–1809; National Archives and Records Administration, National Archives Building, Washington, DC. Hereafter cited as RG 59-NARA.

4. Nathan Sanford Appointment Letter, November 18, 1803, Box 13, RG 59-NARA.

5. See Wood, *Empire of Liberty*, 193–97, 239.

6. Ibid., 640.

7. Fees, Library of Congress, *A Century of Lawmaking for a New Nation: U.S. Congressional Documents and Debates, 1774–1875, Statutes at Large*, 1st Congress, 1st session, Chapter 20, 1789, 92–93. http://memory.loc.gov/ammem/amlaw/lawhome.html. Hereafter cited as *Statutes at Large*-LC. The federal attorney in a district would receive "compensation for his services such fees"; ibid., 5th Congress, 3rd session, Chapter 19, 1799, 625. See Steve Messer, "A History of the United States Attorney's Office in the Southern District of New York," [1], December 17, 2012, http://moglen.law.columbia.edu/twiki/bin/view/AmLegalHist/SteveMesserWikiProject. Sanford would have received a "percentage of the money he won (by fines or civil remedies) for the United States in the cases he brought."

In my sampling of the notes he wrote in his main receipt book, I found that Sanford documented his payment of the New York "District" court fees on December 4, 1804, for example. On January 12, 1808, he paid David Gelston, the collector, for a bond transaction; he paid fees on July 7, 1809, that exceeded $1,000 to Edmond Dunscomb, the district court clerk in New York; see Receipt Book, 1802–1835, vol. 105, GLC-NYPL. Hereafter the "receipt book" is noted in the text, accompanied by the date of the entry. These instances support John Brooke's contention that opportunities for "administrative corruption" abounded, especially where "placeholders depended more on fees than salary for their compensation, as in New York"; Brooke, *Columbia Rising*, 311.

8. Charles Merrill Hough, *The United States District Court for the Southern District of New York, 1789–1919* (Maritime Law Association of the United States, 1934), 23.

9. Ibid., 6–7, 15.

10. Receipts, 1804–34, John Treat Irving Papers Mss., American Antiquarian Society, Worchester, MA.

11. Roper, "Kent's Necrologies"; Kent's description of Irving ended with "& [he] was a Jacksonian in Politics," 229. See Daniel Walker Howe, *What Hath God Wrought, The Transformation of America, 1815–1848* (New York: Oxford University Press, 2007), 4–5, for a discussion of "Jacksonian," often equated at the time with the Democratic Party. See Hough, *Court*, 20n42.

12. Ron Chernow, *Alexander Hamilton* (New York: The Penguin Press, 2004), 339–41.

13. Adams, *Southampton*, 172. See Leonard D. White, *The Jeffersonians: A Study of Administrative History, 1801–1829* (New York: The Macmillan Co., 1951), 154, https://archive.org/details/jeffersoniansast011195mbp.

14. See Founders Online, Washington Papers, http://founders.archives.gov/; see Mather, *Refugees*, 357; see Adams, *Southampton*, 144n*; John Gelston was replaced in 1790 by Henry P. Dering.

15. See Adams, *Bridgehampton*, 131; Mather, *Refugees*, 355–56, 1066.

16. See White, *Administrative History*, 139, 153–54; Chernow, *Alexander Hamilton*, 538–39.

17. The building was demolished in 1815; see "United States Customs House (New York City)," Wikipedia, The Free Encyclopedia, en.wikipedia.org. Hereafter cited as en.wikipedia.org.

18. See White, *Administrative History*, 153–55.

19. David Gelston to Nathan Sanford, atty US N[ew]York, March 11, 1811, Digital Public Library of America, NYPL, Digital Collection, Archives & Manuscripts Division.

20. Wood, *Empire of Liberty*, 666.

21. Fred Kaplan, *John Quincy Adams, American Visionary* (New York: Harper Collins Pub., 2014), 69, 98, 145, 220.

22. John Ferling, *John Adams; A Life* (New York: Holt & Co., 1992), 410, 421.

23. Walter Barrett, *The Old Merchants of New York City* (New York: Carleton, 1863–66), 200–01. See Wood, *Empire of Liberty*, 410, 421; under the Judiciary Act of 1802, a circuit court bench included one United States Supreme Court judge and one district judge. Among his philanthropic activities in 1815, Colden was president of the New York Manumission Society and a director of the American Academy of Arts: see Cornog, *Birth of Empire*, 4.

24. Kermit L. Hall, ed. in chief, *The Oxford Companion to the Supreme Court of the United States* (New York: Oxford University Press, 1992), 624–25.

25. Thomas Lloyd, *Trials of William S. Smith and Samuel G. Ogden: For Misdemeanours, Had in the Circuit Court of the United States for the New-York District, in July 1806* (New York: I. Riley, 1807), 90, https://archive.org/details/trialswilliamss00circgoog.

26. Wood, *Empire of Liberty*, 265–67; Chernow, *Alexander Hamilton*, 560, 566–67; Kaplan, *John Quincy Adams*, 219; Barrett, *Old Merchants*, 203.

27. Lloyd, *Trials*, 101. Ogden's merchant vessel is not the HMS *Leander* discussed by Cornog in *Birth of Empire*. That episode concerned the British ship's activities in New York City waters in April 1806: see 58–59, 84.

28. Nathan Sanford to Mattias B. Tallmadge, February 19, 1806, NYHS.

29. Nathan Sanford to Albert Gallatin, April 14, 1806, AGC-NYHS. As federal attorney responsible for customs violations and illegalities on the high seas, Sanford took direction from Gallatin at the Treasury. Attorney General John Breckinridge served during the months of the trials but was likely in ill health. He died in December 1806.

30. Ibid.

31. Albert Gallatin to Nathan Sanford, July 9, 1806, NYHS.

32. Lloyd, *Trials*, 242.

33. Nathan Sanford to Albert Gallatin, July 24, 1806, AGC-NYHS; Lloyd, *Trials*, 286. The assisting attorney was Pierpont Edwards, a son of Reverend Jonathan Edwards and the federal attorney for the District of Connecticut appointed by President Jefferson in early 1806: see en.wikipedia.org.

34. Thomas Jefferson to Albert Gallatin, August 15, 1806, familytales.org.

35. Lloyd, *Trials*, 217.

36. See Wood, *Empire of Liberty*, 624, 640–41, 646, 659, 680–82; Paul E. Johnson, *Early American Republic, 1789–1829* (New York: Oxford University Press, 2007), 40–43.

37. Cornog, *Birth of Empire*, 102; Adams, *Bridgehampton*, 145–48; Zaykowski, *Sag Harbor*, 65–71. Ebenezer Sage to James Madison, 18 April 1813, https://founders.archives.gov/documents/Madison/03-06-02-0202. Sage was a physician and served in the House from District 1, 1809 to 1815; "Biographical Directory of the United States Congress," http://bioguide.congress.gov/biosearch/biosearch.asp. For Rose's report, see Adams, *Southampton*, 193.

38. See Frederick C. Leiner, "The Squadron Commander's Share: Decatur v. Chew and the Prize Money for the Chesapeake's First War of 1812 Cruise," *The Journal of Military History* 73 no. 1 (January 2009): 73–74. muse.jhu.edu/journal/96.

39. See Donald A. Petrie, *The Prize Game: Lawful Looting on the High Seas in the Days of Fighting Sail* (New York: Berkley Books, 1999), 144–46, 165n2.

40. Hough, *Court*, 23; R. S. Guernsey, *New York City and Vicinity during the War of 1812–'15*, vol. 2 (New York: Charles L. Woodward, 1895), 534.

41. Prize and Related Records for the War of 1812 of the U.S. District Court for the Southern District of New York, 1812–16, RG 21-NARA: see https://www.fold3.com/search/#cat=247. I searched Fold3 limited by the War of 1812. My research did not include the records of privateers, only the cases that involved ships of war. I used both the names Nathan Sanford and Sanford alone, and found matches to fifteen cases that used the printed form for the writ. Given the poor condition of these documents, there were, no doubt, many more case records that did not survive. In the case Jesse Elliott *et al.* (U.S. ship *Eliza*) v. *Caledonia*, fur trader and agent John Jacob Astor signed an affidavit dated March 3, 1813, that he owned the skins. He also made clear in his affidavit that he was a "citizen of the United States of America," challenging the libel that said the commerce involved was pursued by "subjects of the king." I have used the terminology used by the National Archives for case titles and for ships. For ship names, for example, U.S. Frigate *United States*, the usage matches the explanatory note in Donald R.

Hickey, *Don't Give Up the Ship! Myths of the War of 1812* (Champaign: University of Illinois Press, 2006), xxvii.

42. Hickey, *Ship*, 11, 56; see Robert P. Watson, *America's First Crisis: The War of 1812* (Albany: State University of New York Press, 2014), 87–97, for an account of the Battle of Queenston Heights. Watson calls the *Caledonia* a schooner, whereas the writ, in sworn testimony, states that it was a brig. He also dates Elliot's seizure to December 9, when the writ states that it took place on October 9, 199. Hickey places the battle in the Niagara River, whereas the writ says the attack took place on Lake Erie: see Hickey, *Ship*, 56, 155, 332.

43. Wood, *Empire of Liberty*, 681; for Decatur's heroism in Tripoli's harbor in 1804, see ibid., 637.

44. *Berkshire Reporter* (Pittsfield, MA), September 14, 1811.

45. See Leiner, "Decatur," 81, 81n37; Craig R. Scott, "Description," NARA, https://www.fold3.com/page/1916_war_of_1812_prize_cases_1812_1816#description; Samuel H. Williamson, "Seven Ways to Compute the Relative Value of a U.S. Dollar Amount, 1774 to present," *Measuring Worth*, 2015, measuringworth.com/uscompare/. The CPI calculation estimated the worth of $200,000 to be $3,060,000 in 2015. It was the lowest estimate of the different calculations that use a multiplier of fifteen, an approach I will use throughout this book.

46. On its way to New York, the *Macedonian* with its American captors apparently stopped in Newport, RI; see Wood, *Empire of Liberty*, 681. Not all ships were in New York City before a trial in that district began. They had to be in the marshal's custody, however.

47. Hickey, *Ship*, 113–14; Prize Records, RG 21-NARA; Donald R. Hickey, ed., *The War of 1812, Writings from America's Second War of Independence* (Library of America, 2013), 396, 400, 731.

48. See Guernsey, *New York City*, 430–31.

Chapter 4

1. See Wood, *Empire of Liberty*, 276–77, 282–85; Brooke, *Columbia Rising*, 288; Cornog, *Birth of Empire*, 34–36.

2. See Roper, "Kent's Necrologies," 230.

3. Angela Fernandez, "The Ancient and Honorable Court of Dover: Serious Mock, Solemn Foolery, and Sporting Wit in Nineteenth-Century New York State," *Australian & New Zealand Law and History E-Journal*, Referred Paper No. 7 (2012): 219, "The Ancient and Honorable Court of Dover: Mock Trials, Fraternal Orders, and Solemn Foolery in Nineteenth-Century New York State," https://works.bepress.com/angela_**fernandez**/1/download.

4. Cornog, *Birth of Empire*, 5.

5. Brooke, *Columbia Rising*, 93–94, 515n75.

6. See Fernandez, "Ancient and Honorable," for a quotation from the Tammany Society's "Membership List" showing Sanford as a member in 1802 and as Sachem, 1803–1804, 222n81. On Tammany, see Cornog, *Birth of Empire*,

28, 89–90. For Sanford as captain, see also, *Military Minutes of the Council of Appointment of the State of New York, 1783–1821* (State of New York, 1901), 664.

7. Wood, *Empire of Liberty*, 299.

8. Cornog, *Birth of Empire*, 25, 46, 75.

9. Ibid., 5, 37; Brooke, *Columbia Rising*, 247–48.

10. Recommendation, DeWitt Clinton to Department of State, May 3 and May 31, 1802, RG59-NARA; DeWitt Clinton to President Jefferson, May 3, 1802, RG 59-NARA.

11. Cornog, *Birth of Empire*, 39. For the pamphlet war between Clintonians and Burrites, and a description of the July 1802 duel between Clinton and Burrite John Swartwout, see 40–44, 48–49.

12. DeWitt Clinton to President Jefferson, May 31, 1802, RG 59-NARA.

13. Wood, *Empire of Liberty*, 300; Cornog, *Birth of Empire*, 46.

14. Cornog, *Birth of Empire*, 56.

15. DeWitt Clinton to President Jefferson, September 7, 1803, RG 59-NARA; Cornog, *Birth of Empire*, 49–50. According to Charles Elliot Fitch, "Sanford, Nathan," *Encyclopedia of Biography of New York* (New York: The American Historical Society, 1916), 152, Sanford's campaign work for Republicans caught Jefferson's attention and led to his nomination as federal attorney. However, Fitch is incorrect in suggesting that Sanford was "Anti-Clintonian throughout": see 152.

16. See Cornog, *Birth of Empire*, 55, 60, 89.

17. Male suffrage for governor, lieutenant governor, and state senator required a $250 freehold. The Republican candidate for governor won in 1804; the Federalists were so weak that they didn't offer a candidate: Strum, "Property Qualifications," 349.

18. Nathan Sanford to Henry P. Dering, April 18, 1804, Hampton Library, LI Doc 40, Bridgehampton. The requirements for male suffrage for assemblymen and congressmen were a freehold worth between $50 and $250, or renting a tenement for $5 per year. Sanford seems to have used the term "elector" to mean voter until 1821, when changes in suffrage qualifications were made at the state constitutional convention.

19. Wood, *Empire of Liberty*, 382–84.

20. Cornog, *Birth of Empire*,76.

21. Nathan Sanford to DeWitt Clinton, February 27, 1806, DeWitt Clinton Papers, Columbia University, Rare Books & Manuscript Library, New York. Hereafter DWCP-CU; see Cornog, *Birth of Empire*, 73–78; Alexander, *A Political History*, 149–53.

22. Nathan Sanford to DeWitt Clinton, February 27, 1806, DWCP-CU.

23. *Minutes of the Common Council of the City of New York, 1784–1831*, 289, https://archive.org/details/minutescommonco29coungoog.

24. Sean Wilentz, *Rise of American Democracy: Jefferson to Lincoln* (New York: W. W. Norton, 2005), 121; Cushman, *Richard Varick*, 133–34, 210–11.

25. Brooke, *Columbia Rising*, 330–31.

26. *New York American Citizen*, April 5, 1808; *Republican Watch-Tower* (New York City), April 26, 1808.

27. Hough, *Civil List*, 322. Deacon David Hedges served terms in 1786–89, 1804, and 1806–1807, Ibid., 280. Hedges became Sanford's stepfather in 1792.

28. See Wood, *Empire of Liberty*, 649–52; Johnson, *Early American Republic*, 43.

29. See Philip J. Lampi, "The Federalist Party Resurgence, 1808–16: Evidence from the New Nation Votes Database," *JER* 33 (Summer 2013): 259–61; Strum, "Property Qualifications," 351; Cornog, *Birth of Empire*, 91.

30. Alexander, *A Political History*, 171.

31. See Wood, *Empire of Liberty*, 653–58: (performance) bonds were not new with the embargo. In 1790, the collector in Sag Harbor, Henry P. Dering, required a $1,000 bond from the master of the Sloop *Polly* to ensure that the vessel not engage in any "illicit trade" while licensed to sail "between the different Districts of the United States, or to carry on the Bank or Whale Fishery for one year," Coasting Licence, District of Sagg-Harbour [*sic*], October 20, 1790, framed, Whaling Museum, Sag Harbor, NY.

32. See Hough, *Court*, 9.

33. Thompson, *History of Long Island*, 2nd ed. (1843) 2:542.

34. See *Military Minutes*, 1171; *Lampi Collection of American Electoral Returns, 1788–1825* (American Antiquarian Society, 2007) A New Nation Votes, New York 1811 January, Speaker of the Assembly, elections.lib.tufts.edu/terms; New York 1811, Election for State Senate Southern District, ibid.

35. See Cornog, *Birth of Empire*, 86, 88, 90–92, 96, 99–101.

36. For Clinton's relationship to Martin Van Buren in this period, see ibid., 131–32.

37. Ibid., 76, 197n8.

38. 1810 Federal Census, New York Ward 1, New York, New York, NARA Roll, M252_32, p. 2.

39. Eric Homberger, *The Historical Atlas of New York City* (New York: Henry Holt Co., 1998), 46–47, 55, 62–63, 70; Johnson, *Early American Republic*, 80.

40. Johnson, *Early American Republic*, 65.

41. See Hough, *Civil List*, 123; Donald B. Cole, *Martin Van Buren and the American Political System* (n.p.: Princeton University Press, 1984; Eastern National, 2004), 60; Brooke, *Columbia Rising*, 306, 421: the quotation is on page 286. Tompkins was elected governor four times from 1807 to 1817; Clinton followed Tompkins as governor and served from mid-1817 to 1822 and from 1825 until his death in February 1828.

42. Brooke, *Columbia Rising*, 205–6, 313–14: the quotation is on page 205.

43. Strum, "Property Qualifications," 350; *New York Commercial Advertiser*, April 15, 1808; *Political Bulletin and Miscellaneous Repository* (New York City) February 19, 1811; Brooke, *Columbia Rising*, 113.

44. See the *New York Columbian*, April 3, 1816; ibid., April 2, 1817; *Mercantile Advertiser*, April 17, 1819; Henry Wysham Lanier, *A Century of Banking in New York, 1822–1922* (New York: Gilliss Press, 1922), 130, archive.org.

45. See John Lauritz Larson, "An Inquiry into the Nature and Causes of the Wealth of Nations," *JER* 35 (Spring 2015): 2–5.

46. See *Lampi Collection*, New York 1814 Election to Council of Appointment.

47. Jabez D. Hammond, *History of Political Parties in the State of New York from the Ratification of the Federal Constitution to December 1840*, 2 vols. (Cooperstown, NY: H. & E. Phinney, 1847), 1:381–82. The law was passed on October 23, 1814.

48. Ibid., 381–82; ibid. (1846), 2:540 Note A: see Hammond's correction for his statement that Young proposed the restriction on blacks. Although he was not the proposer, Young was among the first to support the freehold requirement for blacks only.

49. Brooke, *Columbia Rising*, 426; the article from the *Commercial Advertiser* was reprinted in the *Cleveland Morning Leader*, February 24, 1863, http://chroniclingamerica.loc.gov/lccn/sn83035143/1863-02-24/ed-1/seq-1.pdf. Kent's previous position as chief justice of the supreme court also placed him on the council.

50. See *Lampi Collection*, New York 1815 Election for U.S. Senator; Nathan Sanford to Martin Van Buren, December 28, 1814, Martin Van Buren Papers, Manuscript Division, LC. Hereafter cited as MVBP-LC; Brooke, *Columbia Rising*, 330.

Chapter 5

1. See Wood, *Empire of Liberty*, 701–6; Johnson, *Early American Republic*, 79–81: the quotation is on page 81.

2. Will, Sandford, 1785; Tax Assessment Rolls, 1800, 1801, 1802, 1803, Manuscript Copies, Suffolk County Historical Society Archives, Riverhead, NY; [Southampton Tax Rate List 1805], *Suffolk County Historical Society Register* 5 (December 1979): 69. Owner and lessee were listed jointly on the tax roll because the lessee paid the property taxes.

3. Like Jesse Pierson, Timothy Halsey was an early area schoolteacher. He lived near Sanford's farm in a circa 1790 timber-frame house that is still standing: see J. Kirkpatrick Flack, "Hay Ground Heritage Area Report" (May 2011), http://southamptontownny.gov/DocumentCenter/View/744; Halsey, *Sketches*, 38.

4. *RTSH*, vol. 3, 379; for the new law, see Henry P. Hedges, "Memories of a Long Life," in *Tracing the Past*, 303. Henry Hedges's recollections of Montauk came from his grandfather, David Hedges. See also, Rattray, *East Hampton*, 374n.

5. Deeds, 1808, Liber D, 116–67; 1817, Liber D, 519–20; 1819, Liber E, 116–67, Suffolk County Registry of Deeds, Riverhead, NY. Sanford was Jeremiah Miller's half-uncle, although the two men were the same age.

6. Deed, Rector of Grace Church to Nathan Sanford, July 12, 1815, Land Papers, Box 286, SFP, GLC-NYPL. See Receipt Book, May 6, 1822; the Grace Church properties were located at the corner of Greenwich Street and Morton Street.

7. Receipt, September 9, 1844, Mary B. Sanford, Miscellaneous Papers, Box 287, SFP, GLC-NYPL; Record of Assessment, Manhattan, First Ward, 1819–34, Municipal Archives, New York; Lanier, *Banking*, 130.

8. Record of Assessment; Lanier, *Banking*, 130. Sanford had begun to rent the "cellar Yard" of 27 Pine Street by 1810: see Receipt Book, May 16, 1810.

9. Law clerk Abraham T. Rose was the nephew-in-law of Sanford's sister: see Sanford, *Sandford/Sanford Families*, 19, 28; George Rogers Howell, *The Early History of History of Southampton L.I., New York* (Albany: Weed, Parsons and Co., 1887), 370; Adams, *Bridgehampton*, 146. See *Portrait and Biographical Record of Suffolk County, Long Island, New York* (New York: Chapman Publishing Co., 1896), 949. One of Abraham T. Rose's uncles was General Rose; the general was a brother-in-law of Nathan Sanford's sister and lived in Bridgehampton, not North Sea, as David Goddard implies. Goddard notes that in 1818 General Abraham Rose became the first president of the "proprietor trustees" in Southampton town: see Goddard, *Colonizing Southampton*, 40–41, 139. Abraham T. (Topping) Rose built a Greek Revival-style mansion in Bridgehampton in 1840; it is now the Topping Rose House, an inn and restaurant.

10. See Folts, "Courts," *Encyclopedia of New York State*, 412; the 1777 state constitution established what became known as the court of errors, an unwieldy institution that heard appeals from the New York State Supreme Court and the court of chancery.

11. Robert E. Wright and David J. Cowen, *Financial Founding Fathers* (Chicago: University of Chicago Press, 2006), 18.

12. See Chernow, *Alexander Hamilton*, 585–89; Cushman, *Varick*, 167–71; Cornog, *Birth of Empire*, 60, 94.

13. Kaplan, *John Quincy Adams*, 186, 194–95, 248, 311, 428, 467–68. Cole, *Martin Van Buren*, 22. By comparison, Martin Van Buren at age twenty-eight in 1810 was earning $10,000 a year from his private law partnership.

14. Roper, "Kent's Necrologies," 230.

15. Cornog, *Birth of Empire*, 8, 92, 199n19; Hammond, *History of Political Parties*, 1:294.

16. Alan Nevins, ed., *The Diary of Philip Hone, 1828–1851* (New York: Dodd, Mead and Company, 1927), 2:525–26; Roper, "Kent's Necrologies," 230. Kent may have used the earlier estimates of $30,000 annual income and multiplied by twelve, the number of years Sanford served as federal attorney. Then perhaps he deducted money for living expenses. Gustavus Myers, *History of Tammany Hall* (New York: Boni & Liverright, 1917), 33, https://archive.org/details/historyoftammany00myeruoft. See *Bicentennial Celebration*, 5.

17. See *Historical Statistics of the United States, Colonial Times to 1970, Bicentennial Edition*, Part 1 (Washington, DC: U.S. Bureau of the Census, 1975), 32: New York State's population based on the federal census was 340,000 in 1790, 1,373,000 in 1820, and 2,429,000 in 1840, two years after Nathan Sanford's death.

18. *Statutes at Large*-LC, 12th Congress, 1st session, Chapter 70, 71. 1812, 719; ibid., 13th Congress, 3rd session, Chapter 95, 1815, 235; see Hough, *Court*,

17–18; *Bicentennial Celebration*, 5: the author notes the reported earnings of Sanford at $100,000 a year. Unlike the decades through the War of 1812, it's not clear whether federal attorneys collected a percentage of civil, especially maritime, case settlements into the 1890s.

19. The reporter referred to "Democratic" Ward Meetings, but I have been unable to document this label for 1808. In March1801, Congress raised the salaries for some district judges. In the New York district court it was set at $1,600: LC-*Statutes at Large*, 6th Congress, 2nd session, Chapter 29, 1801, 121. See Hough, *Court*, 5, for the salary set in 1789 of $1,500 per year for New York's district court judge. The salary for the attorney general of the United States in 1789 was also $1,500: Chernow, *Alexander Hamilton*, 289.

20. The *New-York Herald* reporter had read an article in the April 22, 1808 issue of the *Public Advertiser* that described the Republican meeting.

21. The *Cooperstown Otsego Herald*, April 20, 1811, had reprinted the excerpt from the *New York Columbian*; Cornog, *Birth of Empire*, 89–90.

22. The baby survived and was named Eliza after her mother.

23. Rufus Rockwell Wilson, *Washington: The Capital City and its Part in the History of the Nation* (Philadelphia: Lippincott, 1901), 164.

Chapter 6

1. Quoted in Wood, *Empire of Liberty*, 553.

2. Nathan Sanford to John Trumbull, January 8, 1820, NYHS; John Trumbull to Nathan Sanford, January 12, 1820, NYHS; appropriation, *Statutes at Large*-LC, 16th congress, 1st session, April 11, 1820, 561.

3. See *Lampi Collection*, New York 1815 Election for U.S. Senator, Feb. 7, 1815; see Alexander, *A Political History*, 232–33; for background and a description of personal alliances, see Brooke, *Columbia Rising*, 337–38.

4. See Johnson, *Early American Republic*, 138–39.

5. See, for example, the use of these terms in the letter, Nathan Sanford to Henry Wheaton, January 8, 1816, Literary and Historical Manuscripts, Morgan Library and Museum, New York, NY. In the letter, Sanford described the Senate's discussion of the exclusion of foreign seamen from working with "citizens" on American merchant vessels.

6. See Howe, *What Hath God Wrought*, 80–81, 83; David S. Heidler and Jeanne T. Heidler, *Henry Clay: The Essential American* (New York: Random House, 2010), 123. Madison's Seventh Annual Message to Congress was dated December 5, 1815.

7. No. 42563, December 8, 1817, Early American Imprints, Series II (1801–1819), Shaw-Shoemaker, NYSL, Albany, [1]–2 (hereafter EAI-NYSL); see Wright and Cowen, *Financial*, 117, 125, 130, 136.

8. No. 46133, January 2, 1818, EAI-NYSL.

9. For example, he made the motion that required the printing of 2,000 copies of President James Monroe's annual message that was read to the House and the Senate on November 17, 1818. Two days later he moved that the Senate assign each topic raised in the message, such as foreign relations, and commerce and manufacturing, to the appropriate committee: copies, *Senate Journal*-LC, November 17, 1818, 20, http://memory.loc.gov/ammem/amlaw/lawhome.html. Hereafter cited as *Senate Journal*-LC; message, ibid., November 19, 1818, 22.

10. No. 49754, January 11, 1819, EAI-NYSL.

11. See Chernow, *Alexander Hamilton*, 348–49.

12. See Wood, *Empire of Liberty*, 295–97: the quotation is on page 296.

13. Specie, *Annals of Congress*, LC, Senate, 14th Congress, 1st session, March 25, 1816, vol. 29, 248–49, http://memory.loc.gov/ammem/amlaw/lawhome.html. Hereafter cited as *Annals*-LC; payable on demand, *Senate Journal*-LC, 14th Congress, 1st session, March 26, 1816, 344–45; see Howe, *What Hath God Wrought*, 374.

14. Postponement, *Senate Journal*-LC, 14th Congress, 1st session, April 1, 1816, 366–67; *Annals*-LC, Senate, 14th Congress, 1st session April 1, 1816, vol. 29, 272, 274; gold and silver, *Annals*-LC, Senate, April 2 1816, 373–74: the amendment lost—the vote was twenty-two opposed and fourteen in favor.

15. Howe, *What Hath God Wrought*, 374; Johnson, *Early American Republic*, 139; Robert E. Wright, *The First Wall Street* (Chicago: The University of Chicago Press, 2005), 154–55.

16. Vote on bill, *Senate Journal*-LC. 14th Congress, 1st session, April 3, 1816, 385; see Bray Hammond, *Banks and Politics in America, From the Revolution to the Civil War* (Princeton, NJ: Princeton University Press, 1957), 240; see Howe, *What Hath God Wrought*, 85n67, 86. The four middle states are Maryland, Delaware, Pennsylvania, and New Jersey.

17. Committee, *Senate Journal*-LC, 14th Congress, 1st session, March 1, 1816, 246.

18. Chair, ibid., 16th Congress, 1st session, December 16, 1819, 28. In the fall of 1819, Sanford's name was listed first when the members of the committees were appointed, and he consistently reported out bills from the finance committee, indicating he had become chair.

19. Member, *Senate Journal*-LC, 16th Congress, 1st session, December 8, 1819, 20; bill, Bank of the United States, *Congressional Documents*-LC, S. 13, Senate, 16th congress, 2nd session, December 20, 1820 and Act, ibid., February 20, 1821.

20. Wood, *Empire of Liberty*, 702–8: the quotation is on page 708.

21. Member, *Senate Journal*-LC, 15th Congress, 1st session, December 11, 1817, 26; Sanford was reappointed to the Committee on Commerce and Manufactures November 20, 1818: *Senate Journal*-LC, 15th Congress, 2nd session, 23; member, *Senate Journal*-LC, 16th Congress, 1st session, December 16, 1819, 28; member, *Senate Journal*-LC, 16th Congress, 2nd session, November 20, 1820, 22. He was listed first on the lists for the 15th Congress and is referred to as

chairman. The committee was among the original standing committees which were established in December 1816.

22. Canal, *Senate Journal*-LC, 14th Congress, 2nd session, January 7, 1817, 84–85; Cornog, *Birth of Empire*, 108–13, 117; Brooke, *Columbia Rising*, 424–25.

23. Brooke, *Columbia Rising*, 424.

24. Howe, *What Hath God Wrought*, 216, 220–21, also describes the mixed impact of internal improvements on agriculture by region.

25. Nathan Sanford to Major General Jacob Brown, December 8, 1819, Massachusetts Historical Society, Boston, MA.; for Brown, see C. Edward Skeen, *1816: America Rising* (Lexington: University Press of Kentucky, 2003), 142–43.

26. Wright and Cowen, *Financial*, 43, 50; Wright, *First Wall*, 74–75; see Daniel Peart, "Looking Beyond Parties and Elections: The Making of United States Tariff Policy during the Early 1820s," *JER* 33 (Spring 2013): 99–102 for a discussion of petitioning as a means for influencing legislators.

27. Duties, *Senate Journal*-LC, 14th Congress, 1st session, April 17, 1816, 488, 490; see Howe, *What Hath God Wrought*, 84; Johnson, *Early American Republic*, 139.

28. Sanford married Mary Esther Malbone Isaacs on April 14, 1813: see *Descendants of Jacob Sebor*, 15.

29. *New-York Herald*, May 22, 1816, 4.

30. See Skeen, *1816*, 98; Rosemarie Zagarri, "The Family Factor: Congressmen, Turnover, and the Burden of Public Service in the Early American Republic," *JER* 33 (Summer 2013): 284, 294–95.

31. See Peart, "Tariff Policy," 92; Statistical reports, *Senate Journal*-LC, 15th Congress, 1st session, April 6, 1818, 327; April 11, 1818, ibid., 349.

32. Russell E. Bidlack, "The Book Collection of the Old University of Michigan: The Story of Twelve Volumes," *Quarterly Review Index* 64 (1957–1958): 112–13, http://books.google.com; *An Account of the Receipts and Expenditures of the United States for the Year 1819* (Washington, DC: E. De Krafft, Printer, 1820), 95, http://books.google.com. Seybert served in the House during the years 1809–15 and 1817–19.

33. Johnson, *Early American Republic*, 143–45; Howe, *What Hath God Wrought*, 142–47.

34. See No. S49794, "Mr. Sanford made Report," December 20, 1819, EAI-NYSL, [1]–2. The Report showed that during the embargo of late 1807 the previously expanding exports plummeted. While they regained some strength in 1809, they fell again during the war from June 1812 to December 1814. By the end of September 1818, exports had not returned to their peak of more than $108 million in 1807. For some of the Report's analysis of the export data, see ibid., 3–8. The Treasury continued to deliver their reports to the Senate. On February 19, 1829, during his second term, Sanford moved that 1,000 copies of the secretary of the treasury's report on foreign commerce be printed. The report would ensure the circulation of "accurate information": *Niles Register*, February 28, 1829, 36:12, googlebooks.com. The Internet source for *Register* citations is https://catalog.hathitrust.org/Record/006903835. Citations are from this source except

where otherwise noted. Published in Baltimore, *Niles Register* became a trusted source of information and commentary.

35. For the Report's initial commentary on imports, including how the data was collected and how it might be changed, see No. S49794, EAI-NYSL, 8–12. For quotations, see 12.

36. Ibid., 19.

37. Ibid.

38. Ibid., 29.

39. Bill, *Congressional Documents*-LC, S.11, Senate, 16th Congress, 1st session, December 20, 1819.

40. Bill, *Senate Journal*-LC, 16th Congress, 1st session, February 15, 1820, 158: President Monroe signed the legislation on February 10, 1820.

41. Letter, Secretary of the Treasury to the Speaker of the House, tables attached, Duties on Imports—Comparative Statement, February 9, 1833, ProQuest Congressional, house_doc_96.pdf; see Wood, *Empire of Liberty*, 735–36: the quotation is on page 736. Since Sanford lost his bid for reelection to the Senate in 1821, he did not participate in the debate over the Tariff of 1824.

42. Memorial, *Annals*-LC, Senate, 16th Congress, 1st session, December 27, 1819, 35:38; Peart, "Tariff Policy," 88–93, 99, 104–5, 105n26.

43. See Peart, "Tariff Policy," 105n26, 107. Quotation is on page 107.

44. See Howe, *What Hath God Wrought*, 81, 96–97.

45. Member, Naval Affairs, *Senate Journal*-LC, 15th Congress, 1st session, December 11, 1817, 27; chair, *Senate Journal*-LC, 15th Congress, 2nd session, November 20, 1818, 23. Sanford's name appeared first on the appointee list, and he reported out resolutions, so I have assumed he was chair. Mr. Sanford reported, No. S46297, December 2, 1818, EAI-NYSL.

Chapter 7

1. Sandford, "Rural Connections," 8, 19n27, 20n29.

2. *Slavery in New York*, eds., Ira Berlin and Leslie M. Harris (New York: The New Press, 2005), 16–17, 132–33; 1810 Federal Census, New York Ward 1, New York, New York, NARA Roll, M252_32, p. 2.

3. Receipt Book, January 14, 1803.

4. *Cleveland Morning Leader*, January 10, 1859, http://chroniclingamerica.loc.gov/lccn/sn83035143/issues/1859/. The article described the inauguration of the New Senate Hall on December 6, 1819. The essay used here is probably a reprint from 1819; it appeared two decades after Sanford's death. The Senate leaders of interest listed are James Barbour, Mahlon Dickerson, Richard M. Johnson, Rufus King, William R. King, Nathaniel Macon, Harrison Gray Otis, William Pinckney, Nathan Sanford, and William Smith.

5. Persons escaping, *Senate Journal*-LC, 14th Congress, 2nd session, February 17, 1817, 247–50; see also, public jail, *Annals*-LC, Senate, 14th Congress, 2nd session, February 17, 1817, 30:123.

6. Petition, *Senate Journal*-LC, 15th Congress, 2nd session, December 24, 1818, 101; Importation, Ibid., December 15, 1818, 77; for the committee appointed, see *Annals*-LC, Senate, 14th Congress, 2nd session, December 15, 1818, 33:69; see Howe, *What Hath God Wrought*, 51–52, 57; see Wood, *Empire of Liberty*, 523–27, for a discussion of the terms of the Constitution's ban on the slave trade.

7. See Howe, *What Hath God Wrought*, 147, 150–51. The Tallmadge Amendment was introduced on February 13, 1819; the vote on the amendment in the Senate took place on February 27; the first clause, to prohibit the further introduction of slaves into Missouri lost, twenty-two to sixteen, and the second clause, to free at age twenty-five children born to slaves in Missouri after it became a state, lost as well, thirty-one to seven; *Encyclopedia of American History*, ed. Richard B. Morris (New York: Harper & Brothers, 1961), 159.

8. See Heidler and Heidler, *Clay*, 146–47.

9. Nathan Sanford to Martin Van Buren, February 3, 1820, MVBP-LC.

10. Ibid.; see Howe, *What Hath God Wrought*, 150–52.

11. The boundaries involved in the Thomas amendment are at *Senate Journal*-LC, 16th Congress, 1st session, February 17, 1820, 165–66; amendments, ibid., 166. For all three votes on amendments and the compromise bill, see also *Annals*-LC, Senate, 16th Congress, 1st session, February 17, 1820, 36:427–28.

12. Act, *Senate Journal*-LC, 16th Congress, 1st session, February 17, 1820, 166; *Annals*-LC, Senate, 16th Congress, 1st session, February 17, 1820, 36:430.

13. Amended bill, *Senate Journal*-LC, 16th Congress, 1st session, February 17, 1820, 166–67; Howe, *What Hath God Wrought*, 152, 154. The quotation is on 152. Sanford's reference to the Pacific Ocean is based on a stipulation in the Transcontinental Treaty with Spain signed on February 22, 1819.

14. Howe, *What Hath God Wrought*, 154.

15. See ibid., 155; compromise signed, *Senate Journal*-LC, 16th Congress, 1st session, March 7, 1820, 213. The quotation from President Monroe is in Johnson, *Early American Republic*, 146.

16. Quoted in Howe, *What Hath God Wrought*, 155.

17. New York State resolutions, *Senate Journal*-LC, 16th Congress, 2nd session, November 23, 1820, 26. New York's state constitution did not include a requirement that representatives follow their state legislature's instructions: Skeen, *1816*, 90. However, the legislature "instructed" the senators, who it had elected, while it "requested" that New York's members of the House, elected by the voters, follow the instructions. The vote in the state assembly supporting the instructions was 117 to 4; David N. Gellman and David Quigley, eds., *Jim Crow New York, A Documentary History of Race and Citizenship, 1777–1877* (New York: New York University Press, 2003), 85.

18. Howe, *What Hath God Wrought*, 156.

19. Statehood, *Senate Journal*-LC, 16th Congress, 2nd session, February 28, 1821, 239; see Howe, *What Hath God Wrought*, 156.

20. Congressional pay, *Senate Journal*-LC, 14th Congress,1st session, March 14, 1816, 291–96; Skeen, *1816*, 82.

21. *Huntington Town Records, including Babylon, Long Island, N.Y., 1776–1873*, ed. Charles R. Street, (Huntington: The *Long Islander* Print, 1889), 3:273–77. Sanford had a long relationship with the Town of Huntington. An entry in his receipt book on May 20, 1807, noted that he had received $100 to cover expenses for his trip to Albany in September 1806 "as Counsel to argue motions in Chancery in the suit of the Trustees with Wiliam Nicolls." Like the March 1816 case, this one had concerned the islands, which eventually became part of the Town of Islip.

22. Howe, *What Hath God Wrought*, 86–87.

23. See Wood, *Empire of Liberty*, 717–20; Skeen, *1816*, 86, 93.

24. Electors, *Senate Journal*-LC, 14th Congress, 1st Session, March 20, 1816, 317; Cole, *Martin Van Buren*, 113: in 1824, when a proposal for the popular election of the president resurfaced, Senator Van Buren opposed it, arguing that the practice would reduce the power of the states. Control of elections through Van Buren's party discipline would have also been more difficult.

25. Ibid., 15th Congress, 2nd session, November 25, 1818, 28–31; ibid.,16th Congress, 1st session, January 27, 1820, 125; chart, "Public Officers Elected Statewide," *Encyclopedia of New York State*, 496n.a; see Donald Ratcliffe, "The Right to Vote and the Rise of Democracy, 1787–1828," *JER* 33 (Summer 2013): 250–51.

26. No. S39449, Judge Tallmadge charges, April 8, 1816, EAI-NYSL, 1–2; Sanford to testify, *Senate Journal*-LC, 14th Congress, 1st session, April 12, 1816, 434; see H. Paul Burak, *History of the United States District Court for the Southern District of New York* (New York: Federal Bar Association of New York, New Jersey & Connecticut, 1962), 3–4. I found no evidence that Sanford ever appeared before the House committee.

27. No. S39194, Northern District, February 6,1816, EAI-NYSL; *Statutes at Large*-LC, 14th Congress, 1st session, February 15, 1816, 254; No. S39419, Mr. Sanford submitted, March 7, 1816, EAI-NYSL; see J. Hampden Dougherty, *Constitutional History of the State of New York* (New York: Neale Publishing Co., 1915), 341–42.

28. Wood, *Empire of Liberty*, 418–24.

29. Postponed, LC, *House Journal*, April 17,1816, 668.

30. Rattray, *East Hampton*, 88: the doctor was the first in a line of physicians in East Hampton.

31. Post Office, *Annals*-LC, 14th Congress, 1st session, February 7, 1816, 125; see Howe, *What Hath God Wrought*, 478.

32. Quotations are in Rosalie Miller Baker, "The First Postmaster of East Hampton, Jeremiah Miller," n. d. [c. 1930], JH199, LIC-EHL; Wood, *Empire of Liberty*, 478.

33. 1820 Federal Census, New York Ward 1, New York, New York, p. 67, NARA Roll, M33_77, Image: 45. Sanford may have added one or two of the

servants after his wife's death. The census used the category "free white," meaning not indentured, through the year 1840; by 1840, indenture was highly infrequent and servitude came to denote black slaves. See Wood, *Empire of Liberty*, 345: the Revolution collapsed "all the different dependencies in the society into either freemen or slaves."

Chapter 8

1. See *Lampi Collection*, New York 1821 Election for U.S. Senator: the tally was eighty-eight legislative votes for Van Buren and sixty-three for Sanford; see Craig Hanyan, *DeWitt Clinton and the Rise of the People's Men* (Montreal: McGill-Queen's University Press, 1996), 10–11; Alexander, *A Political History*, 286–87. Historians have referred to the group of Federalists as Clintonian Federalists.

2. Michael Kammen, "The Promised Sunshine of the Future: Reflections on Economic Growth and Social Change in Post-Revolutionary New York," in *New Opportunities in a New Nation: The Development of New York After the Revolution* ed. Manfred Jonas and Robert V. Wells (Schenectady, NY: Union College Press, 1982), 111–12, 125; Johnson, *Early American Republic*, 82, 128–29, 132.

3. See Wood, *Empire of Liberty*, 8–9; John L. Brooke, "'King George Has Issued Too Many Pattents for Us,' Property and Democracy in Jeffersonian New York," *JER* 33 (Summer 2013): 200.

4. Johnson, *Early American Republic*, 127; see Brooke, "King George," 193–94, 211: the quotation is on page 191.

5. John Anthony Casais, "The New York State Constitutional Convention of 1821 and Its Aftermath" (PhD dissertation, Columbia University, 1967), 1–2, 5–7, 25–28; Cornog, *Birth of Empire*, 142–43; Peter J. Galie, "Constitutions and Constitutional Conventions," *Encyclopedia of New York State*, 388.

6. See Nathaniel H. Carter and William L. Stone, eds., *Reports of the Proceedings and Debates of the Convention of 1821, Assembled for the Purpose of Amending the Constitution of the State of New York* (Albany, 1821), 28. Hereafter cited as Carter and Stone, eds., *Reports*. According to the reporters, the publication is a "minute and full journal of the proceedings and debates" with corrections added (page v). Governor DeWitt Clinton was not a delegate.

7. See *New-York Evening Post*, June 23, 1821. In the May 28, 1821 issue of the *Post*, a commentator wrote that if elected, Sanford would be one of the "delegates of elevated character," alongside Chancellor Kent and Stephen Van Rensselaer, since he was not one of the "party men" at Tammany Hall.

8. Brooke, *Columbia Rising*, 383.

9. Carter and Stone, eds., *Reports*, 27, 34–35, 38.

10. Ibid., 207, 210.

11. See Brooke, *Columbia Rising*, 64, 382–83; Ratcliffe, "The Right to Vote," 245; Casais, "Convention of 1821," 2; Folts, "Courts," *Encyclopedia of New York*

State, 412. Nathan Sanford lost his bid in 1814 to sit on the Council of Appointment in an assembly vote, having come in fifth where there were only four openings: see *Lampi Collection*, New York 1814 Election to Council of Appointment.

12. Carter and Stone, eds., *Reports*, 514.

13. Ibid., 517–18.

14. Ibid., 518.

15. Ibid., 521.

16. Ibid., 518. Sanford offered a summary of his thinking in a later debate; see ibid., 610.

17. See ibid., 524–25; Cornog, *Birth of Empire*, 142.

18. Carter and Stone, eds., *Reports*, 627, 630, 636; Appendix, ibid., 690. The quotation is on page 636.

19. See Folts, "Courts," *Encyclopedia of New York State*, 412.

20. Carter and Stone, eds., *Reports*, 485–87: the quotation is on page 486. Sanford's friend Martin Van Buren was not present. Van Buren voted on another resolution earlier on the day of October 19, see 484: he may have left the convention, not wanting to take a stand on the resolution for political reasons. But he chaired the convention the following day. The resolution was defeated by a vote of seventy-three to thirty-three. For excerpts from this portion of the slavery debate, see Gellman and Quigley, *Jim Crow New York*, 194–96. The book offers helpful commentary on the convention of 1821 based on excerpts from Carter and Stone, eds., *Reports*. Anti-black sentiments are traced and emphasized.

21. Carter and Stone, eds., *Reports*, 487–95: the quotations are on page 487. For background on libel in English common law, the politics of the trial of Harry Croswell that began in 1803, and the Act concerning Libels of 1805, see Brooke, *Columbia Rising*, 303–05, 318–19. For James Kent and the libel bill of 1805, the addition of the question of motive at the convention of 1821 (proposed by Sanford, who is not identified by Roper), and Kent's opposition to the change, see Donald [M.] Roper, "James Kent and the Emergence of New York's Libel Law," *American Journal of Legal History*, 17 (1973):226, 229, http://heinonline.org. The language quoted in Peter J. Galie, *Ordered Liberty: A Constitutional History of New York* (New York: Fordham University Press, 1996) pertaining to the role of the jury in acquitting a defendant in a libel case was offered by Sanford as an amendment, but Galie has not attributed it to him: 85.

22. Carter and Stone, eds., *Reports*: the quotations are on pages 491 and 492, respectively.

23. Ibid., 491.

24. Ibid., 495; Casais, "Convention of 1821," 164.

25. Carter and Stone, eds., *Reports*, 38; see *New-York Evening Post*, June 23, 1821.

26. Stephen Van Rensselaer, bioguide.congress.gov/scripts/guidedisplay.pl?index=V000056. See Chernow, *Alexander Hamilton*, 133: Van Rensselaer was "the largest landowner in New York State." He was the Federalist candidate for governor in 1813 but was defeated by Daniel Tompkins.

27. John Cramer, http://bioguide.congress.gov/scripts/biodisplay.pl?index=C000867.

28. Carter and Stone, eds., *Reports*, "Appendix," 687–89. There were 126 delegates in all representing the counties; see ibid., 27–28.

29. See Brooke, "King George," 194; Gellman and Quigley, *Jim Crow New York*, 332n9.

30. Voter qualifications are in Article 2 of the constitution of 1822: see the proceedings of November 7, Carter and Stone, eds., *Reports*, 632 and ibid., Appendix, 661.

31. The quotation on the memorial is from *Journal of the Convention of the State of New York, 1821* (Albany: Cantine & Leake, 1821), 49, Digital Collection, NYSL. The version of the proceedings recorded and printed by Carter and Stone, eds., *Reports*, 134, omits the references to the Declaration of Independence and the New York State Constitution.

32. For the fact that Cramer presented the suffrage report, see Carter and Stone, eds., *Reports*, 236.

33. Ibid., 134–35. The suffrage report is also in "No. 6, In Convention, September 12, 1821," *Committee Reports*, nysl.nysed.gov.

34. Ibid., 178.

35. Ibid, 179.

36. Ibid.

37. Ibid., 179–80.

38. Ibid., 180; David N. Gellman, *Emancipating New York: The Politics of Slavery and Freedom, 1777–1827* (Baton Rouge: Louisiana State University Press, 2006), 207: Gellman cites the committee's proposal as extending suffrage "almost as far as the male population of the state" but fails to attribute the words to Sanford.

39. See Gellman and Quigley, *Jim Crow New York*, 76.

Chapter 9

1. Carter and Stone, eds., *Reports*, 180–81; Sean Wilentz in *The Rise of American Democracy* has misread Sanford's position on race: he lumps Sanford and Ross together on a legislative committee that would give the vote to "white male citizens," excluding blacks (193). As I show here, Sanford voted consistently against black exclusion (see Carter and Stone, eds., *Reports*, 202, for example) until the very end of the suffrage debate, when he supported the compromise that allowed the franchise for only those blacks who owned the required freehold. Also, Sanford's position and the direct quotation from Stephen Van Rensselaer appear in Carter and Stone's transcribed and edited *Reports of the Proceedings* on 178–204, not on 401–27. Debate on "The Elective Franchise" began on September 19, 1821, and was based on the suffrage committee's report. It was not part of the legislative committee's report, as stated in Wilentz, *American Democracy*, 839n31.

2. Wood, *Empire of Liberty*, 680; Brooke, *Columbia Rising*, 464. A patroon was a proprietor of a Dutch land grant.

3. Carter and Stone, eds., *Reports*, 182–83.

4. Ibid., 183.

5. Ibid., 183, 189.

6. Ibid., 198.

7. Ibid., 202. See Elizabeth Stordeur Pryor, "The Etymology of Nigger: Resistance, Language, and the Politics of Freedom in the Antebellum North," *JER* 36 (Summer 2016): 204n1. Pryor maintains that "colored" was a descriptor consciously chosen by black activists in the nineteenth century "to signal racial unity." The example she gives of usage of the term is in a title, "Coloured Citizens," and was "at least as early as 1829 by a black Bostonian," while the white Root had used the term in the phrase, "coloured people," in 1821. Jabez Hammond would later castigate Republicans Root, Young, and Livingston for favoring the elimination of the property requirement for whites while being "zealous to exclude black citizens" from the franchise; Hammond, *History of Political Parties*, 2:21.

8. The Federalists included Peter Jay, a former assemblyman from Westchester County, James Kent, and Rufus King: see Gellman and Quigley, *Jim Crow New York*, 124–27, 138–42.

9. Carter and Stone, eds., *Reports*, 202: the quotation is on 179. "A solid core" of fifteen Federalists and about thirty-five Bucktail Republicans voted to defeat the effort to make the suffrage for whites only: Gellman and Quigley, *Jim Crow New York*, 142. Historians have equated Sanford's role as chair of the suffrage committee with an assumed vote in committee against black male suffrage: see, for example, Cole, *Martin Van Buren*, 70. "Sanford's proposal denied all blacks the vote."

10. Gellman and Quigley, *Jim Crow New York*, 4–5. The quotation is on page 5.

11. See Carter and Stone, eds., *Reports*, 192.

12. Carter and Stone, eds., *Reports*, 215: the quotations are on page 220.

13. Ibid., 224.

14. Ibid., 225.

15. Ibid., 235; see Gellman and Quigley, *Jim Crow New York*, 156, for a description of Tompkins's "selective historical memory" relative to his earlier support for raising regiments of African American soldiers during the War of 1812 and his support for accelerated gradual emancipation. Tompkins was also a member of the New York Manumission Society; Gellman and Quigley, *Jim Crow New York*, 68. The governor's absences from the convention, and, perhaps, his racist outburst, were caused by his "decade of financial privation and heavy drinking," 1815 to his death in 1825; Mark O. Hatfield, with the Senate Historical Office, "Daniel D. Tompkins (1817–1825)," in *Vice Presidents of the United States, 1789–1993* (Washington: U.S. Government Printing Office, 1997), n.p., senate.gov.

16. Mark O. Hatfield, with the Senate Historical Office, "Daniel D. Tompkins (1817–1825)," in *Vice Presidents of the United States, 1789–1993* (Washington, DC: U.S. Government Printing Office, 1997), n.p., senate.gov.

17. Carter and Stone, eds., *Reports*, 235–39: the quotation is on page 239.

18. See Brooke, *Columbia Rising*, 382; see Gellman and Quigley, *Jim Crow New York*, for commentary, 165. The speech is in Carter and Stone, eds., *Reports*, 255–65.

19. Carter and Stone, eds., *Reports*, 270.

20. Ibid., 274–75. The vote to strike the military lost, ninety-two to twenty-six. The vote on striking road work won, sixty-eight to forty-eight. See ibid., 283.

21. In his book, *American Suffrage from Property to Democracy, 1760–1860* (Princeton, NJ: Princeton University Press, 1960), Chilton Williamson cites a letter written on Sunday, September 30, 1821, by Senator Rufus King to his son. In referencing the letter, Williamson has noticed Sanford's leadership on suffrage. Based on the letter, he concludes that "If we can believe Rufus King, only two members of the New York delegation, Nathan Sanford and Jacob Radcliff, favored a more democratic suffrage than that which was adopted": 203, 203n56. Former New York Supreme Court Justice Radcliff's argument for universal suffrage is in Carter and Stone, eds., *Reports*, 286.

22. Ibid., 284.

23. Ibid., 288–89, 329. The quotation is on page 288.

24. Ibid., 329.

25. Ibid., 366–68; see 329. The vote tally is on page 368. On two earlier occasions, Sanford had supported the option of roadwork as a qualifier for suffrage: one was in the Sanford committee report; the other was when the same criterion was proposed later as an amendment. Both proposals required shorter residencies than the three years required here.

26. See Alexander Keyssar, *The Right to Vote, The Contested History of Democracy in the United States*, rev. ed. (New York: Basic Books, 2009), 36–37, 42, for the implication that Sanford consistently supported tax payments. His October 6 vote shows that he changed his thinking over time according to the wording of certain new proposals.

27. For the vote on blacks and the freehold, see Carter and Stone, eds., *Reports*, 369–70.

28. See ibid., 376–77: the vote on October 8 to strike the freehold lost, thirty-three to seventy-one; the quotation is on page 376.

29. Ibid., 364.

30. Ibid., 278: Judge William W. Van Ness (a cousin of William P. and an associate justice on the New York Supreme Court) had suggested earlier that if "we each would yield a little, we might act with unanimity." The quotation from Colonel Young is in ibid., 376. Historians have attributed the "compromise" to various delegates. See Gellman and Quigley, *Jim Crow New York*, 175, who emphasize the role of Martin Van Buren in the compromise by his moving the convention toward limited, white universal suffrage and making "racial exclusion conditional." Brooke, in *Columbia Rising*, 385, acknowledges that "Van Buren's vision prevailed." See ibid., 384, where he argues that Judge William W. Van Ness "crafted the final compromise" with the proviso. I argue that Van Ness merely

reordered the wording of the proviso. See Carter and Stone, eds., *Reports*, 289: Van Ness was not a member of the committee of thirteen where the proposal originated.

31. For the vote that approved the suffrage section up to the proviso that won, eighty-three to thirty-two, see Carter and Stone, eds., *Reports*, 377; for the vote on the entire section, see ibid., 378.

32. Ibid., 553–54. The review began on Saturday, October 27.

33. See ibid., 557: the vote was seventy-two to thirty-two. The report of October 4 had referred ambiguously to the age and residence "last above mentioned" that would be required of blacks. The reference was to the second option for whites—age twenty-one and a three-year residency: the "substitute" specified those requirements for blacks. See ibid., 329,

34. Ibid., 657. Committee member John Ross does not appear in the vote tally for the new constitution published by Carter and Stone, but his name is in the list of voters published in the *Journal of the Convention*, 552.

35. Gellman and Quigley, *Jim Crow New York*, 200. The vote on age and residency requirements for the franchise took place on October 6, 1821.

36. Frederick Douglass, "Address to the People of the United State" (1853), Colored national convention (1853: Rochester, NY), "Proceedings of the Colored national convention, held in Rochester, July 6th, 7th, and 8th, 1853," *ColoredConventions.org*, coloredconventions.org/items/show/458, 11.

37. For example, Gellman and Quigley in *Jim Crow New York* quote Sanford's speech that launched the debate on suffrage but offer no commentary on his role or influence; Brooke in *Columbia Rising* gives no reference to Sanford, although he discusses the convention; see 382–85; Alexander in *Political History* lists Sanford with others as a participant with "eloquence and ability" and makes a fleeting reference to him in the context of court reform; see 298–311: the quotation is on page 298.

38. See Keyssar, *Right to Vote*, 22–42. The quotation is on page 22. Sanford's remarks on suffrage were also referenced by Richard Hofstadter, ed., *Great Issues in American History*, vol. 2, *From the Revolution to the Civil War, 1765–1865* (New York: Random House, 1958), 252.

Chapter 10

1. Carter and Stone, eds., *Reports*, "Appendix," 688.

2. See Cornog, *Birth of Empire*, 139; Howe, *What Hath God Wrought*, 161, 239.

3. Nathan Sanford to Rufus King, January 18, 1822, Manuscript Department, NYHS.

4. V. Maxcy and W.H.B. Lewall to N. Sanford, Samuel Hopkins, Peter Porter, Thomas Gold, August 26, 1822, in McKenna, *Tapping Reeve*, Appendix 6, 201.

5. H. Seymour to J. C. Calhoun, May 9, 1822, in ibid., 202.

6. See *Independent Chronicle and Boston Patriot*, August 9, 1823, 2.

7. Doctor of Laws degree, Nathan Sanford, August 5, 1823, Nathan Sanford Papers, 1799–1834, SC14054, Box 1, NYSL, translated for the author by Dr. Sarah B. Pomeroy; see Messer, "United States Attorney's Office," 1–2.

8. Nathan Sanford's great grandfather Sandford had married Elizabeth More, an alternate spelling of Moore; Clement Moore was a descendant of Elizabeth's grandfather. She is buried in Bridgehampton: see Sanford, *Sandford/Sanford Families*, 13, 15; Kenneth A. Lohf, "Clement Clarke Moore and His Christmas Poem," in Clement C. Moore, *A Visit from St. Nicholas* (A facsimile of the 1848 edition) (New York: Wanderer Books, 1971), n.p.

9. See *Memoires of John Adams Dix, 1821–1828* [database on-line]. Provo, UT: Ancestry.com, Ancestry.com Operations, 2008, 65. Sanford was nominated in January 1823. See also Hammond, *History of Political Parties*, 2:111.

10. Henry Rutgers to Nathan Sandford [*sic*], May 22, 1822, Manuscript Division, LC. Rutgers made large donations to the New Jersey institution that was renamed Rutgers College in 1825 and later became Rutgers University: see "Henry Rutgers," en.wikipedia.org.

11. Adams, *Southampton*, 226n.

12. William H. Crawford to Martin Van Buren, May 19, 1823, MVBP-LC.

13. Ibid.

14. See Cuyler Reynolds, *Albany Chronicles: A History of the City Arranged Chronologically* (Albany, NY: J. B. Lyon, Printers, 1906), 452.

15. *Klinck's Albany Directory* (Albany, NY: E. & E. Hosford, 1823), 62: Sanford was listed as senator in the 1827 edition.

16. George Rogers Howell, Jonathan Tenney, *Bi-centennial History of Albany* (Albany, NY: W. W. Munsell, 1886), 2:651–52, https://archive.org/details/cu31924080795127; John J. McEneny, *Albany: Capital City on the Hudson* (Sun Valley, CA: American Historical Press, 1998), 14; Skeen, *1816*, 98.

17. Eliza Sanford to Edward Sanford, June 10, 1823, Edward Sanford Letters, 1821–1831, GLC-NYPL.

18. Folts, "Courts," *Encyclopedia of New York State*, 412. The court of chancery originated in colonial times and was continued under the state Constitution of 1777; mandatory retirement for the chancellor was still at age sixty—unlike the federal bench where appointments were for life.

19. Letter from Nathan Sanford, August 11, 1823, *Minutes of the Common Council*, 216.

20. See "Hopkins, Samuel Miles (1772–1837)," bioguide.congress.gov/scripts/biodisplay.pl?index=H000780.

21. See *William A. Weaver v. Stephen Whitney, et al.*, in *Reports of cases adjudged and determined in the Court of Chancery of the state of New York: [1814–1850]*, vol. 2 (Rochester, NY, 1888), Images 311–16, *Sabin Americana*. Gale, Cengage Learning. NYPL Databases; *Niles' Weekly Register*, April 3, 1824, 26:72–74.

22. Ibid., 74.

23. Ibid., 89–90, 118: the quotation is on page 90. Other letters were addressed to *Niles Register*, 119–21, 130–32. The *National Intelligencer*, which began publication in Washington in 1800, was America's first national newspaper.

24. The chancery was abolished by the state constitution of 1847.

25. Robert R. Livingston was the first chancellor of New York State, from 1777 to 1801; he died in 1813 and was the older brother of Edward.

26. See "North River Steamboat," en.wikipedia.org; "Gibbons v. Ogden," ibid. The *North River* became known as the steamboat *Clermont*.

27. "Gibbons v. Ogden," ibid.; "Gibbons v. Ogden," http://caselaw.findlaw.com/us-supreme-court/22/1.html.

28. See Howe, *What Hath God Wrought*, 235; R. Kent Newmyer, *The Supreme Court under Marshall and Taney*, 2nd ed. (Wheeling, IL: Harlan Davidson, 2006), 49–51.

29. The quotation is from the last paragraph of the record cited above in http://caselaw.findlaw.com.

30. For *North River v. John Livingston*, see *Reports of cases*, Images 360–83. The quotation is on Image 378; Reynolds, *Albany Chronicles*, 450.

31. *Spafford's 1824 Guide for New York Travellers*, compiled by G. Martin Sleeman (Boonville, NY: Boonville Graphics, 1991), 6.

32. Reynolds, *Albany Chronicles*, 453.

33. Moss Kent to James Kent, March 24, 1824, excerpted in Roper, "Kent's Necrologies," 230n37.

Chapter 11

1. See Hanyan, *DeWitt Clinton*, 74, 175–78, 186. The quotation is on page 175. It is unclear why Sanford did not pursue the governorship. Perhaps he sensed uncertainty in his support beyond a small group within the Bucktail caucus. He may also have felt that he was being used to edge Yates out of office. The Albany Regency was a name invented by Van Buren opponents and assigned to Van Buren and his loyalists who controlled patronage from the state legislature: see Howe, *What Hath God Wrought*, 239, 485.

2. See Cornog, *Birth of Empire*, 151–53.

3. See Howe, *What Hath God Wrought*, 203–7.

4. Ibid., 205–9.

5. See Robert V. Remini, *Henry Clay: Statesman for the Union* (New York: W. W. Norton & Co., 1991), 244; Heidler and Heidler, *Clay*, 171.

6. See Howe, *What Hath God Wrought*, 204–5; see John L. Brooke, "Cultures of Nationalism, Movements of Reform, and the Composite—Federal Polity, From Revolutionary Settlement to Antebellum Crisis," *JER* 29 (Spring 2009): 7.

7. *Niles Register*, November 6, 1824, 27; ibid., February 12, 1825, 382. See also *Lampi Collection*, New York 1824 Vice President of the United States, Electoral College, 1824.

8. For context, see Howe, *What Hath God Wrought*, 207.

9. Ibid., 240; Cornog, *Birth of Empire*, 153–54.

10. See Cornog, *Birth of Empire*, 149–50, 176; the quotation is in Hammond, *History of Political Parties*, 2:211.

11. See "In Assembly, January 16, 1826," "In Senate, March 6, 1826," Search Results, American Antiquarian Society: He was acknowledged as the main author, with judges from the supreme court and several circuits in the state contributing. Sanford did not wait to review the senate's response to the report, which came in early March. americanantiquarian.org/catalog.htm.

12. *Niles Register*, January 21, 1826, 29:324.

13. Howe, *What Hath God Wrought*, 251–55; see Johnson, *Early American Republic*, 152–53.

14. Brooke, "Cultures," 7; see Howe, *What Hath God Wrought*, 210, 305.

15. See Wilentz, *American Democracy*, 307.

16. The quotation from Sanford is in Carter and Stone, eds., *Reports*, 180.

17. Howe, *What Hath God Wrought*, 259.

18. Brooke, *Columbia Rising*, 439, 441–42. The quotations are on pages 441–42.

19. Erastus Root to Martin Van Buren, April 2, 1826, MVBP-LC; Root had fought against giving the franchise to African Americans as a delegate to the state convention, arguing that blacks voted according to their employers' instructions.

20. John Quincy Adams, May 27, 1828, "The Diaries of John Quincy Adams": A Digital Collection, Massachusetts Historical Society, 37:555, masshist.org/jqadiaries (hereafter cited as "Diaries").

21. Root to Van Buren, MVBP-LC; see Cornog, *Birth of Empire*, 177.

22. Nathan Sanford to Samuel Beardsley, September 27, 1826, Manuscript Division, LC.

23. James Sterling Young, *The Washington Community 1800–1828* (New York: Columbia University Press, 1966), 24–25, 42–44; see "Explore Capitol Hill," https://www.aoc.gov/explore-capitol-hill, for the completion of the dome in 1826.

24. Young, *Washington*, 68, 71, 87–89, 98.

25. Edward Conrad Smith, "Sanford, Nathan," *Dictionary of American Biography*, ed. Dumas Malone (New York: Charles Scribner's Sons, 1943), 16:349; Howe, *What Hath God Wrought*, 252: the Interior Department was created in 1849; the Justice Department was created in 1870: *The First 100 Years (1789–1889): The United States Attorneys for the Southern District of New York* (United States Court of Appeals, 2nd Circuit, Historical Committee, 1987), 12.

26. Bill, *Congressional Documents*-LC, S. 19, Senate, 19th Congress, 2nd session, December 20, 1826; *Senate Executive Journal*-LC, 20th Congress, 1st session, March 28, 1828, 603.

27. See David S. Reynolds, *Waking Giant: America in the Age of Jackson* (New York: HarperCollins, 2008), 55.

28. *Niles Register*, March 9, 1826, 30:13; ibid., December 16, 1826, 31:244: Sanford was chair from December 11, 1826, to March 3, 1827; appointments,

Senate Journal-LC, 20th Congress, 1st session, December 10, 1827, 28; ibid., 20th Congress, 2nd session, December 8, 1828, 21; ibid., 21st Congress, 1st session, December 9, 1829, 23; ibid., 21st Congress, 2nd session, December 7, 1830, 5.

29. Treaty, *Senate Executive Journal*-LC, 19th Congress, 2nd session, February 26, 1827, 570–71; conventions of London, ibid., 20th Congress, 2nd session, February 17, 1829, 645; boundary, *Senate Journal*-LC, 20th Congress, 2nd session, February 17, 1829, 131.

30. See Howe, *What Hath God Wrought*, 257–60; see report on memorials, *Senate Journal*-LC, 19th Congress, 2nd session, February 12, 1827, 172.

31. Adams, "Diaries," May 27, 1828.

32. Convention, *Senate Executive Journal*-LC, 21st Congress, 1st session, May 29, 1830, 115; payment, *Senate Journal*-LC, 21st Congress, 2nd session, December 7, 1830, 11; see Howe, *What Hath God Wrought*, 363. The payment is the rough equivalent of $9,750,000 in today's dollars.

33. *Niles Register*, December 12, 1829, 37:254. Sanford was appointed on December 9, 1829; reappointment, *Senate Journal*-LC, 21st Congress, 2nd session, December 7, 1830, 5; see Robert W. Coren, Mary Rephlo, David Kepley, and Charles South, *Guide to the Records of the United States Senate at the National Archives, 1789–1989*, Bicentennial Ed., Document No.100–42 (Washington, DC: National Archives and Records Administration, 1989), 7.7.

34. "Delaware and Hudson Canal," *Ulster [NY] Sentinel*, reprinted in the *Gettysburg Republican Compiler*, August 22, 1827, http://search.ancestry.com/search/db.aspx?dbid=7206.

35. Memorial, *Senate Journal*-LC, 20th Congress, 2nd session, February 16, 1829, 125; vote, *Register of Debates*-LC, Senate, 20th Congress, 1st session, May 13, 1828, 786; letter, Nathan Sanford to Nathaniel P. Tallmadge, February 15, 1828, NYHS.

36. Brooke, *Columbia Rising*, 2; see Howe, *What Hath God Wrought*, 274–75.

37. Mark Schmeller, "The Political Economy of Opinion: Public Credit and Concepts of Public Opinion in the Age of Federalism," *JER* 29 (Spring 2009): 59; Wright, *Financial*, 30–33; see Chernow, *Alexander Hamilton*, 355–56; Richard Sylla, "The Transition to a Monetary Union in the United States, 1787–1795," *Financial History Review* 13, no. 1 (2006): 73–77, http://www.econ.tcu.edu/quinn/finhist/readings/sylla.pdf.

38. Sylla, "Monetary Union," 84.

39. Specie, *Annals*-LC, Senate, 14th Congress, 1st session, March 25, 1816, 29:248–49.

40. Currency, *Senate Journal*-LC, 15th Congress, 2nd session, November 30, 1818, 40.

41. See Howe, *What Hath God Wrought*, 376; *Niles Register*, January 3, 1829, vol. 35, 310; report, *Senate Journal*, 21st Congress, 1st session, May 4, 1830, 283.

42. The quotation is in Howe, *What Hath God Wrought*, 375; coin committee, *Senate Journal*-LC, 21st Congress, 1st session, December 9, 1829, 24: Sanford no doubt chaired the committee.

43. Bill, *Congressional Documents*-LC, S. 49, Senate, 21st Congress, 1st session, January 11, 1830, 1–2.

44. *Niles Register*, February 6, 1830, 37:398.

45. Coin committee, *Senate Journal*-LC, 21st Congress, 2nd session, December 9, 1830, 33; bill, *Congressional Documents*-LC, S. 6, Senate, 21st Congress, 2nd session, December 15, 1830, 1–2: the bill used the terms "pure gold" and "standard gold," with the standard kind allowing more grains of the less pure gold to satisfy the unit requirement. One thousand copies of the report and the bill were printed; *Niles Register*, December 18, 1830, 39:280; bill, *Senate Journal*, 21st Congress, 2nd Session, January 14, 1831, 91. The United States went off the gold standard in 1933.

46. See Howe, *What Hath God Wrought*, 342–48; Johnson, *Early American Republic*, 154–55.

47. Citizens, *Niles Register*, January 9, 1830, 37:331; Indian board, ibid., February 27, 1830, 38:5. Sanford read the memorial in the Senate on February 23; Howe, *What Hath God Wrought*, 348.

48. Indian removal, *Senate Journal*-LC, 21st Congress, 1st session, February 22, 1830, 147–48.

49. Frelinghuysen, *Statutes at Large*-LC, 21st Congress, 1st session, May 26, 1830, 328; Sanford, *Register of Debates*-LC, 21st Congress, 1st session, April 26, 1830, 383.

50. Vote, *Register of Debates*-LC, 21st Congress, 1st session, April 26, 1830, 383; New York's other senator, Charles E. Dudley, also voted for removal, ibid; Howe, *What Hath God Wrought*, 352: the vote in the House was 102 to 97.

Chapter 12

1. Francis P. O'Neill, email to the author, April 8, 2015: the marriage was recorded in the parish registers, located at the Maryland Historical Society. This evidence exposes the myth that Mary Buchanan was given away by President Adams in a White House ceremony: William Bushong, email to the author, February 10, 2014. Mr. Bushong, White House Historical Association, cited three circa 1900 secondary sources that repeated the story.

2. Nathan Sanford to Edward Sanford, Esquire, New York, April 27, 1828, NSP-NYSL; ibid., May 16, 1828.

3. I have reconstructed the family relationship from *Family Tree Maker's Genealogy Site: User Home Page Genealogy Report*, "from Buchanans to Bohanans," http://www.genealogy.com/ftm/d/e/l/David-T-Delgadillo/GENE1-0007.html; Kaplan, *John Quincy Adams*, 274, 326.

4. Adams, "Diaries," May 27, 1828.

5. See Wood, *Empire of Liberty*, 428–29: McKean survived reelection in 1805 as well as a later attempt by radical Republicans to impeach him over the

contentious issue of the role of the courts, as opposed to the legislature, in state government.

6. See "Mary Buchanan Sanford Journal, 1843–1851," October 8, 1843, http://purl.org/net/nysl/nysdocs/263068823.

7. Margaret Bayard Smith, *The First Forty Years of Washington Society*, ed. Gaillard Hunt (New York: Scribner's, 1906) 289, https://archive.org/details/firstfortyyears00huntgoog; Young, *Washington*, 47.

8. Nathan Sanford to Edward Sanford, March 15, 1829, NSP-NYSL; see "from Buchanans to Bohanans."

9. Nathan Sanford to Edward Sanford, December 6,1828, NS Papers, NYSL.

10. Letter, ibid.

11. See Charles Sanford to Edward Sanford, February 17, 1833 [the correct year is 1832], Edward Sanford Letters, 1832–1844, GLC-NYPL. Charles Sanford managed his father's Eagle Neck Farm in Flushing for many years beginning in the early 1830s. It was often rented: see, for example, *Long Island Farmer, and Queens County Advertiser* (Jamaica, NY), February 22, 1842, http://nyshistoric newspapers.org/lccn/sn83031394/issues/1842/.

12. See 1830 Federal Census, Albany Ward 2, Albany, New York, Nathan Sanford, https://www.archives.gov/research/census/publications-microfilm-catalogs-census/1790-1890/part-02.html#1830; Sanford, *Sandford/Sanford Families*, 28, reports partial information on Edward, Eliza's marriage, and Robert; Henry P. Phelps, *The Albany Rural Cemetery* (Albany: Phelps & Kellogg, 1893), 192, 195. It contains information on Mary (b. 1814–d. 1841) and Henry (b. 1816–d. 1832). For Charles, I have used circumstantial evidence to approximate his age and role in life. Eliza was born in 1810 and married John Le Breton in 1826. He died in 1831: see Eliza Le Breton to Edward Sanford, May 10, 1831, Edward Sanford Letters, 1821–1831, GLC-NYPL. Henry wrote from Union College to his sister, Mary: Henry Sanford to Mary Sanford, June 12, 1832, Mary Sanford Gansevoort Papers, General Correspondence, 1832–1846, GLC,NYPL.

13. Mary Sanford to Edward Sanford, September 11, 1831, Edward Sanford Letters, 1821–1831, GLC-NYPL.

14. Hammond, *History of Political Parties*, 2:346–47. Marcy coined the phrase, "To the victor belong the spoils": Howe, *What Hath God Wrought*, 485.

15. *Richmond Enquirer*, May 20, 1831: Sanford's letter to the Tammany Society was dated April 26.

16. Nathan Sanford to William L. Marcy, January 14, 1832, NSP-NYSL.

17. *Johnson's Reports* were compiled by William Johnson for the New York Supreme Court. He also served as reporter at the court of chancery under James Kent. Samuel M. Hopkins followed Johnson as reporter at the chancery when Sanford became chancellor in 1823.

18. See *Catalogue of the Law Library of the Late Chancellor Sanford* (New York: printed by Charles Vinten, [1839]), Manuscripts and Archives Division, NYPL.

19. Library, *Niles Register*, December 16, 1826, 31:244: the committee was appointed on December 10, 1826; see J. Roderick Heller III, *Democracy's Lawyer, Felix Grundy of the Old Southwest* (Baton Rouge: Louisiana State University Press, 2010), 188: in addition to Sanford, the library committee included Senator Marcy and Felix Grundy, senator from Tennessee. President Jackson signed the authorization on July 14, 1832.

20. J. Munsell, ed., *Collections on the History of Albany, from its Discovery to the Present Time* (Albany, NY: J. Munsell, 1867), 36; Howell, *Southampton*, 752.

21. Invitation, Mrs. Sanford to Jared L. Rathbone, January 9, 1830, Legal Papers, Box 287, SFP, GLC-NYPL. Rathbone became mayor of Albany.

22. Mary Sanford to Edward Sanford, February 3, 1832, Edward Sanford Letters, 1832–1844, GLC-NYPL. For Livingston and Tallmadge identifications, see en.wikipedia.org.

23. Alice P. Kenney, *The Gansevoorts of Albany, Dutch Patricians in the Upper Hudson Valley* (Syracuse, NY: Syracuse University Press, 1969), 151, 154–58, 182.

24. Ibid., 198–202; for context, see Howe, *What Hath God Wrought*, 502–04.

25. Phelps, *Albany Rural Cemetery*, 192: Peter Gansevoort's family gravestone lists the names of Peter and Mary's "infant children Mary, Isaac, and Herman." See also Kenney, *Gansevoorts*, 182–84. The births took place from 1835 to 1840. Only two of Mary's children survived into adulthood. Mary died of tuberculosis in 1841.

26. No stock dividends appear in my sampling of the receipt book after 1823.

27. *Minutes of the Common Council*, August 1, 1825, March 26, 1827, April 23, 1827.

28. *Historical Guide to the City of New York* (New York: F. A. Stokes, 1913), 307. Sanford no doubt worked with an agent. The avenue referenced is today's Jamaica Avenue.

29. Nathan Sanford to John A. King, February 15, 1823, NYHS.

30. See *Journeys on Old Long Island*, 53, 59n3. The quotation is on page 53.

31. Henry D. Waller, *History of the Town of Flushing, Long-Island, New York* (Harrison, NY: Harbor Hills Books, 1975; reprint of 1899), 184–86, 192.

32. Nathan Sanford to Robert W. Mott, January 17, 1829, NYHS.

33. *Sag Harbor Corrector*, July 7, 1827, 4: the notice about the auction calls Sanford a "Subscriber" to the newspaper.

34. The receipts are in Sanford's receipt book, July 23, 1830; March 23, 1831; December 26, 1834; January 13, 1835. The rent payment was on November 26, 1831. The last entry in the receipt book was made on December 9, 1835. The Mechanics' and Farmers' Bank where Sanford left his papers was in Albany. Sanford would also have received cash to spend on the mansion from the sale of his Albany residence, although it is not clear whether he owned the townhouse outright.

35. See Henry Sanford to Mary Sanford, June 12, 1832, Mary Sanford Gansevoort Papers, General Correspondence, 1832–1846, GLC-NYPL.

36. See "Mary Buchanan Sanford Journal, 1843–1851," where Mary wrote in 1851 that she had left Albany sixteen years earlier. The quotations are in "Flushing," an article reprinted from the *New York Commercial* in the *Long Island Farmer*, May 27, 1835, 2. Sanford is buried in the Saint George's Episcopal Church cemetery in Flushing.

37. See Chancellor's Enrolled Decrees and Papers after 1800, case G145, Box 92, NYS Archives, Series J0063: hereafter cited as Final Decree-NYS Archives. Eagle Neck Farm, long managed by Charles Sanford, occupied a portion of the property.

38. The quotation is in *Historical Guide*, 307.

39. William S. Pelletreau, "Chancellor Nathan Sandford [*sic*]," *Sag-Harbor Espress*, May 21, 1908; Jason Crowley, email to the author, January 7, 2016: Tuckahoe Marble quarried in Westchester County, New York, may have been used.

40. "Flushing," 2.

41. Benjamin F. Thompson, *History of Long Island; Containing an Account of the Discovery and Settlement* (New York: E. French, 1839), 377–78, http://history.pmlib.org/ClassicLIHisDocCollections. The quotation is on page 377.

42. See Final Decree-NYS Archives, "No. Nine" for the April 26, 1836 mortgage—the bond carried a 6% interest rate; see "No. Ten" for the May 2, 1836, $5,000 bond at the same interest rate.

43. Mortgage note, Nathan Sanford and Mary Sanford, Mechanics' Bank, New York, June 6, 1836, Land Papers, Box 286 [18–21], SFP, GLC-NYPL.

44. Mary Sanford to Edward Sanford, April 10, 1833, Edward Sanford Letters, 1832–1844, GLC-NYPL. The stepchildren always addressed Mary Buchanan Sanford as "Mother."

45. Passport application, Nathan Sanford, November 3, 1837, U. S. Passport Applications, 1795–1925 [database on-line], http://search.ancestry.com/search/db.aspx?dbid=1174; see Wm Barrow to Chas Sanford, November 27, 1837, LL B-14, LIC-EHL: Barrow was Sanford's doctor; he sent his respects to Mrs. Sanford and asked Charles to let him know "As soon as you hear from your Father," indicating that he was away; see Kenney, 182. Travel to a Caribbean island was practiced in the eighteenth century, as well. In 1751, George Washington accompanied his older half-brother Laurence to Barbados in the hope that the climate would cure his case of tuberculosis.

46. Samuel B. Romaine to Nathan Sanford, December 27, 1837, Box 287, 119–20, SFP, GLC-NYPL. The letter addressed the "Greenwich property," another name for the Grace Church lots.

47. Mary [Buchanan] Sanford to Mary Sanford, March 13, 1838, Mary Sanford Gansevoort Papers, General Correspondence, 1832–1846, GLC-NYPL.

48. Sanford had probably lived with one lung since about the age of thirty. His four children were Edward, Charles, Mary, and Robert; Eliza had died prior to 1838. The Le Breton girls became wards of the court. Mary had two surviving children by the fall of 1838, Henry and Catherine: see Kenney, 182–83.

49. Estate Inventory, October 23, 1838, vol. 103, GLC-NYPL. The inventory report was not issued until March 29, 1839; Edward Sanford to Mary S.

Gansevoort, October 10, 1839, Legal Papers, Box 128, SFP, GLC-NYPL; for alcohol consumption patterns, see Howe, *What Hath God Wrought*, 167.

50. *Long Island Farmer*, November 14, 1838, 3.

51. The Index to *Letters of Administration, 1791–1900*, Queens County, New York, contained no listing for Nathan Sanford: Edward's use of the term "administrator" must have been based on an informal agreement between him and his father.

52. Office of Assistant Register of the Court of Chancery, January 31, 1839, Legal Papers, Box 128, GLC-NYPL. This part of the GLC collection contains personal letters; it also contains copies of disparate documents related to the case. Robert and the two orphaned Le Breton granddaughters were underage and could not participate in the proceedings.

53. Edward Sanford to Mary S. Gansevoort, October 10, 1839, ibid.; Edward Sanford to Charles Sanford, November 14, 1839, LL B-14, LIC-EHL.

54. Enclosure in letter, Edward Sanford to Mary S. Gansevoort, October 10, 1839, Legal Papers, GLC-NYPL.

55. Chancellor Reuben Walworth opened the trial on November 16, 1838. The Final Decree is dated May 16, 1843. See Anderson A. Robbins, "Distinguished Bridgehamptonite," *The Long Island Forum* 16, no. 8 (August 1953): 142.

56. Final Decree-NYS Archives; Sanford Hall, as the Mansion House was also called, was purchased in 1844–45 by Dr. James Macdonald and Allan Macdonald, who converted it into a private institution for the mentally ill: see Allan Macdonald, "Life of Dr. Macdonald," *The American Journal of Insanity* 6 (1849): 85, https://archive.org/details/psyamericanjourn06ameruoft. Macdonald family papers are at Yale University.

57. Obituary reprinted in *Niles National Register*, November 10, 1838, vol. 55, 166, https://babel.hathitrust.org/cgi/pt?id=njp.32101064077363;view=1up;seq=5.

58. Thompson, *History of Long Island*, 2nd ed. (1843) 2:543.

59. *Brooklyn Eagle*, August 1, 1893, https://bklyn.newspapers.com/title_1890/the_brooklyn_daily_eagle/.

60. For the quotation, see Kaplan, *John Quincy Adams*, 210.

Selected Bibliography

Adams, James Truslow. *Memorials of Old Bridgehampton*. Port Washington, NY: Ira J. Friedman, 1962. First published 1916.

———. *History of the Town of Southampton*. Bridgehampton, NY: Hampton Press, 1918.

Alexander, DeAlva Stanwood. *A Political History of the State of New York*. Vol. 1, *1774–1832*. New York: Henry Holt, 1906. Reprint. Elibron Classics, 2006.

Ashton, Susanna. "A Corrupt Medium: Stephen Burroughs and the Bridgehampton, New York, Library." *Libraries & Culture: A Journal of Library History* 38, no. 2 (Spring 2003): 93–120.

Barrett, Walter. *Old Merchants of New York City*. New York: Carleton, 1863–66.

Bassford, Amy Osborn. Description of Clinton Academy. [circa 1960]. LIC-EHL.

Berlin, Ira and Leslie M. Harris, eds. *Slavery in New York*. New York: New Press, 2005.

Berger, Bethany. "It's Not About the Fox: The Untold History of *Pierson V. Post*." *Duke Law Journal* 55, no. 6 (April 2006): 1089–1143. http://heinonline.org.

Boonshaft, Mark. "The Litchfield Network: Education, Social Capital, and the Rise and Fall of a Political Dynasty, 1784–1833." *Journal of the Early Republic* 9 (Winter 2014): 561–95.

Breen, T. H. *Imagining the Past: East Hampton Histories*. Reading, MA: Addison-Wesley Publishing, 1989.

Brooke, John L. "Cultures of Nationalism, Movements of Reform, and the Composite—Federal Polity, From Revolutionary Settlement to Antebellum Crisis." *Journal of the Early Republic* 29 (Spring 2009): 1–33.

———. *Columbia Rising: Civil Life on the Upper Hudson from the Revolution to the Age of Jackson*. Chapel Hill: University of North Carolina Press, 2010.

———. "'King George Has Issued Too Many Pattents for Us,' Property and Democracy in Jeffersonian New York." *Journal of the Early Republic* 33 (Summer 2013): 187–217.

Burak, H. Paul. *History of the United States District Court for the Southern District of New York*. New York: Federal Bar Association of New York, New Jersey & Connecticut, 1962.

Burroughs, Stephen. *Memoirs of the Notorious Stephen Burroughs of New Hampshire*. New York: Dial Press, 1924.

Bushman, Richard L. *The Refinement of America: Persons, Houses, Cities*. New York: Alfred A. Knopf, 1992.

Casais, John Anthony. "The New York State Constitutional Convention of 1821 and Its Aftermath." PhD diss., Columbia University, 1967.

Catalogue of the Law Library of the Late Chancellor Sanford. New York: printed by Charles Vinten, 1839.

Chernow, Ron. *Alexander Hamilton*. New York: Penguin Press, 2004.

Clowes, Ernest S. *Wayfarings: A collection chosen from pieces which appeared under that title in the Bridgehampton news, 1941–1953*. Bridgehampton, NY, 1953.

Coleman, Steven R. "Political Journalism in the 1790s: *Frothingham's Long Island Herald*." *Long Island Historical Journal* 4, no. 1 (Fall 1991): 92–104.

Cornog, Evan. *The Birth of Empire: DeWitt Clinton and the American Experience, 1769–1828*. New York: Oxford University Press, 1998.

Countryman, Edward. "From Revolution to Statehood." In *The Empire State, A History of New York*, ed. Milton M. Klein. Ithaca, NY: Cornell University Press, 2001.

Curts, Paul H., ed. *Bridgehampton's Three Hundred Years*. Bridgehampton: Hampton Press, 1956.

Davidson, Cathy N. *Revolution and the Word: The Rise of the Novel in America*. New York: Oxford University Press, 1986.

Diamond, Beatrice. *An Episode in American Journalism: A History of David Frothingham and His Long Island Herald*. Port Washington, NY: Kennikat Press, 1964.

Douglass, Frederick. "Address to the People of the United States." Proceedings of the Colored National Convention, held in Rochester [NY], July 6th, 7th, and 8th, 1853. http://coloredconventions.org/items/show/458.

Dukeminier, Jesse, and James E. Krier. *Property*. 2nd ed. Boston: Little, Brown, 1988.

Dwight, Timothy. *Travels in New England and New York*. Edited by Barbara Miller Soloman. Vols. 1, 3. Cambridge, MA: Belknap Press of Harvard University Press, 1969.

Ferguson, Robert A. *Law and Letters in American Culture*. Cambridge, MA: Harvard University Press, 1984.

Ferling, John. *John Adams: A Life*. New York: Holt, 1992.

Fernandez, Angela. "The Ancient and Honorable Court of Dover: Serious Mock, Solemn Foolery, and Sporting Wit in Nineteenth-Century New York State." *Australian & New Zealand Law and History E-Journal*, Referred Paper No. 7 (2012): 194–239. "The Ancient and Honorable Court of Dover: Mock Trials, Fraternal Orders, and Solemn Foolery in Nineteenth-Century New York State." https://works.bepress.com/angela_**fernandez**/1/download.

———. "Copying and Copyright Issues at the Litchfield Law School." University of Toronto, Legal Studies Research Paper No. 08-13 (July 14, 2008): 1–25. http://ssrn.com/abstract=1160023.

———. "The Lost Record of *Pierson v. Post*, the Famous Fox Case." *Law and History Review* 27, no. 1 (2009): 149–78. http://jstor.org/stable/27641649

———. "*Pierson v. Post*: A Great Debate, James Kent, and the Project of Building a Learned Law for New York State." *Law and Social Inquiry* 34, 2 (2009): 301–36.

Fitch, Charles Elliot. "Sanford, Nathan." *Encyclopedia of Biography of New York*. New York: The American Historical Society, 1916.

Folts, James D. "Courts, State." *Encyclopedia of New York State*. Edited by Peter Eisenstadt. Syracuse, NY: Syracuse University Press, 2005.

Galie, Peter J. *Ordered Liberty: A Constitutional History of New York*. New York: Fordham University Press, 1996.

Gellman, David N., and David Quigley, eds. *Jim Crow New York: A Documentary History of Race and Citizenship, 1777–1877*. New York: New York University Press, 2003.

Goddard, David. *Colonizing Southampton: The Transformation of a Long Island Community, 1870–1900*. Albany, NY: Excelsior Editions, State University of New York Press, 2011.

Guernsey, R. S. *New York City and Vicinity during the War of 1812–'15*. Vol. 2. New York: Charles L. Woodward, 1895.

Halsey, William Donaldson. *Sketches from Local History*. [1935]. Reprint. Southampton, NY: Yankee Peddler Book Co., 1966.

Hammond, Bray. *Banks and Politics in America from the Revolution to the Civil War*. Princeton, NJ: Princeton University Press, 1957.

Hammond, Jabez D. *History of Political Parties in the State of New York from the Ratification of the Federal Constitution to December 1840*. Vols. 1–2. Cooperstown, NY: H. & E. Phinney, 1846–47.

Hanyan, Craig. *DeWitt Clinton and the Rise of the People's Men*. Montreal: McGill-Queen's University Press, 1996.

Hedges, Henry P. *Tracing the Past: Writings of Henry P. Hedges, 18171911, Relating to the History of the East End*. Edited by Tom Twomey. New York: Newmarket Press, 2000.

Heidler, David S., and Jeanne T. Heidler. *Henry Clay: The Essential American*. New York: Random House, 2010.

Heller, J. Roderick, III. *Democracy's Lawyer: Felix Grundy of the Old Southwest*. Baton Rouge: Louisiana State University Press, 2010.

Hickey, Donald R. *Don't Give Up the Ship! Myths of the War of 1812*. Urbana: University of Illinois Press, 2006.

———, ed. *The War of 1812: Writings from America's Second War of Independence*. New York: Library of America, 2013.

Historical Statistics of the United States: Colonial Times to 1970, Bicentennial Edition, Part I. Washington, DC: U.S. Bureau of the Census, 1975.

Homberger, Eric. *The Historical Atlas of New York City*. New York: Henry Holt, 1998.

Hone, Philip. *The Diary of Philip Hone, 1828–1851*. Edited by Alan Nevins. Vol. 2. New York: Dodd, Mead, 1927.

Hough, Charles Merrill. *The United States District Court for the Southern District of New York, 1789–1919*. New York: Maritime Law Association of the United States, 1934. http://history.nysd.uscourts.gov/.

Hough, Franklin B. *New York Civil List from 1777 to 1858*. Albany, NY: Weed, Parsons, 1858.

Howe, Daniel Walker. *What Hath God Wrought: The Transformation of America, 1815–1848*. New York: Oxford University Press, 2007.

Howell, George Rogers. *The Early History of Southampton L.I., New York*. 2nd ed. Albany, NY: Weed, Parsons, 1887.

Johnson, Paul E. *Early American Republic, 1789–1829*. New York: Oxford University Press, 2007.

Kammen, Michael. "The Promised Sunshine of the Future: Reflections on Economic Growth and Social Change in Post-Revolutionary New York." In *New Opportunities in a New Nation: The Development of New York After the Revolution*. Edited by Manfred Jonas and Robert V. Wells. Schenectady, NY: Union College Press, 1982.

Kaplan, Fred. *John Quincy Adams: American Visionary*. New York: Harper Collins, 2014.

Kenney, Alice P. *The Gansevoorts of Albany: Dutch Patricians in the Upper Hudson Valley*. Syracuse, NY: Syracuse University Press, 1969.

Keyssar, Alexander. *The Right to Vote: The Contested History of Democracy in the United States*. Rev. ed. New York: Basic Books, 2009.

Lampi, Philip J. "The Federalist Party Resurgence, 1808–16: Evidence from the New Nation Votes Database." *Journal of the Early Republic* 33 (Summer 2013): 255–81.

Lanier, Henry Wysham. *A Century of Banking in New York, 1822–1922*. New York: Gilliss Press, 1922.

Larson, John Lauritz. "An Inquiry into the Nature and Causes of the Wealth of Nations," *Journal of the Early Republic* 35 (Spring 2015): 1–23.

Leiner, Frederick C. "The Squadron Commander's Share: Decatur v. Chew and the Prize Money for the Chesapeake's First War of 1812 Cruise." *The Journal of Military History* 73, no. 1 (January 2009): 69–82. http://muse.jhu.edu/journal/96.

Mann, Bruce H. *Republic of Debtors, Bankruptcy in the Age of American Independence*. Cambridge, MA: Harvard University Press, 2002.

Mather, Frederic Gregory. *The Refugees of 1776 from Long Island to Connecticut*. Albany, NY: J. B. Lyon Co., 1913.

McKenna, Marian C. *Tapping Reeve and the Litchfield Law School*. New York: Oceana Publications, 1986.

Minty, Christopher. "'A List of Persons on Long Island': Biography, Voluntarism, and Suffolk County's 1778 Oath of Allegiance." *Long Island History Journal* 24, no. 2 (2015): 1–13. http://lihj.cc.stonybrook.edu.

Morgan, Edmund S. *American Heroes: Profiles of Men and Women Who Shared Early America*. New York: W. W. Norton, 2009.

Myers, Gustavus. *History of Tammany Hall.* New York: Boni & Liverright, 1917. https://archive.org/details/historyoftammany00myeruoft.

Naylor, Natalie A., ed. *Journeys on Old Long Island: Travelers' Accounts, Contemporary Descriptions, and Residents' Reminiscences, 1744–1893.* Interlaken, NY: Empire State Books, 2002.

Newmyer, R. Kent. *The Supreme Court under Marshall and Taney.* 2nd ed. Wheeling, IL: Harlan Davidson, 2006.

Peart, Daniel. "Looking Beyond Parties and Elections: The Making of United States Tariff Policy during the Early 1820s." *Journal of the Early Republic* 33 (Spring 2013): 87–108.

Petrie, Donald A. *The Prize Game: Lawful Looting on the High Seas in the Days of Fighting Sail.* New York: Berkley Books, 1999.

Pope, Charles Henry. *The Pioneers of Massachusetts: A Description List, Drawn from the Records of the Colonies, Towns and Churches, and other Contemporaneous Documents.* 1900. Reprint. Baltimore, MD: Genealogical Publishing, 1991.

Prime, Nathaniel S. *A History of Long Island From Its First Settlement by Europeans to the Year 1845.* New York: Robert Carter, 1845.

Pryor, Elizabeth Stordeur. "The Etymology of Nigger: Resistance, Language, and the Politics of Freedom in the Antebellum North." *Journal of the Early Republic* 36 (Summer 2016): 203–45.

Ratcliffe, Donald. "The Right to Vote and the Rise of Democracy, 1787–1828." *Journal of the Early Republic* 33 (Summer 2013): 219–54.

Rattray, Jeannette. *East Hampton History Including Genealogies of Early Families.* Garden City, NY: Country Life Press, 1953.

Reeves, Henry A. "Commerce, Navigation and Fisheries of Suffolk County." In *Bi-Centennial History of Suffolk County.* Babylon, NY, 1885.

Remini, Robert V. *Henry Clay: Statesman for the Union.* New York: W. W. Norton, 1991.

Reynolds, Cuyler. *Albany Chronicles: A History of the City Arranged Chronologically.* Albany, NY: J. B. Lyon Printers, 1906.

Roper, Donald M. "The Elite of the New York Bar as Seen from the Bench: James Kent's Necrologies." *New-York Historical Society Quarterly* 56, no. 3 (July 1972): 199–237. http://nyhistory.org/library/digital-collections.

Sandford, Ann H. "Rural Connections: Early Republic Bridgehampton and Its Wider World, 1790–1805." *Long Island Historical Journal* 15 (Fall 2002/Spring 2003): 1–22.

———. "Bridgehampton's 'Accidental' Settling, 1650–1700." Paper delivered at the New York State History Conference, Cooperstown, NY, June 2007.

———. "Rural Wealth and American Property Law: The Sagaponack and Bridgehampton Connections, 1802 and 1805." Bridgehampton Museum's *The Bridge* (Summer 2011): 18–21.

Sanford, Grover Merle. *The Sandford/Sanford Families of Long Island.* Baltimore, MD: Gateway Press, 1975.

Skeen, C. Edward. *1816: America Rising*. Lexington: University Press of Kentucky, 2003.

Smith, Edward Conrad. "Sanford, Nathan." *Dictionary of American Biography* [DAB]. Edited by Dumas Malone. Vol. 16. New York: Charles Scribner's Sons, 1943.

Smith, Margaret Bayard. *The First Forty Years of Washington Society*. Edited by Gaillard Hunt. New York: Scribner's, 1906. https://books.google.com/books?id=cKEdAAAAMAAJ.

Stevens, Robert. *Perspectives in American History*. Edited by Donald Fleming and Bernard Bailyn. Vol. 5. Cambridge, MA: Charles Warren Center for Studies in American History, 1971.

Strong, John A. *"We Are Still Here!": The Algonquian Peoples of Long Island Today.* Interlaken, NY: Empire State Books, 1998.

Strum, Harvey. "Property Qualifications and Voting Behavior in New York, 1807–1816." *Journal of the Early Republic* 1 (Winter 1981): 347–371. http://jstor.org/stable/3122826.

Sylla, Richard. "The Transition to a Monetary Union in the United States, 1787–1795." *Financial History Review* 13, no. 1 (2006): 73–95.

Taylor, Alan. *William Cooper's Town, Power and Persuasion on the Frontier of the Early American Republic*. New York: Vintage Books, 1996.

Thompson, Benjamin F. *History of Long Island; Containing an Account of the Discovery and Settlement*. New York: E. French, 1839. http://history.pmlib.org/ClassicLIHisDocCollections.

———. *History of Long Island from Its Discovery and Settlement to the Present Time*. 2nd ed. Vol. 2. New York: Gould, Banks, 1843. http://history.pmlib.org/ClassicLIHisDocCollections.

———. *History of Long Island from its Discovery and Settlement to the Present Time*, 3rd ed. Vol. 2. Revised by Charles J. Werner. New York: Robert H. Dodd, 1918. history.pmlib.org/ClassicLIHisDocCollections

Watson, Robert P. *America's First Crisis: The War of 1812*. Albany, NY: State University of New York Press, 2014.

White, Leonard D. *The Jeffersonians: A Study of Administrative History, 1801–1829*. New York: Macmillan, 1951. https://archive.org/details/jeffersoniansast011195mbp.

Wilentz, Sean. *Rise of American Democracy: Jefferson to Lincoln*. New York: W. W. Norton, 2005.

Williamson, Samuel H. "Seven Ways to Compute the Relative Value of a U.S. Dollar Amount, 1774 to Present." *Measuring Worth* (2015). http://measuringworth.com/uscompare/.

Wood, Gordon S. *Empire of Liberty: A History of the Early Republic, 1789–1815*. New York: Oxford University Press, 2009.

Wright, Robert E. *The First Wall Street*. Chicago: The University of Chicago Press, 2005.

Wright, Robert E., and David J. Cowen, *Financial Founding Fathers*. Chicago: University of Chicago Press, 2006.

Young, James Sterling. *The Washington Community 1800–1828*. New York: Columbia University Press, 1966.

Zagarri, Rosemarie. "The Family Factor: Congressmen, Turnover, and the Burden of Public Service in the Early American Republic." *Journal of the Early Republic* 33 (Summer 2013): 283–316.

Zaykowski, Dorothy Ingersoll. *Sag Harbor—The Story of an American Beauty*. Sag Harbor, NY: Sag Harbor Historical Society, 1991.

Index